THE UNITED STATES SUPREME COURT'S ASSAULT ON THE CONSTITUTION, DEMOCRACY, AND THE RULE OF LAW

The United States Constitution was drafted by principled men who aspired to form "a more perfect union," in which the individual pursuits of free men triumphed over the collective power of government. The Founders recognized the intuitive, almost instinctual, human craving for liberty driven by the power of the human spirit, the promise of free will, the preservation of self-autonomy, and the primacy of the people. The Founders' vision for American democracy embodied equality, not elitism, championed fairness, not favoritism, and emphasized autonomy, not aristocracy.

Unfortunately, the "heady days of the here and now" and the "transcendent dimensions of liberty" have blinded many to the Founders' vision. We have become a nation of men, not laws, governed by an unelected Supreme Court and an unaccountable federal government. We are a country defined by party, not patriotism, by selfishness, not sacrifice, and by corruption, not compassion. Today, the United States does not resemble the country in which the Founders lived and continues to drift from the values upon which the Constitution rests. American democracy now resides in the shadows of elitism, under the intolerable burden of inequality and a false promise of liberty. Until this changes, the future will not be brighter than the past, and the winds of change will stall under the weight of cynicism. In *The United States Supreme Court's Assault on the Constitution, Democracy, and the Rule of Law*, Adam Lamparello and Cynthia G. Swann analyze the United States Supreme Court's landmark rulings and propose a framework for interpreting the Constitution that gives power to the people, not the privileged, and recognizes that "when the past no longer illuminates the future . . . the Founders' dream for a 'more perfect union' vanishes".

Adam Lamparello is a law professor and attorney who has taught at Loyola University College of Law in New Orleans, Louisiana and Mercer University School of Law in Macon, Georgia.

Cynthia Swann is a law professor and attorney who has over twenty years of practice experience in Washington, D.C., and who has taught at the Appalachian School of Law.

Controversies in American Constitutional Law

Series Editors:

Jon Yorke and Anne Richardson Oakes

Centre for American Legal Studies, School of Law, Birmingham City University, UK

Controversies in American Constitutional Law presents and engages with the contemporary developments and policies which mold and challenge US constitutional law and practice. It deals with the full spectrum of constitutional issues, publishing work by scholars from a range of disciplines who tackle current legal issues by reference to their underlying legal and political histories and the philosophical perspectives that they represent. Its cross-disciplinary approach encourages analysis of past, present, and future challenges to the idea of US constitutionalism and the power structures upon which it rests. The series provides a forum for scholars to challenge the boundaries of US constitutional law and engages with the continual process of constitutional refinement for the protection of individual rights and liberties, within an evolving framework of legitimate government.

CALS promotes research, scholarship, and educative programs in all areas of US law, and is the home of the *British Journal of American Legal Studies.* Faculty members have extensive experience in submitting *amicus curiae* briefs to the United States Supreme Court and lower federal courts, and advising on criminal justice issues in many states. CALS coordinates the largest British law undergraduate internship program to the United States. Through this program and members' research, CALS has created relationships with more than 100 partners in over 25 states. CALS faculty advise public bodies, provide professional training, and speak at conferences across the United States.

Recent titles in this series:

Controversies in Equal Protection Cases in America: Race, Gender and Sexual Orientation
Anne Richardson Oakes
ISBN 978-1-4094-5427-4

Controversies in Tax Law: A Matter of Perspective
Edited by Anthony C. Infanti
ISBN 978-1-4724-1492-2

Controversies in Innocence Cases in America
Edited by Sarah Lucy Cooper
ISBN 978-1-4094-6354-2

THE UNITED STATES SUPREME COURT'S ASSAULT ON THE CONSTITUTION, DEMOCRACY, AND THE RULE OF LAW

Adam Lamparello
Cynthia Swann

Routledge
Taylor & Francis Group
LONDON AND NEW YORK

First published 2017
by Routledge
4 Park Square, Milton Park, Abingdon, Oxon OX14 4RN
605 Third Avenue, New York, NY 10017

Routledge is an imprint of the Taylor & Francis Group, an informa business

British Library Cataloguing in Publication Data
A catalogue record for this book is available from the British Library

Library of Congress Cataloging in Publication Data
Names: Lamparello, Adam, author. | Swann, Cynthia G., author.
Title: The United States Supreme Court's assault on the Constitution, democracy and the rule of law / Adam Lamparello and Cynthia Swann.
Description: Abingdon, Oxon ; New York, NY : Routledge, 2016. | Series: Controversies in American constitutional law
Identifiers: LCCN 2016029036 | ISBN 9781138222434 (hardback) | ISBN 9781138222441 (pbk) | ISBN 9781315407760 (epub) | ISBN 9781315407753 (mobipocket)
Subjects: LCSH: United States. Supreme Court. | Political questions and judicial power—United States. | Constitutional law—United States. | Rule of law—United States.
Classification: LCC KF8748 .L24 2016 | DDC 342.73—dc23
LC record available at https://lccn.loc.gov/2016029036

ISBN: 978-1-138-22243-4 (hbk)
ISBN: 978-1-138-22244-1 (pbk)
ISBN: 978-1-315-40778-4 (ebk)

Typeset in Galliard
by Apex CoVantage, LLC

CONTENTS

LEGAL TABLES

Cases	Page
Atkins v. Virginia	15
Allgeyer v. Louisiana	150
Austin v. Michigan Chamber of Commerce	22
Baker v. Carr	111
Baskin v. Bogan	98
Baze v. Rees	9
Bowers v. Hardwick	89, 91, 95, 104
Brown v. Board of Education	69
Bush v. Gore	76
Central Hudson Gas & Electric Corporation v. Public Utilities Commissions	233
Chaplinsky v. New Hampshire	233
Chevron, Inc., v. Natural Resources Defense Council	49
Citizens United v. FEC	11
City of Renton v. Playtime Theaters	233
Clinton v. New York	37
Dred Scott v. Sandford	158
General Electric Co. v. Gilbert	135
Gideon v. Wainright	201
Griswold v. Connecticut	13
Geduldig v. Aiello	136
Kelo v. City of New London	139
Kiyoshi Hirabayashi v. United States	54
Korematsu v. U.S.	53
Lawrence v. Texas	89
Lochner v. New York	149
Loving v. Virginia	70
McCutcheon v. FEC	32

Constitutional provisions

ACKNOWLEDGEMENTS

Adam Lamparello would like to thank Scott Payne and Lydia Lamont for their helpful revisions to earlier versions of this book.

PREFACE

The landmark cases that undermined U.S. constitutional law

> *Justice Douglas, you must remember one thing. At the constitutional level where we work, 90 percent of any decision is emotional. The rational part of us supplies the reasons for supporting our predilection.*
>
> —Chief Justice Charles Evans Hughes

***

The process by which the United States Supreme Court decides cases, and the reasoning underlying its decisions, matter more than the outcomes it reaches. In some cases, when the desirability of an outcome motivates the Court's decisions, democracy is weakened, separation-of-powers principles are undermined, and centralization replaces decentralization. In short, outcome-based decision making harms citizens of all political persuasions – except the wealthiest – and undermines principles of equality, liberty, and self-determination. For these reasons, the Supreme Court should embrace an interpretive framework that promotes equal participation in the democratic process, fosters accountability, and facilitates robust democratic discourse among citizens of all backgrounds. Currently, the Court's decisions in many landmark cases, although commendable in many respects, are failing in this regard. In *The United States Supreme Court's Assault on Democracy, the Constitution, and the Rule of Law*, we propose a solution that strives to restore integrity to the Court's decision-making process; this process eschews ideology and a focus on the utility of outcomes in favor of a jurisprudence that gives all citizens a meaningful voice in governance.

By way of background, when commentators discuss the Supreme Court's landmark decisions, spirited debate often ensues concerning which decisions constitute the 'best' and 'worst' in the Court's history. Predictably, this debate frequently splits along ideological lines, with progressive commentators praising landmark decisions such as *Roe v. Wade* and *Obergefell v. Hodges*, and conservative commentators lamenting decisions such as *Planned Parenthood v. Casey* and *Lawrence v. Texas.* By focusing on one's ideological predilections, these debates necessarily are limited to questioning the *outcomes* that the Court reached, rather than the *processes* by which the Court arrived at the results. In a number of cases, all of which are discussed *infra*, the Court's decision-making process harmed citizens of all political persuasions because they undermined federalism and separation-of-powers principles, inhibited participatory democracy, and reinforced democratic and political inequality.

Stated simply, in many landmark decisions, most jurists would find the reasoning by which the Court reached its respective outcomes – often by bare 5–4 majorities – deeply problematic. The arguably worst decisions in the Court's history were produced through one of the five following means:

- Prohibiting the legislative and executive branches from remedying corruption and unfairness in the political and democratic process and experimenting with solutions to make government more responsive to citizens
- Erroneously deferring to the legislative and executive branches and leaving citizens vulnerable to cognizable legal harms
- Expanding judicial review at the expense of democratic discourse while simultaneously failing to provide sufficient guidance to lower courts, elected representatives, and other agencies of government
- Weakening individual rights and promoting class-based inequality
- Disregarding states' authority and individual autonomy

In *The United States Supreme Court's Assault on Democracy, the Constitution, and the Rule of Law*, the authors posit that when the emphasis is on the processes (e.g., the legal reasoning) leading to a decision, debates concerning the 'best' and 'worst' Supreme Court decisions will transcend ideological lines. Such debates will result in a richer consideration of the Court's case law, a more nuanced understanding of the Court's relationship to our democratic government, and a broader consensus concerning which decisions are truly the worst in the Court's history and why.

This book has two distinct features that distinguish it from others focusing on the Supreme Court's jurisprudence. First, it is nonideological and provides a detailed critique of Supreme Court cases that would likely garner agreement from progressive and conservative thinkers alike. It also sets forth a proposal to enhance the integrity of the legal decision-making process, and in so doing effectuate political and democratic equality for citizens of all political persuasions and socioeconomic backgrounds. At bottom, *The United States Supreme Court's Assault on Democracy, the Constitution, and the Rule of Law* is a book that promotes intellectual honesty as the bedrock to sound judicial decision making. It is divided into seven parts and composed of thirty chapters. Parts I–V address the five themes listed earlier and sets forth a list of the worst decisions in the Court's history. The chapters within each part are dedicated to a single Supreme Court decision, in which we analyze the Court's reasoning and explain why it undermined, among other things, federalism, separation of powers, and democratic governance. Additionally, we explain why these decisions compromised the relationship between the Court and coordinate branches, the federal government and the states, and citizens and their elected representatives.

The following chart sets forth the decisions identified as the worst in the Court's history and the reasons why they negatively affected democracy.

Case	*Holding*	*Impact on Democracy*
Citizens United v. Federal Election Commission	Prohibitions on corporate expenditures within 30 and 60 days of presidential and primary elections violate the First Amendment.	Undermined participatory democracy and prevented the coordinate branches from remedying corruption (i.e., unfair access to and influence over public officials) in the electoral process.
McCutcheon v. Federal Election Commission	Aggregate limits on individual contributions violate the First Amendment.	Undermined participatory democracy and prevented the coordinate branches from remedying corruption (i.e., unfair access to and influence over public officials) in the electoral process.
Clinton v. New York	The Line Item Veto Act violates the Presentment Clause.	Encroached on coordinate branches' lawmaking power.
U.S. Term Limits v. Thornton	Statutes establishing term limits for federal elected officials violate the Constitution.	Contributed to entrenched and unaccountable majorities.
Chevron, Inc., v. Natural Resources Defense Council	Agency interpretations of statutes and constitutional provisions are entitled to substantial deference if the language of a provision can reasonably support the interpretation.	Deferred too heavily to federal agencies.
Korematsu v. U.S.	The executive branch may, in a time of war and for national security purposes, subject Japanese Americans to internment.	Failed to check arbitrary exercise of executive power.
Griswold v. Connecticut	A state law banning contraception violates the right to privacy, which is found in constitutional "penumbras" that emanate from the text.	Ignored the Constitution's text and embraced top-down lawmaking through creation of an unenumerated 'right to privacy.'
Roe v. Wade	The right to privacy under the Fourteenth Amendment's Due Process Clause includes a right to first-trimester abortions.	Manipulated the Fourteenth Amendment's Due Process Clause, embraced top-down lawmaking, and expanded the unenumerated "right to privacy."

(*Continued*)

Case	*Holding*	*Impact on Democracy*
Planned Parenthood v. Casey	States may not impose an "undue burden" on a woman's right to access abortion services.	Manipulated the Fourteenth Amendment's Due Process Clause, embraced top-down lawmaking through invention of a right to "define the mysteries of existence."
Lawrence v. Texas	State laws banning sodomy among same-sex couples violate the "substantive sphere of liberty" under the Fourteenth Amendment's Due Process Clause.	Manipulated the Fourteenth Amendment's Due Process Clause, embraced top-down lawmaking through a definition of liberty "in its spatial and more transcendent dimensions."
Obergefell v. Hodges	Same-sex marriage bans violate same-sex couples' right to liberty and "equal dignity" under the Fourteenth Amendment's Due Process Clause.	Manipulated the Fourteenth Amendment's Due Process Clause, embraced top-down lawmaking through invention of a right to "equal dignity." The ruling should have been based on the Equal Protection Clause.
The Slaughterhouse Cases	The Privileges and Immunities Clause only encompasses rights expressly enumerated in the Constitution.	Left citizens vulnerable to arbitrary exercises of the state police power.
Milliken v. Bradley	States are not required to desegregate public schools unless the state previously had a policy of intentional segregation.	Entrenched inequality into the law by making it more difficult to desegregate schools and remedy disparities in the quality of public education.
San Antonio Independent School District v. Rodriguez	Funding for public education may be based on property tax revenues.	Undermined *Brown v. Board of Education* and made it more difficult for states to desegregate the schools.
McCleskey v. Kemp	The death penalty is not unconstitutional merely because it is disproportionately imposed on African Americans.	Permitted the death penalty's imposition despite strong evidence that race was a factor in deciding whether to seek the death penalty.
General Elec. Co. v. Gilbert	Employers are not required to cover conditions related to pregnancy in their health insurance plans.	Discriminated against women by excluding pregnancy-related conditions from benefits plans.

Case	*Holding*	*Impact on Democracy*
Kelo v. City of New London	States may seize private property to serve private interests, provided that the seizure serves a public purpose.	Embraced an overly broad view of state power and subjected citizens to seizures of private property to benefit private interests.
Lochner v. New York	Laws regulating the number of hours that certain employees work (for the purpose of addressing harmful working conditions) violate an individual's right to freely enter into contracts.	Encroached on the states' police power by preventing states from addressing abusive labor practices.
Wickard v. Filburn	The Commerce Clause permits Congress to regulate purely local economic activity if it has a substantial effect on interstate commerce.	Embraced an overly broad view of Congress's power under the Commerce Clause

In a separate chapter, we explain why two controversial and heavily criticized decisions in the Court's recent history – *Bush v. Gore* and *National Federation of Independent Investors v. Sebelius*, are justifiable as a matter of constitutional law, regardless of whether one agrees with the outcome. We also discuss why *Dred Scott v. Sandford* did not make the list.

Part VI identifies several of the best Supreme Court decisions and explains why they furthered democracy's core values, including separation of powers, federalism, checks and balances, and protecting politically marginalized groups. Part VII sets forth a proposal advocating that the Court should have an instrumental role in creating a process-based, pro-democracy, and pragmatic jurisprudence. In Part VII, we provide a comprehensive framework that should inform the Justices' judicial philosophies, regardless of ideology, and promote an equal and participatory democracy. Specifically, we advocate for a process-oriented theory of judicial review under which the utility of an outcome, no matter how desirable, can never be justified unless the reasoning comports with the Constitution's text, its original purposes, and democratic vision. We also advance a theory of constitutional interpretation in which rights are not viewed as absolute, but as contextual, such that the protections afforded to individual rights should be predicated, in part, on the effects that their exercise will have on third parties. The final chapter offers concluding thoughts and argues that a pro-democracy jurisprudence is the foundation on which equality rests and the path by which to restore collective and equal liberty for all citizens.

We hope that this book challenges you to think beyond politics and ideology and to conclude that the best outcome any court can reach is one that is reached through fair and honest decision making and that promotes equal justice – and liberty – under the law.

Adam Lamparello
Cynthia Swann

Introduction

RELEVANT CONSTITUTIONAL PROVISIONS AND LEGAL TERMS

In the chapters that follow the authors analyze how the Court has interpreted various provisions in the United States Constitution and examine the theories relied upon by the Justices to develop constitutional meaning. What follows is a summary of relevant constitutional provisions and important legal terms discussed throughout this book (as defined by the authors) and an introductory discussion concerning the two most popular theories of constitutional interpretation.

***

Relevant constitutional provisions

U.S. Const., Art. I, Section 7, Cl. 2 & 3

The Presentment Clause

Every Bill which shall have passed the House of Representatives and the Senate, shall, before it become a Law, be presented to the President of the United States: If he approve he shall sign it, but if not he shall return it, with his Objections to that House in which it shall have originated, who shall enter the Objections at large on their Journal, and proceed to reconsider it. If after such Reconsideration two thirds of that House shall agree to pass the Bill, it shall be sent, together with the Objections, to the other House, by which it shall likewise be reconsidered, and if approved by two thirds of that House, it shall become a Law. But in all such Cases the Votes of both Houses shall be determined by Yeas and Nays, and the Names of the Persons voting for and against the Bill shall be entered on the Journal of each House respectively. If any Bill shall not be returned by the President within ten Days (Sundays excepted) after it shall have been presented to him, the Same shall be a Law, in like Manner as if he had signed it, unless the Congress by their Adjournment prevent its Return in which Case it shall not be a Law.

Every Order, Resolution, or Vote to which the Concurrence of the Senate and House of Representatives may be necessary (except on a question of Adjournment) shall be presented to the President of the United States; and before the Same shall take Effect, shall be approved by him, or being disapproved by him, shall be repassed by two thirds of the Senate and House of Representatives, according to the Rules and Limitations prescribed in the Case of a Bill.

U.S. Const., Art. I, Section 8

The taxing and spending power

The Congress shall have Power To lay and collect Taxes, Duties, Imposts and Excises, to pay the Debts and provide for the common Defence and general Welfare of the United States; but all Duties, Imposts and Excises shall be uniform throughout the United States.

U.S. Const., Art. I, Section 8, Cl. 3

The Commerce Clause

[The Congress shall have Power] To regulate Commerce with foreign Nations, and among the several States, and with the Indian Tribes.

U.S. Const., Art. III, Section 2

Judicial review

The judicial Power shall extend to all Cases, in Law and Equity, arising under this Constitution, the Laws of the United States, and Treaties made, or which shall be made, under their Authority; – to all Cases affecting Ambassadors, other public ministers and Consuls; – to all Cases of admiralty and maritime Jurisdiction; – to Controversies to which the United States shall be a Party; – to Controversies between two or more States; – between a State and Citizens of another State; – between Citizens of different States; – between Citizens of the same State claiming Lands under Grants of different States, and between a State, or the Citizens thereof, and foreign States, Citizens or Subjects.

U.S. Const., Amend. I

Congress shall make no law respecting an establishment of religion, or prohibiting the free exercise thereof; or abridging the freedom of speech, or of the press; or the right of the people peaceably to assemble, and to petition the Government for a redress of grievances.

U.S. Const., Amend. IV

The right of the people to be secure in their persons, houses, papers, and effects, against unreasonable searches and seizures, shall not be violated, and no warrants shall issue, but upon probable cause, supported by oath or affirmation, and particularly describing the place to be searched, and the persons or things to be seized.

U.S. Const., Amend. V

No person shall be held to answer for a capital, or otherwise infamous crime, unless on a presentment or indictment of a Grand Jury, except in cases arising in the land or naval forces, or in the Militia, when in actual service in time of War or public danger; nor shall any person be subject for the same offence to be twice put in jeopardy of life or limb; nor shall be compelled in any criminal case to be a witness against himself, nor be deprived of life, liberty, or property, without due process of law; nor shall private property be taken for public use, without just compensation.

U.S. Const., Amend. VI

In all criminal prosecutions, the accused shall enjoy the right to a speedy and public trial, by an impartial jury of the State and district wherein the crime shall have been committed, which district shall have been previously ascertained by law, and to be informed of the nature and cause of the accusation; to be confronted with the witnesses against him; to have compulsory process for obtaining witnesses in his favor, and to have the Assistance of Counsel for his defence.

U.S. Const., Amend. VIII

Excessive bail shall not be required, nor excessive fines imposed, nor cruel and unusual punishments inflicted.

U.S. Const., Amend. IX

The enumeration in the Constitution, of certain rights, shall not be construed to deny or disparage others retained by the people.

U.S. Const., Amend. X, Section 1

The powers not delegated to the United States by the Constitution, nor prohibited by it to the States, are reserved to the States respectively, or to the people

U.S. Const., Amend. XIV, Section 1

All persons born or naturalized in the United States, and subject to the jurisdiction thereof, are citizens of the United States and of the State wherein they reside. No State shall make or enforce any law which shall abridge the privileges or immunities of citizens of the United States; nor shall any State deprive any person of life, liberty, or property, without due process of law; nor deny to any person within its jurisdiction the equal protection of the laws.

***

Relevant legal terms

Democratic form of government

Broadly speaking, in a democracy, whether direct (where the people vote on policy initiatives) or indirect (where elected representatives enact legislation that governs all citizens in a state or country), the will of the majority is paramount. In essence, the majority is considered the governing body, leaving the minority with little, if any, legal protections. For this reason, democracies can easily devolve into the "tyranny of the majority," in which the minority is neither free nor equal under the law.

Republican form of government

In a republic, power resides in the people as individuals, and citizens have *inalienable* rights that the majority cannot infringe. As a result, in a republic, protections for minority rights are typically stronger, as the focus is on liberty and equality for *all* citizens.

American democracy ("democracy")

American democracy is a hybrid of democratic and republican forms of government, in which the will of the majority (and the branches of state and federal governments) is constrained by provisions in the Constitution regarding the structure of governance (e.g., separation of powers, checks and balances) and the rights granted to all citizens (e.g., freedom of speech).

Originalism

Broadly speaking, originalism is a theory of interpretation stating that judges should interpret the Constitution's text based on the commonly understood meaning of the words at the time they were adopted and in a manner that is consistent with the original purpose of a particular provision.

Living constitutionalism

Living constitutionalism is a competing theory on interpretation stating that the Constitution is a "living" or "evolving" document, such that constitutional meaning changes over time based on contemporary values and norms, particularly to address legal issues that the Founders could not foresee.

Judicial restraint

A principle that, where alternative constructions of the Constitution's text are possible, the Court should adopt the interpretation that will result in upholding, rather than invalidating, a law, and that in some circumstances the Court should defer to the coordinate branches at the state and federal level when a relevant constitutional provision is ambiguous or when the Constitution is silent on an issue.

Judicial activism

A principle that the Court should invalidate arbitrary federal and state laws, including those that infringe on basic civil liberties, even if such laws do not violate an enumerated constitutional right, for the purpose of protecting minority rights and politically marginalized groups.

Textualism

Textualism is a theory of interpretation stating that the words in a statute or constitutional provision should be given their ordinary meaning and that other factors, such as legislative intent or the objectives underlying a law, are not valid methods of interpretation.

***

The competing approaches to constitutional interpretation: originalism versus living constitutionalism

Background

Before examining the differences between, and the utility of, originalism and living constitutionalism, it is important to identify the sources of legal authority that the Court often relies upon when reaching a decision. Typically, when interpreting constitutional provisions or statutes, the Justices will consider (1) the text, and strive to give the words their most reasonable and intended meaning; (2) the purpose(s); (3) the Court's precedent; (4) the historical record, including evidence that reveals the Founders' original intent; (5) the nation's traditions and practices; and (6) the pragmatic consequences of a decision, including the impact on citizens, the workability of a particular rule, and the effect on future cases. Furthermore, based on their judicial philosophies, the Justices may afford greater emphasis to some sources, and the relevance of these sources will vary depending on, among other things, whether the text in question is ambiguous, whether the purpose(s) underlying a constitutional provision or statute is ascertainable, and whether the historical record is sufficiently reliable or indicative of the Founders' intent.

Significantly, however, the Justices can have interpretive difficulties when relying on these sources and the effect can be to complicate, rather than clarify, the decision-making process. For example, a constitutional provision or statute can have many, and often conflicting, purposes. Also, when a constitutional provision or statute has several purposes, identifying the proper purpose turns in substantial part on the context within which it is applied (e.g., the legal question at issue). Similarly, the purpose of a constitutional provision or statute will vary depending on the level of generality with which it is stated, and the manner in which a Justice frames a purpose can be used to manipulate or disregard the text. In this way, relying on purposes, especially where the text's meaning is fairly straightforward, invites subjectivity into the decision-making process and therefore has the potential to undermine the legitimacy of an outcome.

Assume, for example, that the government enacts a law permitting law enforcement officers to search the digital cameras of motorists who are arrested on public highways. The purpose of the statute is to ensure that the arrestee cannot destroy evidence that may exist on the camera and relate to the crime of arrest. This statute is subsequently challenged on the ground that it violates the Fourth Amendment to the United States Constitution, which states as follows:

> The right of the people to be secure in their persons, houses, papers, and effects, against unreasonable searches and seizures, shall not be violated, and no warrants shall issue, but upon probable cause, supported by oath or affirmation, and particularly describing the place to be searched, and the persons or things to be seized.

In deciding whether the law violates the Fourth Amendment, the Court must consider whether the warrantless search of an arrestee's camera is "unreasonable" in light of the amendment's purpose. The Court must also identify the purpose underlying the Fourth Amendment. What, exactly, is that purpose? Some would argue that the Founders *generally* sought to protect individual privacy rights and that the warrant requirement is intended to limit the circumstances within which law enforcement may conduct searches. Given this purpose, the law at issue violates the Fourth Amendment because it authorizes law enforcement to conduct searches of digital cameras without a warrant. Others may argue that the Founders *specifically* intended to safeguard privacy rights *in the home* and only sought to protect the "papers and effects" traditionally found in the home. Under this view, the law would not necessarily violate the Fourth Amendment because it authorizes searches of individuals who are arrested in a *public* place.

This example demonstrates that the manner in which a Justice interprets a constitutional provision or statute depends on how a Justice frames the underlying purpose in a provision or statute. This, in turn, directly informs the meaning that a Justice will give to the words in a text, particularly where the text is ambiguous or susceptible to alternative interpretations. For this reason, an interpretive framework that is primarily purpose driven should be avoided, especially if it would result in giving the text a meaning that its words cannot reasonably bear.

The same holds true when a Justice considers the pragmatic consequences of a decision. Excessive emphasis on "consequences," or what some call "pragmatism," can lead a Justice to manipulate or disregard the text to reach an outcome that accords with his or her subjective policy preferences. Likewise, when considering the historical record, a Justice may be tempted to "cherry-pick" from the record to support a desired outcome. A Justice may also rely selectively on the country's traditions, as well as the Court's prior jurisprudence, to support a decision that is inconsistent with, or contrary to, a reasonable reading of the text.

Stated simply, when a Justice relies predominantly on purposes, pragmatism, and consequences, the outcome is likely to be tainted with the stain of illegitimacy because it results from an intellectually dishonest decision-making process. For these reasons, coupled with the importance of ensuring judicial restraint and respect for the democratic process, the Justices should begin, and in many cases end, with an interpretation of the text that gives the words their fairest – and intended – meaning and that is consistent with a constitutional provision's or statute's original purposes.

Originalism versus living constitutionalism

Originalism and living constitutionalism are the most common – and competing – methods of constitutional interpretation. Advocates of living constitutionalism assert that the Constitution's meaning changes over time to reflect contemporary societal values and to resolve legal issues that the Founders could not foresee, including those affecting civil rights and liberties. Although this view is fairly benign as an abstract proposition, in practice living constitutionalism enables the Court to manipulate, even disregard, the Constitution's text to achieve desired outcomes. An outcome-driven jurisprudence can lead to, among other things, an abuse of judicial power, the usurpation of Congress's lawmaking authority, and a rule of law that is based on judges' personal policy predilections.

Notwithstanding, there are circumstances in which living constitutionalism can be a valid interpretive theory. Its utility – and legitimacy – in this regard depends on whether:

- The text in question is ambiguous
- The text is reasonably susceptible to alternative interpretations
- The text is silent on an issue
- The purpose(s) of a constitutional provision, when read in conjunction with the words, supports a particular interpretation

When the text is ambiguous

As a threshold matter, courts must first ascertain whether a constitutional provision (or a statute) can properly be characterized as ambiguous. The answer depends in substantial part on the text, its original purposes, and the legal question at issue. For example, the Free Speech Clause of the First Amendment prohibits the government from "abridging . . . the freedom of speech." This language begs the question of precisely when governmental conduct constitutes an "abridgement" of speech. It is also unclear whether "speech" is limited to specific categories of expressive activity (e.g., verbal utterances) or includes nonverbal conduct, such as monetary contributions to a political candidate. Equally unclear is whether the definition of a speaker is limited to individuals or encompasses corporations. Consequently, when evaluating whether a law violates the First Amendment, the Court must identify criteria to resolve these ambiguities and, ultimately, to ascribe meaning to the Constitution's words.

Of course, this does not necessarily mean that the Free Speech Clause of the First Amendment is always ambiguous. The presence of ambiguity depends on the legal question that the Court confronts in a given case. For example, a law prohibiting all speech that is critical of Congress or the president would unquestionably violate the First Amendment because it is an outright ban on, and necessarily an abridgement of, speech. On the other hand, a law prohibiting anti-abortion protestors from protesting within twenty feet of abortion facilities does not necessarily constitute an impermissible "abridgement" of speech. After all, if the government passes a law regulating the time, place, and manner in which speech can be expressed, does that always constitute an "abridgement" of speech? The answer is unclear and requires the Court to interpret the word "abridgement" in light of the First Amendment's original purposes (to promote decentralized governance and a robust marketplace of ideas); the ordinary meaning of the word "abridgment"; the Court's prior jurisprudence, history and tradition; and the likely consequences of a particular interpretation. As this example demonstrates, ambiguity arises when the text does not provide sufficient guidance to assess the constitutionality of a specific law.

Constitutional ambiguity exists in many provisions of the United States Constitution. For example, the religion clauses of the First Amendment provide that "Congress shall make no law respecting an establishment of religion, or prohibiting the free exercise thereof." This language provides no guidance regarding the circumstances in which the government impermissibly "establishes" or prohibits the "free exercise" of religion. Certainly, a law declaring that Catholicism is the nation's official religion would undoubtedly constitute an "establishment" of religion, but if a law authorized members of Congress to say a nondenominational prayer before the beginning of each legislative session, would that likewise be an "establishment" of religion? Regarding the "free exercise" of religion, a law requiring all citizens to attend a Catholic mass every Sunday would unquestionably infringe on an individual's right to freely exercise religion. On the other hand, if Congress enacted a law banning the slaughter of animals, would that violate the rights of religious groups that engage in ritual animal sacrifice?

In addition, the purposes of a constitutional provision can be ambiguous. For example, the Fourth Amendment, which prevents the government from conducting "unreasonable searches and seizures," protects individual privacy rights, most notably concerning the "papers" and "effects" typically found in a home. As a result, legislation permitting law enforcement officers to randomly and without warning search any area of a private residence – absent any suspicion of criminal activity – would certainly violate the Fourth Amendment. Conversely, a statute authorizing law enforcement officers to monitor the outgoing calls of individuals suspected of criminal activity would not necessarily violate the Fourth Amendment because neither the language nor the purpose of the Fourth Amendment conclusively supports a finding that the conduct is unreasonable. After all, one could argue that an outgoing telephone call, which reveals nothing more than the number dialed, is entirely different from searches of a wallet, diary, or computer, all of which may contain the "papers" and "effects" traditionally afforded Fourth Amendment protection. The Court would thus be required to consider, among other things, whether monitoring outgoing phone calls is sufficiently intrusive to constitute an invasion of an individual's privacy and whether the government's interest in preventing criminal conduct outweighs this intrusion. As this example reveals, the text and purpose of the Fourth Amendment is, at least in some cases, indeterminate, and its meaning depends on the Court's interpretation of its words.

By implication, when confronted with constitutional ambiguity, the Court cannot adopt a strictly originalist approach because the text – and, in some instances, the purpose(s) – can be interpreted in various ways to reach different outcomes. In such circumstances, however, the Court can rely on aspects of originalism and living constitutionalism to evaluate a statute's constitutionality. To illustrate the intersection between originalism and living constitutionalism, consider the text of the Eighth Amendment:

> Excessive bail shall not be required, nor excessive fines imposed, nor cruel and unusual punishments inflicted

Undoubtedly, the words "cruel" and "unusual" are quite broad and, in some instances, will not guide the Court when evaluating the permissibility of particular punishments. In these circumstances, an examination of the historical record can often reveal the Founders' original intent. In the Eighth Amendment context, the record indicates that the Founders' intent was to prohibit punishments that inflict unnecessary pain. As Justice Clarence Thomas stated in *Baze v. Rees*, "the evidence we do have from the debates on the Constitution confirms that the Eighth Amendment was intended to disable Congress from imposing torturous punishments."

Nevertheless, it is difficult to determine precisely when pain is "unnecessary." For example, does "unnecessary" suggest that a punishment is cruel and unusual if a less painful method of punishment is available to achieve the same objective (e.g., causing death via lethal injection as opposed to the electric chair)? Or does "unnecessary" mean that more painful methods of punishment are permissible provided they are not unduly harsh? The answers to these questions are inescapably relative because they depend upon, among other things, comparing the punishment in question to other existing punishments, evidence regarding the severity of pain that a specific punishment inflicts, and upon a subjective determination regarding whether a punishment is sufficiently harsh to violate the Eighth Amendment.

Therefore, when a court is confronted with the question of whether a particular method of execution, such as hanging or the electric chair, violates the Eighth Amendment, the broad phrasing of the text and its purposes requires the Court to exercise independent judgment. In such a circumstance, what other sources of legal authority should the Court consider to ensure that its decision-making process is legitimate and not grounded in politics or subjectivity? Certainly, the historical record leading to the Eighth Amendment's adoption, including deliberations during the drafting process, can inform the Justices. Similarly, developments in the Court's case law, including standards that have been developed to assess whether a punishment violates the Eighth Amendment, may counsel in favor of a particular result.

Moreover, the Court can – and should – consider the pragmatic, moral, and social implications of its decision *provided* they lead to an outcome that is consistent with a reasonable interpretation of the Eighth Amendment's text and original purpose. After all, moral considerations are certainly relevant to determining whether a punishment is cruel and unusual. For example, a judge may rely on contemporary definitions of "cruel" and "unusual," and may consider modern societal attitudes or understandings concerning the permissibility and acceptability of specific types of punishments.

Based on these and other factors, a judge may conclude that the electric chair is cruel and unusual because alternative and less painful methods of execution exist (e.g., lethal injection), and because the electric chair has, at least in some cases, resulted in prolonged suffering prior to death. The fact that the Founders may not have considered the electric chair to be cruel and unusual (had it existed at the time) is not germane because the existing punishments during and before the Founders' era (e.g., public hangings and burning at the stake) would have made the electric chair appear a more humane alternative. In contemporary society, however, punishments such as burning at the stake would unquestionably be considered barbaric (and therefore unnecessary), and the availability of lethal injection as a method of execution, although not without its problems, could certainly lead a judge to hold that the electric chair, which is far more violent and painful, is cruel and unusual.

This analysis reflects a hybrid approach that incorporates elements of originalism and living constitutionalism into judicial decision making. Indeed, even though the judge's decision incorporated contemporary moral and pragmatic considerations, such as whether "unnecessary pain" requires the state to impose the most humane method of execution, they enabled the judge to reach a reasonable outcome that was arguably consistent with the Eighth Amendment's text and original purpose. Put differently, constitutional ambiguity can blur the line between living constitutionalism and originalism and, ironically, show how originalism and living constitutionalism can serve complementary, not contradictory, purposes, ensure a fair decision-making process, and enhance the legitimacy of an outcome.

On the other hand, constitutional ambiguity should not be viewed as giving judges the authority to rely solely or even predominantly on moral and pragmatic considerations to invalidate laws that they subjectively deem cruel and unusual, particularly if doing so is neither supported by the text nor consistent with its purposes. Consequently, the argument that primarily moral readings of the Constitution (regardless of the text) are necessary to protect minority rights and traditionally disenfranchised groups, which in turn enables these groups to more fully participate in democracy, has merit only if it results in an honest interpretation of the Constitution. On the other hand, moral readings of the Constitution, if they lead a judge to disregard or manipulate the text, are inherently illegitimate because morality-based decisions are inescapably subjective. For example, one might argue from an ontological point of view that the correctness of a decision should depend in substantial part on its utility, including the likelihood that it will achieve equality and liberty for all citizens. This contention erroneously assumes that a moral consensus can be reached regarding the utility of a particular outcome and the precise definition of liberty and equality. Consider the following:

- Is it immoral to allow citizens to burn the American flag?
- Is it immoral to force grammar school students to recite the Pledge of Allegiance?
- Is it immoral to allow public schools to use corporal punishment on children?

These questions do not yield a definitive answer because they depend on subjective assessments regarding what is "good" or "beneficial" for society.

Furthermore, one may have fundamentally different conceptions of liberty and equality. For example, one may believe that liberty is best expressed through self-determination. As a result, when faced with constitutional ambiguity, a judge adopting this view would likely defer to the legislative branch and uphold democratically enacted laws, even if the judge views such laws as unwise. On the other hand, one may define liberty as protecting the intrinsic dignity of every human being. A judge embracing this conception would likely invalidate legislation that, in the judge's personal opinion, deprives an individual or group of dignity. Accordingly, disregarding or manipulating the Constitution would likely be seen as a necessary means to a virtuous end (outcome), even though the basis for that outcome – dignity – is capable of many definitions. These examples support the proposition that primarily moral readings of the Constitution enable judges "to roam where unguided speculation might take them," which results in decisions based on personal viewpoints, not on a faithful interpretation of the Constitution. Put simply, the text is there for a reason: to safeguard against the abuse of judicial power and, concomitantly, usurpation of the democratic process. After all, just as one man's terrorist is another man's freedom fighter, one judge's view of justice many be another's prescription for injustice.

The inherent flaws in embracing a primarily moral reading of the Constitution is underscored by the fact that the most controversial cases in the Court's recent history, including *Roe v. Wade*, *Planned Parenthood v. Casey*, *Citizens United v. FEC*, and *Bush v. Gore*, were decided by a single vote and deeply divided the Justices. The reason is that each decision was predicated largely on moral principles. To be clear, the Court should not be prohibited from considering the utility of an outcome, including its impact on the civil rights and liberties of traditionally disenfranchised and politically powerless groups. It is to say that, in the context of judicial decision making, pragmatic concerns do not justify disregarding or engaging in dishonest interpretations of the Constitution's text. There also exist competing constitutional concerns, such as separation of powers, federalism, checks and balances, and decentralization, to prevent unelected judges from inventing law based on their personal values and therefore become a de facto oligarchy. Accordingly, the Court has a legal duty to construe the text in a manner that the words and original purpose can support. If the text is susceptible to alternative constructions, as in the Eighth Amendment context, the Court would not err if it relied in part on moral considerations to assess the utility of an outcome. Conversely, if moral considerations drive the Court to ignore or manipulate the Constitution's text, the outcome itself would not be legitimate, regardless of its utility. *Griswold* is a textbook example of an illegitimate decision.

For this reason, exclusive reliance on living constitutionalism, especially if used as a justification to disregard the text, can lead to illegitimate outcomes and create the perception that the Court's decisions are politically driven. For example, if a state authorized the death penalty for the crime of child rape, the Eighth Amendment would not support the conclusion that such penalty is cruel and unusual. Although it could be argued that such a penalty is "unusual" because most states do not authorize the death penalty for child rape, it would not be "cruel" to do so if the method of execution (e.g., lethal injection) itself comported with the Eighth Amendment.

Unfortunately, in *Kennedy v. Louisiana*, a case where the Court relied almost exclusively on "living constitutionalism" a bare 5–4 majority held that the Eighth Amendment prohibits states from executing defendants convicted of raping a child under the age of twelve. In an opinion authored by Justice Anthony Kennedy, the majority held that "evolving standards of decency that mark the progress of a maturing society" as evidenced by a survey of state laws, public opinion polls, jury verdicts, and the Court's "reasoned judgment," supported a prohibition on executions unless the crime for which the defendant was convicted resulted in death. Unlike a decision holding that the electric chair violates the Eighth Amendment, the Court's holding in *Kennedy* rests predominantly on an arbitrary standard. For example, are state laws and public opinion polls accurate barometers of an "evolving standard of decency"? Are there not situations where reasonable minds can differ on matters of policy, with neither more "decent" than the other? Is it not true that one's view of "decency" is invariably subjective? The Court's decision underscores the difference between incorporating elements of living constitutionalism into a decision (e.g., the electric chair example) and basing a decision primarily on a vague "standard" that allows the Court to rely on whatever "evolving standards" fit with the Justices' moral dispositions. To avoid this problem, when courts consider if punishments that did not exist in the Founders' era are cruel and unusual, the Court should be guided – and limited – by the text and its purposes.

Also, allowing nine unelected judges to base constitutional interpretation on moral considerations would result in a rule of law that is rooted in relativity and subjectivity. In fact, if one truly believes that moral considerations should be a dominant factor in constitutional interpretation, then why not permit renowned philosophers to decide whether abortion and assisted suicide are fundamental rights?

Whether the text is susceptible to a particular interpretation

In some circumstances, the text and its purpose(s) may support alternative interpretations. For example, the Fifth Amendment states in relevant part that no citizen "shall be compelled in any criminal case to be a witness against himself." The Court has interpreted this provision to permit criminal defendants to avoid testifying at trial (and be subject to cross-examination by the prosecution). Although this rule is unquestionably supported by the Fifth Amendment's text, other issues arising thereunder are more difficult to resolve. If the government enacted a law stating that a jury may infer guilt from the defendant's silence at trial, would it violate the Fifth Amendment? Some might argue that this law does not technically compel a defendant to be a "witness" at trial, and therefore does not infringe on a defendant's Fifth Amendment right. Others may argue that the law penalizes defendants for invoking their Fifth Amendment right or indirectly coerces defendants to testify, thus constructively depriving defendants of the right itself.

When alternative interpretations of a constitutional provision are possible, the Court should adopt the interpretation that will strengthen the democratic process and safeguard the Constitution's underlying values, including decentralization, federalism, separation of powers, self-determination, and bottom-up lawmaking. On the other hand, the Court should not manufacture ambiguity where it does not exist, and instead should strive to ascribe a meaning that the text and its original purpose(s) can reasonably support. As an example, consider the Due Process Clause of the Fourteenth Amendment.

No state shall deprive any person of life, liberty, or property, without due process of law

The Fourteenth Amendment's plain language leaves little room to debate its meaning: the state may not deprive citizens of life, liberty, or property unless the state provides appropriate procedures to guard against the arbitrary deprivation of these rights. Accordingly, the phrase "due process of law" qualifies the preceding language and therefore protects procedural, not substantive, rights. Citizens may challenge state action under the amendment by arguing that the state's procedures were inadequate, and courts may disagree on whether the procedures adopted in a given case provide "due process of law." On the other hand, a plain reading of the Fourteenth Amendment undercuts the assertion that it can be a legitimate source of substantive constitutional rights.

To be sure, the Fourteenth Amendment's meaning would change if it only stated that "No state shall deprive any person of life, liberty or property." In this situation, courts might disagree about whether life, liberty, or property encompasses various rights, such as abortion. But that is not what the Fourteenth Amendment says. If citizens want to change the language of the Fourteenth Amendment, they can do so by amending the constitution.

Also, inferring substantive rights from the Fourteenth Amendment leads to an entirely illogical result. If, as the Court held in *Griswold v. Connecticut*, the Fourteenth Amendment protects a right to privacy, then the Court is essentially saying that no processes whatsoever could be sufficient to deprive a woman of this right. Under that interpretation, the Court has, as a practical matter, severed the words "due process of law" from the Fourteenth Amendment and transformed its meaning in a manner that is wholly inconsistent with what the Founders intended. Ultimately, when the Court in *Griswold* interpreted the Fourteenth Amendment to protect *substantive* rights to privacy, it ascribed a meaning that the words could not possibly support, *and* it expressly altered the very meaning of the provision. By manipulating the Fourteenth Amendment in this manner, the Court disregarded the constraints on its Article III reviewing authority and gave itself the power to disregard the text in other cases to expand, limit, or create new "rights" as it sees fit.

The so-called "right" of privacy is a perfect example illustrating this point. The word "privacy" is nearly impossible to define with precision and can be interpreted to protect countless new "rights" that bear no relationship, directly or indirectly, to a particular constitutional provision. May a cocaine addict argue that the right to privacy protects his or her choice to use drugs? Can polygamists seek refuge under the right to privacy? Can individuals claim that the right to privacy protects assisted suicide? In answering these questions, it is not sufficient merely to argue that the Court would never venture to construe the language in such an expansive way. One hundred years ago, the same reasoning would have been applied to argue that the Court would never create a right to abortion and a right to same-sex marriage. Well, look where we currently stand. Those rights currently exist even though they resulted from decisions that were as startling in their breadth as they were dishonest in their reasoning. And as the Court drifts further and further away from the text, democracy fades further and further away into the shadows of oligarchy.

This discussion underscores the problem with creating new rights from broadly defined constitutional "penumbras" or from liberty "in its spatial and more transcendent dimensions." In *Roe v. Wade*, *Planned Parenthood v. Casey*, and *Obergefell v. Hodges*, the Court relied in part on the so-called right to privacy to create unenumerated "rights" that were contrary to, rather than consistent with, the language and purpose of the Fourteenth Amendment. That, in a nutshell, is the problem with outcome-based decision making. It creates a nation of men, not laws, who mandate "the liberty of all" from the top down by inventing new rights under the thin and all-too-transparent veneer of constitutional legitimacy. After all, imagine if a state or federal statute was interpreted under the "living constitution" framework. This would allow judges to singlehandedly change the meaning of *any* law based on contemporary norms or the whims of public opinion, and therefore usurp the legislature's lawmaking authority. No reasonable jurist would accept the legitimacy of such an approach, and no intellectually honest jurist should countenance its application when the Justices interpret the United States Constitution.

Whether the text is silent on a particular issue

In some cases, the Constitution provides no guidance whatsoever. For example, not a single provision even remotely addresses whether women have a right to first-trimester abortions, whether citizens have a right to assisted suicide, whether the government may enact a limit of two children per family, or whether the government may require citizens who are HIV positive to disclose this fact to potential sexual partners.

When confronted with such questions, the Court should never rely on living constitutionalism because it would give the Justices nearly unfettered authority to invalidate legislation (or create new rights) based on subjective values. Perhaps the reason for this silence is that the Founders may have neither foreseen nor contemplated a particular right, chosen not to mention a right because it was not deemed worthy of constitutional protection, or believed that those rights not enumerated in the Constitution should be decided by the people democratically. In the vast majority of cases, it will be difficult, if not impossible, to identify the reason. In such a circumstance, the outcome of a decision assumes greater importance because, if the Court decided to hear a case where the text is silent, its decision will have a substantial impact on the structure of governance, including federalism, separation of powers, and the democratic process. As such, the Court should be cautious in its approach and strive to issue decisions that promote a participatory democracy at the state and federal level, that defer to the legislative and executive branches, and that enhance the fairness of the political and electoral process. As discussed later, these concerns should have led the Court in *Citizens United* to uphold the limits on corporate expenditures, to uphold the aggregate limit on individual contributions in *McCutcheon*, to uphold the Line Item Veto Act in *Clinton*, and to allow the abortion right to evolve democratically in *Roe v. Wade*.

Of course, there are exceptions to this rule. First, there may be situations where the legislative and executive branches are unable or unwilling to address a particular issue. For example, in *Shelby County v. Holder*, the Court invalidated Sections Four and Five of the Voting Rights Act, which required states with a history of discrimination against minority voters to seek federal preclearance before enacting changes to their voting laws. The Court's decision was surprising to many, in part because the Senate had previously voted 98–0 to reauthorize the act, making invalidation of the act appear to be an example of judicial overreaching. Notwithstanding, as Justice Antonin Scalia stated during oral argument, Congress was incapable of addressing the act's flaws for fear of political fallout:

> I don't think there is anything to be gained by any Senator to vote against continuation of this act. And I am fairly confident it will be reenacted in perpetuity

> unless – unless a court can say it does not comport with the Constitution . . . *It's – it's a concern that this is not the kind of a question you can leave to Congress.* There are certain districts in the House that are black districts by law just about now. And even the Virginia Senators, they have no interest in voting against this. The State government is not their government, and they are going to lose – they are going to lose votes if they do not reenact the Voting Rights Act. Even the name of it is wonderful: The Voting Rights Act. Who is going to vote against that in the future?[1]

As Justice Scalia noted, had the Court not intervened, the act would have continued in perpetuity, leaving states harmed by potentially unconstitutional provisions without any means by which to seek a legal remedy.

Second, the Court may intervene where dysfunction in the democratic process makes it difficult, if not impossible, for voters to participate in or seek policy changes through the legislature. This can occur in situations where entrenched majorities are so powerful that minority groups have no political power (the "tyranny of the majority"), where states simply refuse to implement laws that are either decided by the people or courts, or where states enact legislation that indirectly eviscerates an established constitutional right.

In *Atkins v. Virginia*, for example, the Court established a categorical ban on the execution of intellectually disabled criminal defendants.[2] The Court held that when determining if a defendant is intellectually disabled, the state should consider the defendant's IQ along with evidence of adaptive and developmental disabilities. Subsequently, the state of Florida enacted a statute requiring, as a condition of proving intellectual disability, that a defendant have an IQ of 70 or below, even though IQ tests have a standard error of measurement of plus or minus 5 points. All defendants with IQs above 70 were eligible for the death penalty, regardless of any other evidence relating to adaptive or developmental disability. The practical effect of Florida's law was that some defendants who would have been considered intellectually disabled under *Atkins* would be executed. In this circumstance, the Court appropriately intervened and held that Florida's law ran afoul of *Atkins* and violated the Eight Amendment's ban on cruel and unusual punishment.

Third, although the Court should invalidate laws that are arbitrary on their face and subject citizens to injustice or deprive them of basic liberties, it should not create constitutional rights that no interpretation of the text, such as the Fourteenth Amendment, can support. This is true, *a fortiori*, because the Ninth Amendment provides that the Constitution should not be interpreted to "deny or disparate other rights *retained* by the people." This language suggests that the Constitution is not the sole source of fundamental rights and that citizens possess additional *unenumerated* rights. Consequently, in limited circumstances, the Ninth Amendment can provide the basis upon which to invalidate arbitrary legislation that infringes on basic civil liberties.

1 See Transcript of Oral Argument at 47–48, Shelby Cty. v. Holder, 133 S. Ct. 2612 (2013) (No. 12-96), available at http://www.supremecourt.gov/oral_arguments/argument_transcripts/12-96_7648.pdf (emphasis added).

2 536 U.S. 304 (2002).

In the majority of cases, these exceptions are not present. As discussed in Chapter 8, when the Court in *Roe v. Wade* created a right to first-trimester abortions, this issue was being hotly contested among legislatures in many states, with some deciding to legalize and others choosing to outlaw abortion. The fact that some states did not legalize abortion, by itself, was not a reason to justify the Court's intervention, and certainly not the ultimate decision. That is the essence of the democratic process – some citizens win, and some lose, and all citizens have the right to continually seek policy changes through the legislature.

Likewise, when the Court decided *Obergefell v. Hodges* and created a right to same-sex marriage, states were debating this issue democratically, and many states, through either the legislature or state Supreme Court, recognized a right to same-sex marriage. By intervening, the Court removed this issue from the democratic process and from the people.

Whether the purpose of a law, when taken together with the language, supports a particular interpretation

The Court should eschew reliance on living constitutionalism to issue decisions that contravene the purpose of a law or constitutional provision. Consider the following hypothetical statute as an example:

> Citizens are prohibited from smoking cigarettes in a public place. Violations will result in a fine of $500.00.

Note: For the purposes of this example, assume that the aim of this provision was to protect citizens from the dangers of secondhand smoke.

Courts interpreting this provision will encounter ambiguity only in determining whether a citizen was smoking a cigarette in a public place. For example, if a person smokes a cigarette inside of their car while parked in a deserted lot, are they in a public place? Courts may disagree about this while also maintaining consistency with the purpose of the statute. By the same token, what if someone is smoking a pipe in a crowded movie theater? There would be no question that the person was in a public place, but it is not clear whether secondhand smoke from a pipe causes harm to third persons in the same manner as secondhand smoke from a cigarette. Given the statute's language and purpose, how should the Court rule if an individual is fined $500 for smoking a pipe in a public place?

The Court should reverse the conviction. A pipe is not a cigarette. If the legislature intended to include pipes, it could have. Because it did not, the courts have no authority to ascribe a meaning to the word "cigarette" that it will not bear. Some living constitutionalists would argue that the conviction should be upheld because the "spirit" of the law is to protect citizens from the deleterious effects of secondhand smoke, and that a pipe is reasonably equivalent to a cigarette and causes similar harms. A contrary holding would require the courts to rewrite the statute and to make, not interpret, the law in violation of their Article III power. The fact that some living constitutionalists would have no problem with such a result is perhaps the best evidence why living constitutionalism is anathema to the founding principles upon which democracy and decentralization rest: federalism, separation of powers, checks and balances, and bottom-up lawmaking.

Put differently, reversing the conviction would promote judicial restraint and reinforce a basic principle of constitutional interpretation. When determining the meaning of a law or constitutional provision, courts must consider the words as evidence of the statute's purpose and not ascribe to the words a meaning that they cannot support, even if such meaning would arguably further the statute's purpose, and certainly not if a court thinks it should be interpreted to reach a desirable outcome. In the previous example, perhaps a court would have reached a better outcome if it affirmed the defendant's conviction. But the Court has no power to reach this conclusion; affirming the conviction would constitute an abuse of that power. This is why the process of decision making is vitally important. If courts reached whatever conclusions they deemed most desirable, they would slowly erode the fabric of American constitutional democracy and concentrate power in the only branch of government that is not elected and not accountable to the people. The following diagram summarizes the interplay between living constitutionalism and originalism, including when the use of either theory is inappropriate.

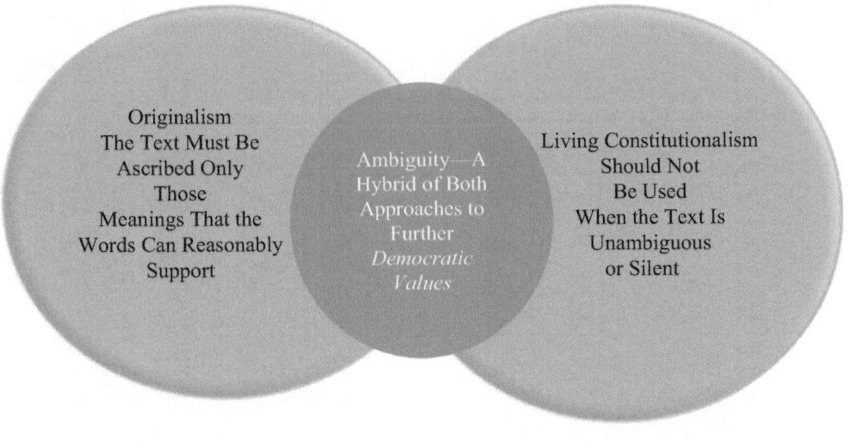

As discussed in the chapters that follow, the debate between living constitutionalism and originalism has profound implications for the fundamental values on which democracy is based: decentralization, federalism, separation of powers, checks and balances, and bottom-up lawmaking. Before proceeding to those chapters, up next are the constitutional provisions that are examined in this book and that have been the subject of substantial disagreement among the Justices.

PART I

The cases that prohibited the legislative and executive branches from remedying corruption and unfairness in the political and democratic process

We can have democracy in this country, or we can have great wealth concentrated in the hands of a few, but we can't have both.

—Louis D. Brandeis

1

CITIZENS UNITED V. FEC

Congress shall make no law respecting an establishment of religion, or prohibiting the free exercise thereof; or abridging the freedom of speech, or of the press; or the right of the people peaceably to assemble, and to petition the government for a redress of grievances.

—United States Constitution, Amend. I

Summary

- The Court's opinion in *Citizens United* created a First Amendment hierarchy that favored the wealthy and enabled them to have disproportionate influence in the democratic process.
- The Court's opinion is contrary to, rather than consistent with, the First Amendment's original purposes and embraces individual liberty over collective liberty.
- The Court should have deferred to the coordinate branches' policy decision, or refused to grant *certiorari*, because the First Amendment's text did not address the issue of whether corporations were speakers or whether speech was money.
- Ironically, a different outcome in *Citizens United* would not have remedied an inherent flaw in free societies: democracy and equality are not compatible.
- The Court should embrace a jurisprudence that links processes with outcomes by rooting decisions in a reasonable interpretation of the text, narrowly defining rights, and preferring severance over invalidation of a law in its entirety.

***

Introduction

Many commentators criticize the Court's decision in *Citizens United*, arguing that it inflicted substantial damage to the integrity of the democratic process.[1] In a 5–4 decision,

1 The quoted material in this chapter is taken from Citizens United v. Federal Election Commission, 558 U.S. 310 (2010).

the Court invalidated a law that strove to reduce the influence of money in politics and equalize all speakers' ability to meaningfully influence and gain access to public officials. At first glance, *Citizens United* appears to have enshrined inequality into the democratic process because the Court's holding allows corporations to use general treasury funds to make independent expenditures to political candidates. This gives some corporations a louder – and more powerful – voice in the electoral and political process, provides corporations with favored access to elected officials, and renders the votes of millions of citizens at the ballot box more symbolic than real.

Perhaps the most problematic aspect of *Citizens United* was the Court's interference with the coordinate branch's ability to rectify the corruption and inequality that plague state and federal elections. The Court should have deferred to the legislative and executive branches' judgment, as both branches were intimately familiar with the problem the law sought to address (i.e., corruption) and because the text of the First Amendment was indeterminate, in that it did not conclusively resolve the questions whether corporations should be considered speakers or whether money constitutes speech. In the face of textual ambiguities, the salutary and pro-democracy objectives that the law furthered, and the coordinate branches' familiarity with the issue, the Court should have refused to grant *certiorari*. In so doing, the Court would have safeguarded its institutional legitimacy and permitted the people's elected representatives to define constitutional meaning where the textual provision is susceptible to differing interpretations.

***

The decision

In *Citizens United*, a nonprofit organization challenged §203 of the Bipartisan Campaign Reform Act of 2002. The act prohibited "corporations and unions from using their general treasury funds to make independent expenditures for speech that is an 'electioneering communication' or for speech that expressly advocates the election or defeat of a candidate."[2] An electioneering communication was defined as "any broadcast, cable, or satellite communication" that "refers to a clearly identified candidate for Federal office" and is made within 30 days of a primary election.[3] The act also provided that the communication must be "publicly distributed," which in "the case of a candidate for nomination for President" means that the communication "[c]an be received by 50,000 or more persons in a State where a primary election . . . is being held within 30 days."[4]

By way of background, in *Austin v. Michigan Chamber of Commerce* the Court had previously upheld limits on electioneering, reasoning that "political speech may be banned based on the speaker's corporate identity."[5] In *Citizens United*, however, the Court overruled *Austin* and held that the act violated the corporation's First Amendment rights. The Court based its decision on three grounds.

2 Id. at 318–319.
3 Id. at 321.
4 Id.
5 558 U.S. 346.

First, the act constituted an outright ban on speech, and the type of speech that was banned – advertisements and books advocating for political candidates or issues – constituted "classic examples of censorship."[6] The Court noted that

> [a]s a 'restriction on the amount of money a person or group can spend on political communication during a campaign,' that statute 'necessarily reduces the quantity of expression by restricting the number of issues discussed, the depth of their exploration, and the size of the audience reached.'[7]

Second, the Court held that the act would have compromised the integrity of the democratic process. The majority explained that speech "is an essential mechanism of democracy, for it is the means to hold officials accountable to the people" and underscored "[t]he right of citizens to inquire, to hear, to speak, and to use information to reach consensus is a precondition to enlightened self-government and a necessary means to protect it."[8]

Third, the Court rejected the antidistortion rationale enunciated in *Austin*, which upheld limits on electioneering for the purpose of "curb[ing] the political influence of 'those who exercise control over large aggregations of capital.'"[9] In prior cases, Congress had specifically relied on the principle that the "differing structures and purposes" of corporations and unions "may require different forms of regulation in order to protect the integrity of the electoral process."[10] The Court rejected this justification, holding "[t]he fact that speakers may have influence over or access to elected officials does not mean that these officials are corrupt."[11] Writing for the majority, Justice Kennedy stated:

> Favoritism and influence are not . . . avoidable in representative politics. It is in the nature of an elected representative to favor certain policies, and, by necessary corollary, to favor the voters and contributors who support those policies. It is well understood that a substantial and legitimate reason, if not the only reason, to cast a vote for, *or to make a contribution to, one candidate over another is that the candidate will respond by producing those political outcomes the supporter favors.* Democracy is premised on responsiveness.[12]

In so holding, the Court rejected the argument that "the Government has an interest 'in equalizing the relative ability of individuals and groups to influence the outcome of elections.'"[13] The Court explained that the "First Amendment's protections do not

6 Id. at 337.
7 Id. at 339 (quoting Buckley v. Valeo, 424 U.S. 1, 19 (1976)) (per curiam).
8 Id.
9 Id. at 348 (quoting Massachusetts Citizens for Life, Inc., 479 U.S. 238, 249 (1986)) (internal citation omitted) (brackets added).
10 Id. (quoting California Medical Ass'n v. Federal Election Comm'n, 453 U.S. 182, 201 (1981)).
11 Id. at 359.
12 Id. (quoting McConnell v. Federal Election Comm'n, 540 U.S. 93, 297 (2003)) (Kennedy, J., dissenting) (emphasis added).
13 Id. at 350 (quoting Buckley, 424 U.S. at 48).

depend on the speaker's 'financial ability to engage in public discussion.'"[14] As the majority asserted, "the rule that political speech cannot be limited based on a speaker's wealth is a necessary consequence of the premise that the First Amendment generally prohibits the suppression of political speech based on the speaker's identity."[15] In the majority's view, such a result would interfere "with the 'open marketplace' of ideas protected by the First Amendment."[16] For these reasons, the Court held that the only permissible basis upon which Congress can regulate corporate expenditure is to prevent elected officials from securing "a political *quid pro quo [i.e., a bribe]*."[17]

***

Analysis

> *If there was one decision I would overrule, it would be Citizens United. I think the notion that we have all the democracy that money can buy strays so far from what our democracy is supposed to be. So that's No. 1 on my list.*
>
> *The Court's interference with that decision of the political branches seemed to me out of order. The Court should have respected the legislative judgment. Legislators know much more about elections than the Court does. And the same was true of Citizens United. I think members of the legislature, people who have to run for office, know the connection between money and influence on what laws get passed.*

Justice Ruth Bader Ginsburg

The Free Speech Clause of the First Amendment provides that Congress "shall make no law . . . abridging the freedom of speech."[18] On its face, this broadly phrased language is ambiguous because reasonable jurists would likely disagree regarding whether a law "abridges" speech. For example, does an abridgment of speech occur if the government regulates the time, place, and manner in which speech is disseminated? Does the government abridge speech by outlawing the manufacture and sale of violent video games? In fact, what constitutes "speech"? Does speech refer merely to verbal utterances on matters of political and social importance, or does speech encompass nonverbal expressions, such as campaign contributions? Additionally, who qualifies as a speaker? Must the speaker be an individual or group, or do speakers include corporate entities?

Given the First's Amendment's ambiguous language, when assessing the constitutionality of §203 the Court had three options at its disposal. First, the Court could have refused to grant *certiorari* and deferred to the coordinate branches. Second, the Court could have upheld the act on the ground that it prevented corporations from gaining undue access to and influence over elected officials and therefore preserved the integrity of the electoral process. Third, the Court could have invalidated the act by holding that the First Amendment protects corporations as speakers, that corporate expenditures constitute speech, and that restricting such expenditures constitutes

14 Id. (quoting Buckley, 424 U.S. at 49).
15 Id.
16 Id. at 354 (quoting New York State Bd. of Elections v. Lopez Torres, 552 U.S. 196, 208 (2008)).
17 Id. at 356 (quoting Buckley, 424 U.S. at 26) (emphasis added) (brackets added).
18 See U.S. Const., Amend. I.

an impermissible abridgment of a corporation's free speech rights. If the Court had chosen either of the first two options, corporations would not have had the ability to rely on expenditures to gain political favoritism, and corruption (or the appearance thereof) in the political process would have been reduced. Unfortunately, by choosing the third option, the Court: (1) enshrined inequality and favoritism into democracy; (2) diminished the practical value of most citizens' free speech rights; and (3) undermined the original purpose of the First Amendment. What's worse, an examination of the historical record leading to the First Amendment's adoption reveals that the Court's decision was inconsistent with the amendment's original purposes.

The original purpose of the First Amendment

> *Democracy must be built through open societies that share information. When there is information, there is enlightenment. When there is debate, there are solutions. When there is no sharing of power, no rule of law, no accountability, there is abuse, corruption, subjugation and indignation.*
>
> —Atifete Jahjaga

The historical record reveals that the First Amendment is designed to further two core purposes: decentralization and uninhibited debate on matters of political and social importance.

Decentralization

A primary purpose underlying the First Amendment is to effectuate decentralized governance and therefore give each state the authority to determine the scope of free speech protections:

> The Founders believed that they could ensure individual liberty by limiting the federal government's power, leaving as the domain of the states all but the categories of federal authority specifically enumerated in the Constitution. *They counted on the states to maintain this allocation – to combat centralization – through the political process.* The Framers of the Bill of Rights well understood that the states' ability to perform this role depended crucially upon First Amendment protection from federal government censorship.[19]

The focus on decentralization underscores the Founders' broader view that the Constitution's *structural* constraints were inextricably linked to achieving individual and collective liberty:

> From the Founding to the Civil War, the purpose and effect of the First Amendment was to leave regulation of speech to the states. This particular concern with

19 David Yassky, Eras of the First Amendment, 91 COLUM. L. REV. 1699, 1713 (1991) (emphasis added).

> the power of the central government reflected the larger theory of the Founders. In the original constitutional vision, *liberty was tied to the independence of the states*. This theory was embedded in the constitutional structure. The separation of powers, the enumeration of powers in Article I, Section 8, and the Bill of Rights all aimed at checking the federal government, thereby ensuring that states would remain the primary loci of lawmaking authority.[20]

In this way, "[t]he First Amendment was a central component of the federal structure," as it "protected not only the rights of individual citizens, but also the prerogatives of the states, and, most important, the vitality of the state-based political process."[21]

Uninhibited speech on matters of political and social importance

In *Snyder v. Phelps*, the Court emphasized that the First Amendment is designed to effectuate robust public debate and the free expression of diverse viewpoints. Writing for the majority, Chief Justice Roberts stated that "speech on 'matters of public concern' . . . is 'at the heart of the First Amendment's protection,'" and that the right to freely express one's views reflects "a profound national commitment to the principle that debate on public issues should be uninhibited, robust, and wide-open."[22] Stated simply, speech "concerning public affairs is . . . the essence of self-government," and therefore "occupies the highest rung of the hierarchy of First Amendment values, and is entitled to special protection."[23] In essence, the Founders were mindful of protecting unpopular, offensive, and distasteful speech, which they viewed as essential to creating a vibrant marketplace of ideas where all views could be expressed without the fear of suppression or reprisal. As a result, the state or federal government may not, among other things, restrict speech on the basis of its content or a disagreement with the speaker's point of view.

The Court's decision in light of the First Amendment's original purposes

Given the First Amendment's indeterminate language, the correctness of the Court's conclusion must be considered in light of its core purposes: to effectuate decentralization and foster the robust and uninhibited exchange of ideas on matters of political, social, and economic import. Against this backdrop, the Court's holding that corporations are speakers and that money is speech is inconsistent with the First Amendment's original purposes.

20 Id. at 1711–1713 (emphasis added).

21 Id.

22 562 U.S. 443, 451–452 (2011) (quoting Dun & Bradstreet, Inc. v. Greenmoss Builders, Inc., 472 U.S. 749, 758–759 (1985) (plurality opinion) (internal citation omitted); New York Times, Co., v. Sullivan, 376 U.S. 254, 270 (1964)).

23 Id. at 452 (quoting Garrison v. Louisiana, 479 U.S. 64, 74–75 (1964); Connick v. Myers, 461 U.S. 138, 145 (1983)) (internal quotation marks omitted).

Regarding decentralization, although the statute at issue in *Citizens United* was enacted at the federal rather than state level, the principles underlying decentralization nonetheless counseled in favor of upholding the restrictions on corporate expenditures. The primary concern underlying decentralization is to ensure that the federal government does not impermissibly infringe on the powers reserved to the states and the people. The Founders believed that the federal government's authority should be limited to the powers expressly enumerated in the Constitution and that all other power was reserved to the states and their citizens. In the First Amendment context, this arguably means that the states should have the authority to determine the scope of free speech protection, particularly in light of the unique policy concerns confronting different states.

The Court's decision disregarded the decentralization rationale in its entirety, in substantial part because of the incorporation doctrine, which states that certain provisions in the Bill of Rights, although initially applicable only to the federal government, are also binding on the states. The First Amendment is one of several provisions in the Bill of Rights that the Court has incorporated into the states. As a practical matter, therefore, the Court's holding that corporations were speakers, that money was speech, and that preventing unfair access to and influence in government did not justify restrictions on corporate expenditures materially interfered with every state's ability to regulate corporate speech. After *Citizens United*, no state may enact legislation that distinguishes between corporations and individuals as speakers, that differentiates between expenditures and "pure" speech, or that is dedicated to reducing unfair access to and influence in the political process. Thus, the Court's decision in *Citizens United* did not merely prevent the federal government from eradicating the actual or apparent corruption that corporate expenditures engender. It prohibited *all* states from enacting legislation to address corruption or, at the least, favoritism, in the *states'* electoral processes.

Concerning the interest in fostering a robust marketplace of ideas, the Court's decision inhibited, rather than facilitated, a diverse and free exchange of viewpoints. The Court allowed the "voices" of wealthy corporations to be so influential that it effectively diminished the power, impact, and influence of other citizens' voices. At bottom, the Court's decision transformed the marketplace of ideas into a forum that favored the most powerful speakers over the most vulnerable and that accorded political influence to those with the most resources, not necessarily the best ideas.

It was precisely for this reason that the Court's pre–*Citizens United* decisions upheld legislation that sought to address the undue access and influence that large corporate contributions can purchase. In *McConnell*, for example, the Court stated as follows:

> We have repeatedly sustained legislation aimed at "the corrosive and distorting effects of *immense aggregations of wealth that are accumulated with the help of the corporate form* and that have little or no correlation to the public's support for the corporation's political ideas."[24]

The Court's rationale in *McConnell* should have persuaded the majority in *Citizens United* to hold that the interest in equalizing speakers' voices ensures that the diverse

24 McConnell, 540 U.S. at 205 (internal citations omitted; emphasis added).

and divergent voices of all citizens meaningfully contribute to public discourse. As Justice John Paul Stevens argued in dissenting from the majority's holding, "[a] democracy cannot function effectively when its constituent members believe laws are being bought and sold," because such a perception compromises "the integrity of the marketplace of political ideas."[25] In failing to adopt this rationale, the Court undermined the First Amendment's original purposes and enshrined inequality into the electoral process because substantial monetary contributions are the vehicle by which corporations obtain access to politicians that ordinary citizens cannot. At bottom, no democracy can flourish in a system that entrenches inequality into the fabric of public debate or that countenances political favoritism on the basis of wealth and privilege.

Admittedly, a contrary holding in *Citizens United* would have restricted the speech of only one particular group – corporations – based solely on its identity. The Court deemed such restriction a violation of the First Amendment:

> The Government may commit a constitutional wrong when by law it identifies certain preferred speakers. By taking the right to speak from some and giving it to others, the Government deprives the disadvantaged person or class of the right to use speech to strive to establish worth, standing, and respect for the speaker's voice. The Government may not by these means deprive the public of the right and privilege to determine for itself what speech and speakers are worthy of consideration. The First Amendment protects speech and speaker, and the ideas that flow from each.[26]

This argument is flawed because the law at issue in *Citizens United* did not involve "taking the right to speak from some and giving it to others."[27] Rather, the powerful influence of "substantial aggregations of wealth" on the electoral process (and elected officials) compromises middle and low-income voters' ability to "use speech to strive to establish worth, standing, and respect for the speaker's voice."[28] After all, few could credibly argue that corporations are a "disadvantaged person or class."[29] If anything, the Court's decision ensured that the already-disadvantaged class (middle- and low-income voters) would remain disadvantaged – and all but disenfranchised.

Favoritism in the political process v. *quid pro quo* corruption

The Court should have reaffirmed *Austin*'s antidistortion rationale, which was affirmed in *McConnell v. FEC*, where the Court held that "[w]e have not limited [the anticorruption] interest to the elimination of cash-for-votes exchanges."[30] Before *McConnell*, the Court in *Buckley* likewise concluded that Congress could "legitimately conclude that the avoidance of the appearance of improper influence is also critical . . . if

25 Citizens United, 558 U.S. at 453 (Stevens, J., dissenting).
26 Id. at 340–341.
27 Id. at 340.
28 Id. at 437 (Stevens, J., dissenting); Id. at 340.
29 Id. at 340.
30 540 U.S. at 95.

confidence in the system of representative Government is not to be eroded to a disastrous extent."[31]

When corporations use money to gain influence over elected officials, it can lead to the very evil – *corruption* – that Congress sought to proscribe. Ironically, although the Court held that Congress could regulate speech to prevent *quid pro quo* corruption, the decision actually *disincentivized* political actors from *ever* taking bribes because the majority's opinion countenanced a softer yet equally effective form of corruption – using money to indirectly *purchase* votes.

Common sense supports this proposition. After all, given the extraordinarily high cost of running for elected office, politicians will, at least in some instances, make policy decisions to benefit the donors who have funded their campaigns, including those who offer substantial contributions. For example, if the National Rifle Association donates $150,000 to a senatorial candidate, one would expect that the candidate, if elected, will vote "No" on legislation seeking to regulate the purchase and sale of handguns.

The problem with this type of governance, which *Citizens United* expressly endorsed, is that elected representatives become loyal to a small fraction of wealthy donors rather than to the people writ large. As a practical matter, elected officials enter office not free to vote their conscience on matters of social and public policy, but obligated to return "favors" to the donors who are in substantial part responsible for their election. This renders government less democratic and transparent, and transforms democracy into a plutocracy driven by a codependency between elected officials and wealthy donors. The following table lists the top ten donors of presidential candidate Hillary Clinton's campaign.

"Person"	*Amount*
1 Soros Fund Management	$7,039,000
2 Laborers Union	$4,000,250
3 Euclidean Capital	$3,502,700
4 Pritzker Group	$2,814,343
5 Saban Capital Group	$2,531,995
6 Paloma Partners	$2,505,400
7 Herb & Marion Sandler/Sandler Foundation	$2,502,700
8 Women's Self-Worth Foundation	$2,502,700
9 Priorities USA/Priorities USA Action	$2,151,000
10 Newsweb Corp	$2,013,500

The upshot is that the votes of average citizens at the ballot box are more symbolic than real, depriving them of power and a government that should be for and by the people. Justice John Paul Stevens echoed these sentiments in *Citizens United*, stating that Congress has "a compelling constitutional basis, if not . . . a democratic duty, to take measures designed to guard against the potentially harmful effects of corporate spending in local and national races."[32] Moreover, preventing Congress from regulat-

31 424 U.S. at 27.
32 558 U.S. at 394.

ing corporate speech "threaten[ed] to undermine the integrity of elected institutions across the Nation."[33] Put simply, unfair access to and influence over elected officials is a form of corruption.

Corporations are "people" and therefore speakers under the First Amendment

The Court erred by failing to make a distinction, for First Amendment purposes, between corporations and individuals. In so doing, the Court disregarded its prior holding in *First National Bank of Boston v. Belotti*, where the majority suggested that "a corporation's right to speak on issues of general public interest implies no comparable right in the quite different context of participation in a political campaign for election to public office."[34] This is true, *a fortiori*, when one considers the effect of corporate speech on the integrity and fairness of the electoral process.

Of course, some may argue that the Court's decision was a paradigmatic example of process-based reasoning. If the Court was truly focused on reaching a desirable outcome, it certainly would have upheld the restrictions, and therefore furthered principles of democratic governance. By refusing to do so, the Court eschewed a desirable outcome in favor of a decision that respected First Amendment values.

This argument lacks merit because it misperceives the interplay between process-based decision making and pragmatic considerations. As stated earlier, an intellectually honest interpretation of the Constitution does not mean that the Court can *never* consider the utility of a particular outcome. This is especially true when, as in *Citizens United*, the text is ambiguous. After all, not a single word in the First Amendment supports the conclusion that corporations should be regarded as people. In addition, neither the underlying purposes of the First Amendment nor the history leading to its adoption suggests that the Founders intended corporations to be regarded as speakers. Given these facts, why would the Court construe constitutional ambiguity in a manner that undermined fairness in the electoral process, that allowed corporations to have undue influence in governance, and that transformed the marketplace of ideas into a monopoly of ideas?

***

Questions

Should Citizens United have been decided differently? Was the outcome in Citizens United correct but the reasoning erroneous? If so, write the opinion.

Should money be considered speech?

33 Id. at 396 (brackets added).
34 435 U.S. 765, 788, fn. 26 (1978).

Should corporations be considered persons under the First Amendment?

The majority based its holding in substantial part on the fact that it furthered, rather than undermined, the democratic process. Given the effects of money in politics, how can this conclusion be justified?

2

MCCUTCHEON V. FEC

Congress shall make no law respecting an establishment of religion, or prohibiting the free exercise thereof; or abridging the freedom of speech, or of the press; or the right of the people peaceably to assemble, and to petition the government for a redress of grievances.
—United States Constitution, Amend. I

Summary

- In *McCutcheon*, the Court invalidated a portion of the Bipartisan Campaign Reform Act of 1971 that set aggregate limits on individual contributions to political candidates.
- The Court held that Congress may only regulate contributions to prevent *quid pro quo* corruption and held that restrictions designed to prevent individuals from gaining access to and influence over public officials was not permissible.
- The Court held that Congress may not restrict speech for the purpose of equalizing speakers' voices.
- After *McCutcheon*, wealthy individuals will continue to have disproportionate influence in the political process and gain favored access to elected officials, therefore compromising the integrity of lawmaking institutions.

***

Introduction

In *McCutcheon*, a plurality of the Court prohibited Congress from remedying "soft" corruption in the political process (i.e., undue access to and influence over elected officials), and in so doing undermined the integrity of democratic decision making and compromised the core purpose of the First Amendment.[1] In a 5–4 decision, the Court

1 The quoted material in this chapter is taken from McCutcheon v. Federal Election Commission, 572 U.S., 134 S. Ct. 1434 (2014).

held that the interest in preventing wealthy individuals from gaining unfair access to or influence over elected officials did not justify aggregate spending limits on individual contributions. As a result, the Court adopted an overly narrow definition of corruption and sanctioned a governance structure in which elected officials are accountable to a small percentage of wealthy donors, not ordinary citizens. Consequently, the plurality's decision in *McCutcheon* contributed to political inequality by making it harder for ordinary citizens to meaningfully participate in democracy, and made it likely that the influence of money, not the strength of ideas, would continue to undermine the fairness and integrity of the electoral process.

***

The decision

The *McCutcheon* Court addressed whether limits on aggregate contributions by individuals, which was first passed in the Federal Election Campaign Act of 1971 and amended by the Bipartisan Campaign Reform Act of 2002, violated the First Amendment. Specifically, in the 2013–2014 election cycle, the act permitted individuals "to contribute up to $2,600 per election to a candidate ($5,200 total for the primary and general elections); $32,400 per year to a national party committee."[2] The base limits also "apply with equal force to contributions that are 'in any way earmarked or otherwise directed through an intermediary or conduit' to a candidate."[3]

In a 5–4 decision, the Court held that this provision prevented individuals "from fully contributing to the primary and general election campaigns of ten or more candidates."[4] Writing for the majority, Chief Justice John Roberts began his analysis by emphasizing that the First Amendment applies equally to all citizens, regardless of whether the individual is "on the one hand, a 'lone pamphleteer [] or street corner orator [] in the Tom Paine mold,' or is, on the other, someone who spends 'substantial amounts of money in order to communicate [his] political ideas through sophisticated' means."[5]

Chief Justice Roberts explained that an "aggregate limit on *how many* candidates and committees an individual may support through contributions is not a 'modest restraint' [on speech] at all."[6] Furthermore, the "Government may no more restrict how many candidates or causes a donor may support than it may tell a newspaper how many candidates it may endorse."[7] In so holding, Chief Justice Roberts rejected the argument that the interest in equalizing free speech supported aggregate limits on individual contributions:

> We have consistently rejected attempts to suppress campaign speech based on other legislative objectives. No matter how desirable it may seem, it is not an acceptable governmental objective to 'level the playing field,' or to 'level electoral

2 Id. at 1442.
3 Id.
4 Id. at 1438.
5 Id. at 1448 (internal citations omitted) (brackets in original).
6 Id. (emphasis in original) (brackets in original).
7 Id.

> opportunities,' or to 'equaliz[e] the financial resources of candidates' . . . The First Amendment prohibits such legislative attempts to 'fine-tun[e]' the electoral process, no matter how well intentioned . . . As we framed the relevant principle in *Buckley*, 'the concept that government may restrict the speech of some elements of our society in order to enhance the relative voice of others is wholly foreign to the First Amendment.'[8]

Put simply, the desire to equalize speakers' voices rests on an impermissible "legislative . . . determination that particular speech is useful to the democratic process."[9]

Chief Justice Roberts also held that Congress may only restrict contributions for the purpose of "preventing corruption or its appearance," and *not* to prohibit individuals from influencing elected officials.[10] For Chief Justice Roberts, "the possibility that an individual who spends large sums may garner 'influence over or access to elected officials or political parties' does not justify a restriction on speech."[11] As such, "the Government may not seek to limit the appearance of *mere* influence or access" because access or influence alone "will not cause the electorate to lose faith in our democracy."[12] In Chief Justice Roberts's view, this approach was consistent with the principle that the Court should "err on the side of protecting political speech rather than suppressing it."[13]

As a result, Congress may not prevent individuals from "[s]pending large sums of money in connection with elections" if it is "not in connection with an effort to control the exercise of an officeholder's duties."[14] Instead, Congress may only restrict corporate expenditures to prevent *quid pro quo corruption* (i.e., bribes), or the "appearance of corruption stemming from public awareness of the opportunities for abuse inherent in a regime of large individual financial contributions."[15]

***

Analysis

> *I regard freedom of expression as the primary right without which one cannot have a proper functioning democracy.*
>
> —Lord Hailsham

Like *Citizens United*, the Court's decision has deeply troubling implications for the political and democratic process because it failed to recognize that wealth has a subversive effect on federal elections. Indeed, by prohibiting Congress from imposing

8 Id. at 1450 (quoting Arizona Free Enterprise Club's Freedom Club PAC v. Bennett, 564 U.S., 131 S. Ct. 2806, 2825–2826 (2011)).
9 Id. at 1449.
10 Id. at 1441.
11 Id. at 1451 (quoting Citizens United, 588 U.S. at 359).
12 Id.
13 Id. (quoting Federal Election Comm'n v. Wisconsin Right to Life, 551 U.S. 449, 457 (2007)).
14 Id. at 1450.
15 Id. (internal citation omitted).

aggregate contribution limits to reduce unequal access to and influence in the political process, the Court prohibited Congress from addressing a pervasive form of corruption that extends beyond the *quid pro quo*. As a result, elections will continue to be dominated by wealth, inequality, and favoritism and the voices of ordinary citizens will remain silent.

The unfair access and influence problem – again

The biggest flaw in *McCutcheon* was the Court's conclusion that the interest in preventing undue influence over and access to elected representatives was not sufficiently compelling to justify aggregate individual contribution limits. Contrary to the Court's reasoning, undue influence and access *is* a form of corruption because it compromises the integrity of elections and gives wealthy donors disproportionate influence over elected officials.

In his dissenting opinion, Justice Stephen Breyer correctly argued that corruption is properly "understood not only as *quid pro quo* bribery, but as privileged access to and pernicious influence upon elected representatives."[16] Justice Breyer recognized that the "justification for aggregate contribution restrictions is strongly rooted in the need to assure political integrity and ultimately in the First Amendment itself," particularly because the "threat to that integrity posed by the risk of special access and influence remains real."[17] At bottom, Justice Breyer understood that corruption extends to an unspoken relationship between an individual donor and elected representative: the purpose of a contribution is not to advocate for a candidate or an idea. It is to purchase a vote regarding policies that matter to the donor, not necessarily citizens writ large.

Instead of permitting Congress to implement a solution that addressed this threat, the plurality's decision "substitute[d] judges' understandings of how the political process works for the understanding of Congress; [and] . . . fail[ed] to recognize the difference between influence resting upon public opinion and influence bought by money alone."[18]

Undermining the original purposes of the First Amendment – again

In *McCutcheon*, the plurality summarized its view of the First Amendment – and citizen participation in democracy – as follows:

> The First Amendment 'is designed and intended to remove governmental restraints from the arena of public discussion, putting the decision as to what views shall be voiced largely into the hands of each of us . . . in the belief that no other approach would comport with the premise of individual dignity and choice upon which our political system rests.'[19]

16 Id. at 1469 (Breyer, J., dissenting).
17 Id. at 1480.
18 Id. at 1481 (brackets added).
19 Id. at 1448 (quoting Cohen v. California, 403 U.S. 15, 24 (1971)).

The majority emphasized that "the First Amendment safeguards an *individual's right to participate* in the public debate through political expression and political association."[20] On an abstract level, the Court is correct because restrictions that are applied to a discrete group of citizens (i.e., wealthy individuals) necessarily limit their ability to fully exercise the right to free speech. As a practical matter, however, the majority's decision created a "speech hierarchy" that gave a dominant "voice" to a small percentage of wealthy citizens and diminished the voices of middle- and lower-income citizens nationwide. In so doing, the majority's decision frustrates, rather than furthers, First Amendment values because it countenanced a system where money, not true political speech, is the door through which access and influence are obtained.

***

Questions

Should Congress be allowed to regulate speech for the purpose of preventing access to or influence over public officials?

Should the Court be more willing to defer to congressional attempts to remedy flaws in the democratic process? If so, what standards should be used to determine whether deference is appropriate in a given case?

Do the text and original purpose of the First Amendment contemplate that speakers' messages will have similar influence, or just merely guarantee the right to speech, regardless of effect?

20 Id.

3

CLINTON V. NEW YORK

> *Every Bill which shall have passed the House of Representatives and the Senate, shall, before it become a Law, be presented to the President of the United States: If he approve he shall sign it, but if not he shall return it, with his Objections to that House in which it shall have originated, who shall enter the Objections at large on their Journal, and proceed to reconsider it. If after such Reconsideration two thirds of that House shall agree to pass the Bill, it shall be sent, together with the Objections, to the other House, by which it shall likewise be reconsidered, and if approved by two thirds of that House, it shall become a Law.*
>
> —U.S. Const., Art I., Sec. 7, Cl. 1 ("The Presentment Clause")

Summary

- In *Clinton*, the Court invalidated the Line Item Veto Act and prohibited the coordinate branches from experimenting with a solution that would have reduced wasteful government spending.
- The Court should have deferred to the coordinate branches' judgment because the text of Article I, Section 7 of the Constitution (the Presentment Clause) was ambiguous, and therefore did not compel the Court to invalidate a workable solution that promoted fiscal responsibility.
- The Court's decision is arguably inconsistent with its prior decisions regarding Congress's power to delegate lawmaking powers to federal agencies.

***

Introduction

In *Clinton*, the Supreme Court invalidated the Line Item Veto Act even though the language of Article I, Section 7 – the Presentment Clause – was ambiguous on its face and therefore did not necessarily support invalidating the act.[1] In the face of such ambiguity, the Court should have (1) refused to grant *certiorari*; or (2) upheld the act, deferred to the coordinate branches' judgment, and placed a substantial emphasis on the fact that the Line Item Veto enhanced fiscal accountability in government. By failing to do so, the Court undermined the coordinate branches' ability to experiment with solutions to problems that the Founders did not foresee and that the Presentment Clause did not prohibit.

***

The decision

The Line Item Veto Act provided the president with the "power to 'cancel in whole' three types of provisions that have been signed into law: '(1) any dollar amount of discretionary budget authority; (2) any item of new direct spending; or (3) any limited tax benefit.' "[2] The act also provided that, when selecting items for "cancellation" the president "must consider the legislative history, the purposes, and other relevant information about the items."[3] Specifically, the president must determine that a cancellation will "(i) reduce the Federal budget deficit; (ii) not impair any essential Government functions; and (iii) not harm the national interest."[4] Upon cancelling a particular spending item, the president was required to notify Congress, which had the authority to issue "a 'disapproval bill' " that would render the cancellation "null and void."[5]

The Court invalidated the cancellation provision despite acknowledging that "[a]lthough the Constitution expressly authorizes the President to play a role in the process of enacting statutes, it is silent on the subject of unilateral Presidential action that either repeals or amends parts of duly enacted statutes."[6] Thus, reasonable minds could differ regarding the permissibility of allowing the president to cancel a provision in a ***duly enacted*** law. Despite this ambiguity, the Court invalidated the act, stating as follows:

> There are powerful reasons for construing constitutional silence on this profoundly important issue as equivalent to an express prohibition. The procedures governing the enactment of statutes set forth in the text of Article I were the product of the great debates and compromises that produced the Constitution itself. Familiar historical materials provide abundant support for the conclusion that the power to enact statutes may only "be exercised in accord with a single, finely wrought and exhaustively considered, procedure."[7]

1 The quoted material in this chapter is taken from Clinton v. New York, 524 U.S. 417 (1998).
2 Id. at 436 (quoting 2 U.S.C. §691(a)).
3 Id.
4 Id.
5 Id. at 436–437 (quoting 2 U.S.C. §691(d)).
6 Id. at 439.
7 Id. at 439–440 (quoting INS v. Chadha 462 U.S. 919, 951 (1983)).

In the Court's view, because the president's cancellation powers resulted in "truncated versions of two bills that passed both Houses of Congress," they failed to comply with "the 'finely wrought' procedure that the Framers designed."[8]

***

Analysis

> *There is hardly a political question in the United States which does not sooner or later turn into a judicial one.*
>
> —Alexis de Tocqueville

In *Clinton*, the legislative and executive branches collectively agreed on a solution that would have addressed a persistent and seemingly intractable problem (excessive spending) and fostered fiscal responsibility and accountability in governance. By invalidating the act, the Court overstepped its reviewing authority and undermined the separation of powers, a result not compelled by the ambiguous language in Article I, Section 7. Given this ambiguity, the Court should have deferred to the coordinate branches on a matter that was uniquely within their expertise.

Textual ambiguity supports deference, not intervention

At the outset, the majority conceded that "[m]any members of both major political parties who have served in the Legislative and the Executive Branches have long advocated the enactment of such procedures for the purpose of 'ensur[ing] greater fiscal accountability in Washington.'"[9] In fact, the Court acknowledged that the Constitution was *silent* on whether the cancellation provision was constitutional, yet nonetheless proceeded to invalidate bipartisan legislation that strove to remedy a pervasive problem affecting the national economy.

Accordingly, the Court should have exercised restraint and afforded the coordinate branches sufficient latitude to experiment with a solution that made government work better for the people. Instead, the Court's decision ensured that the wasteful spending of taxpayer money would continue, not cease, just as in *Citizens United*, where the Court's decision enabled wealthy corporations to continue dominating the electoral process.

The Court's fidelity to the text is the product of convenience rather than conviction. In other cases, such as *Griswold v. Connecticut* and *Roe v. Wade*, the Court manipulated the Constitution's text to reach desired outcomes – and to expand or create new unenumerated rights – that no honest reading of the Fourteenth Amendment could support. Considering its outcome-focused approach in cases such as *Griswold* and *Roe*, it is odd that the Court would rely so heavily on ambiguous language in the text to reach such an undesirable outcome. As Justice Scalia stated in his dissenting

8 Id. at 440.
9 Id. at 447 (internal citation omitted).

opinion, the Presentment Clause (Art. I, Section 7) "does not demand the result the Court reaches."[10] The majority missed an opportunity to promote a principle that was nowhere to be found in *Griswold*: when the text is ambiguous or subject to alternative but reasonable interpretations, deference to the coordinate branches, in some circumstances, is itself a desirable outcome.

Justice Stephen Breyer echoed these sentiments in his dissenting opinion, emphasizing "the genius of the Framers' *pragmatic* vision, which this Court has long recognized in cases that find constitutional room for necessary *institutional innovation.*"[11] Quoting Chief Justice John Marshall, Breyer stated as follows:

> To have prescribed the means by which government should, in all future time, execute its powers, would have been to change, entirely, the character of the instrument, and give it the properties of a legal code. It would have been an unwise attempt to provide, by immutable rules, for exigencies which, if foreseen at all, must have been seen dimly, and which can be best provided for as they occur.[12]

The Court disregarded Justice Marshall's admonition – and as such government remains less, not more, accountable to the people.

Undermining the separation of powers

Invalidating the Line Item Veto Act undermined separation-of-powers principles, the purpose of which is to provide a "safeguard against the encroachment or aggrandizement of one branch at the expense of the other."[13] Although the Constitution gives the legislature and executive branches enforcement and lawmaking power, respectively, by cancelling a particular provision in already enacted legislation, the president was following and therefore enforcing the law. As Justice Breyer noted in his dissenting opinion:

> [O]ne cannot say that the Act 'encroaches' upon Congress' power, when Congress retained the power to insert, by simple majority, into any future appropriations bill, into any section of any such bill, or into any phrase of any section, a provision that says the Act will not apply.[14]

Equally as important, Congress retained the right to disapprove of the president's cancellations and was not truly ceding lawmaking powers to the executive branch.

Additionally, the Court's decision was arguably inconsistent with precedent holding that Congress may delegate rule-making power to agencies of government. For example, the Court has ruled on numerous occasions that Congress may create and

10 Id. at 464 (Scalia, J., dissenting).
11 Id. at 472 (Breyer, J., dissenting) (emphasis added).
12 Id. (quoting McCulloch v. Maryland, 4 Wheat. 316, 4 L. Ed. 579 (1819)).
13 Id. at 482 (internal citation omitted).
14 Id.

empower federal agencies to promulgate rules governing education, air transportation, and environmental policy. As a practical matter, such rules have the force of law. The Court similarly upheld a statute in which Congress created a commission to draft federal sentencing guidelines, and for over twenty years those guidelines required judges, absent extraordinary circumstances, to impose mandatory prison sentences on criminal defendants. Arguably, it is inconsistent for the Court to invalidate legislation that gives the president a power not to make law, but merely to cancel limited portions of already enacted laws that Congress retains the power to overrule.

Simply put, based on the Presentment Clause's ambiguous language, the important interests served by the Line Item Veto Act, and its jurisprudence in the nondelegation context, the Court erred by failing to provide "constitutional room for necessary institutional innovation."[15]

***

Questions

When confronted with constitutional ambiguity, should the Court focus primarily on the utility of an outcome?

Does constitutional ambiguity preclude judicial objectivity? If not, what factors motivate a judge to reach a particular outcome when confronted with ambiguous language?

Do you agree with Justice Kennedy's or Justice Breyer's conception of liberty?

15 Id. at 472 (Breyer, J., dissenting).

4

U.S. TERM LIMITS V. THORNTON

No Person shall be a Representative who shall not have attained to the Age of twenty five Years, and been seven Years a Citizen of the United States, and who shall not, when elected, be an Inhabitant of that State in which he shall be chosen.

—U.S. CONST., ART I., SEC. 2, CL. 2

No Person shall be a Senator who shall not have attained to the Age of thirty Years, and been nine Years a Citizen of the United States, and who shall not, when elected, be an Inhabitant of that State for which he shall be chosen.

—U.S. CONST., ART I., SEC. 3, CL. 3
—("the Qualification Clauses")

Summary

- The Court's decision in *Term Limits* rang a death knell for the states' ability to address, and possibly cure, the problems spawned by long-term congressional membership, including, among other things, its negative impact on job performance and voter participation.
- The Court was offered, but declined to embrace, a reading of the law at issue that would have avoided ruling on its constitutionality.
- In the face of textual silence and ambiguous historical data, and despite the pro-democracy objectives that the law clearly articulated, the Court determined to use the case as a platform for espousing its views on federalism.

***

Introduction

Term Limits offered the Court an opportunity to affirm and strengthen the democratic process at one of its most fundamental levels. Presented with the question of whether the states, through their voters, may appropriately choose who will represent them in Congress, and in so doing respond to the growing belief that entrenched incumbencies damage the integrity of the electoral system, the Court ruled in the negative. Relying on silent, if not ambiguous, text and inconsistent historical materials, the Court opted to ignore the substantive issue before it – the efficacy of term limits for congressional members – in favor of engaging in a battle with the dissent over federalism. The Court's indifference to the significant concerns expressly addressed by the proposed term limits and its willingness to silence the voices of the voting public through an unnecessary interpretation of constitutional text indicates a troubling willingness on the part of the Court to assume for itself the power to speak on behalf of voters.

The decision

In *Term Limits*, the Court considered the constitutionality of an amendment to the Arkansas constitution that denied ballot access to any otherwise-eligible federal congressional candidate having already served three terms in the House of Representatives or two terms in the Senate. Affirming a state trial court decision that found the term-limits provision unconstitutional, the Arkansas Supreme Court concluded that the states have no authority to restrict the length of service of congressional members. Specifically, it concluded that the requirements for congressional service expressly enumerated in the Qualification Clauses of the U.S. Constitution regarding age, citizenship, and residency were fixed and could not be altered by the states. The Supreme Court agreed in a 5–4 vote, holding that the Arkansas amendment violated the federal constitution.

The Court saw the constitutional challenge as involving two issues: (1) whether the Constitution itself forbids the states from adding to or altering the qualifications specifically identified in its text; and, (2) if so, whether the ballot access provision actually implicated the Qualification Clauses at all, given that candidates could still run for election through a write-in process. The Court answered the first question in the affirmative. In so doing, it relied in large part on its reasoning in *Powell v. McCormack*,[1] a case in which the Court had previously considered whether Congress has the power to impose qualifications on its members other than those stated in the text of the Constitution. Concluding that it does not, the Court in *Powell* engaged in a lengthy consideration of the history of the clauses, opined about the Founding Fathers' likely intent in drafting them, and ultimately determined that the qualifications articulated in the Qualification Clauses are fixed and not subject to change. Inherent in the Court's determination that Congress lacks such power was its reliance on certain "basic principles of our democratic system"[2] – in particular, that "the people should choose whom they please to govern them."

Acknowledging that *Powell*'s conclusion that Congress is without power to add qualifications for membership did not speak to whether the states had such power, the Court again drew on historical evidence regarding the Framers' intent, including the

1 The quoted material in this chapter is taken from U.S. Term Limits v. Thornton, 514 U.S. 779 (1985).
2 Id. at 548.

convention and ratification debates. Rejecting the argument that the power to add qualifications was a part of the states' original powers, the Court opined that the election of representatives to the national legislature was instead a new right, thus precluding any argument that state-initiated additions to the qualifications already stated in the text of the Constitution were part of the original powers preserved by the Tenth Amendment. Finally, the Court opined that even if the states had retained some power in this regard, such power was subsequently "divested" through the Framers' intent that the Constitution be the exclusive source for identifying qualifications for congressional members. In this regard, the Court articulated its view of precisely who the "people" are within the meaning of Constitution, concluding that permitting individual states to adopt their own qualifications for congressional candidates would be consistent with the "Framers' vision of a uniform National Legislature representing the people of the United States."[3]

As to the contention that the Qualification Clauses were not implicated by the Arkansas amendment, the Court quickly concluded that the intent of the amendment was to "achieve a result that is forbidden by the Federal Constitution,"[4] namely "to prevent the election of incumbents."[5] The "slight chance of victory" for reelection as a write-in candidate evidenced, in the Court's view, an evasion of the Qualification Clauses that the Framers would not have countenanced.[6]

Justice Thomas's dissent vigorously disputed the majority's argument, asserting that the Constitution's silence as to whether the states could impose additional or different eligibility requirements on congressional candidates opens the door for the states to so act.

Analysis

> *It is one of the happy incidents of the federal system that a single courageous state may, if its citizens choose, serve as a laboratory; and try novel social and economic experiments without risk to the rest of the country.*
>
> —Justice Louis Brandeis, *New State Ice Co. v. Liebmann, 285 U.S. 262, 311 (1932)*

There can be little dispute that the Arkansas law at issue was designed as an "experiment" to address the perceived problems associated with entrenched incumbencies. Following a general election, the voters of Arkansas adopted the "Term Limitation Amendment" at the heart of the case. The preamble to the amendment specifically provided:

> The people of Arkansas find and declare that elected officials who remain in office too long become preoccupied with reelection and ignore their duties as representatives of the people. Entrenched incumbency has reduced voter participation and has led to an electoral system that is less free, less competitive, and less

3 Id. at 783.
4 Id. at 829.
5 Id. at 830.
6 Id. at 831.

> representative than the system established by the Founding Fathers. Therefore, the people of Arkansas, exercising their reserved powers, herein limit the terms of elected officials.[7]

At the time of the *Term Limits* decision, more than twenty other states had adopted language that likewise sought to limit the length of congressional terms and thereby reinvigorate the electoral process, enhance voter participation in our democratic system, and address the substantive problems spawned by long-term congressional membership.

The Court's decision to pull the plug on the states' attempts to experiment with the term-limit solution is problematic on several levels. First, the Court could have and should have declined to opine on the constitutionality of the law in the first instance. This is because the Arkansas amendment could fairly be construed as not implicating the Qualification Clauses of the Constitution at all. Specifically, the Court could have determined that the amendment did not act as an absolute bar to an incumbent seeking reelection, but instead merely made it more difficult to do so. In this regard, the Arkansas amendment could be fairly construed as a permissible ballot-access restriction – a construction that would have avoided any need for the Court to weigh into what was clearly an attempt by Arkansas (and other states) to fashion a remedy to the entrenched incumbency problem by experimenting with the concept of term limits.

Likewise, the Court could have concluded that there is nothing in the text of the U.S. Constitution that would invalidate the amendment. Indeed, the Court candidly acknowledged that the text is silent as to the power of the states to add to or otherwise change the qualifications for those individuals seeking membership in Congress. The Court could have, then, declined to impose a reading that invalidated the amendment and that effectively ended any further attempts by the states to legislate a solution to the problems spawned by long-term congressional membership.

The Court similarly could have limited the scope of its opinion to finding that the amendment, although unconstitutional, might be cured through narrower tailoring. In this regard, the Court could have suggested that the Arkansas term limits apply only for a certain period of time, thereby leaving open the possibility that a candidate could seek reelection after having stepped out of the political ring for a period sufficient to eliminate the perceived problems posed by entrenchment. The Court also could have suggested that the term limits be expanded beyond those set out in the amendment for a period sufficient to permit congressional members to develop competency and expertise, yet short enough to protect against the evils the amendment expressly sought to address.

Rather than take any of these more measured approaches, however, the Court instead permanently undermined the ability of the states, through their legislative process, to cure an acknowledged problem that threatens the democratic process. As the dissent noted, there is an irony in the Court's contention that, by holding the term-limit provision unconstitutional, it was securing the right of the people "to choose whom they please to govern them."[8] And, of course, although the Court claimed that it "is not our province" to resolve the "long standing debate" regarding the efficacy of

7 Id. at 784.
8 Id. at 879 (Thomas, J., dissenting) (internal citation omitted).

congressional term limits, it did precisely that by leaving a constitutional amendment as the only way for a state to weigh in on the qualifications of the members it sends to Congress.

***

Questions

Should the Court have declined to rule on the constitutionality of the provision, given that the provision could reasonably be understood to not implicate the Qualification Clauses in the first instance?

Was the Court justified in using the Term Limit case as a platform for fleshing out its view of federalism?

Should the Court have addressed the merits of the competing arguments regarding congressional term limits and taken the effect of its ruling into account in formulating its opinion?

What are the differences between how the dissent and majority understand who constitutes "the people," and what ramifications does that have for our system of government going forward?

PART II

The cases in which the court inappropriately deferred to the legislative and executive branches

Popularity makes no law invulnerable to invalidation. Americans accept judicial supervision of their democracy – judicial review of popular but possibly unconstitutional statutes – because they know that if the Constitution is truly to constitute the nation, it must trump some majority preferences.

—George Will

5

CHEVRON, INC. V. NATURAL RESOURCES DEFENSE COUNCIL

I say, that Power must never be trusted without a check.

—John Adams

Summary

- The Court's decision in *Chevron* afforded the administrative branch an inappropriate degree of deference.
- The Court improperly relinquished its obligation to "say what the law is."
- The framework announced by the Court for identifying when deference is due, and the nature of that deference, is confusing, largely unworkable, and has left courts to determine, inconsistently, what kind of oversight is appropriate in a given case.

***

Introduction

In *Chevron*, and in the context of construing the meaning of the term "stationary source" in the Clean Air Act, the Court articulated a framework for governing the degree of deference to be afforded a federal agency in interpreting and implementing statutes. The framework – a seemingly simple two-step scheme – asks first whether Congress has clearly spoken to the issue in question. If so, the reviewing court is to give effect to Congress's expressed intent. Any agency interpretation in conflict with that intent is invalid. If, on the other hand, Congress's intent is unclear, or if it has remained silent, then step two of the framework requires that the reviewing court defer to any reasonable agency interpretation of the statutory language at issue. This analysis has proven to be anything but simple and flies in the face of an elemental component of our democratic system: that the executive, legislative, and judicial branches serve as checks and balances against one another. In addition to introducing a confusing and inconsistently applied framework for reviewing agency interpretations and decisions, the *Chevron* decision essentially invited courts to woodenly defer to agency action and to relinquish their obligation to "say what the law is."

***

The decision

At issue in *Chevron* was the meaning of a term found in a regulation promulgated by the Environmental Protection Agency (EPA) under the Clean Air Act, and relevant to a permit program designed to decrease air pollution emissions from "any new or modified major stationary sources." The EPA had determined that the phrase "stationary sources" – a term that Congress did not explicitly define in the context of the permit program – could be construed to allow states to treat all pollution-emitting devices within the same industrial grouping as if they were contained in a so-called "bubble." That construction was subsequently challenged on the ground that it was contrary to prior rulings by the U.S. Court of Appeals for the District of Columbia that the "bubble concept" was inapplicable in the context of the permit program in question, thereby invalidating the regulation. The Court reversed the prior rulings of the Court of Appeals, finding that the Court had erroneously invalidated the EPA regulation because it had adopted a "static judicial definition of the term 'stationary source' when it had decided that Congress itself had not commanded that definition."[1]

In so doing, the Court framed what has come to be known as the two-step *Chevron* test. The test, which is to be used to review an agency's construction of a statute that it administers, was formulated as follows:

> First, always, is the question whether Congress has directly spoken to the precise question at issue. If the intent of Congress is clear, that is the end of the matter; for the court, as well as the agency, must give effect to the unambiguously expressed intent of Congress. If, however, the court determines Congress has not directly addressed the precise question at issue, the court does not simply impose its own construction on the statute, as would be necessary in the absence of an administrative interpretation. Rather if the statute is silent or ambiguous with respect to the specific issue, the question for the court is whether the agency's answer is based on a permissible construction of the statute.[2]

Once Congress delegates the authority to administer a program or statutory scheme to an agency, that delegation "necessarily requires the formulation of policy and the making of rules to fill any gap left, implicitly or explicitly, by Congress."[3] Thus, the test provides that in any instance in which Congress has either not spoken or has not clearly stated its intent, the default is for the reviewing court to defer to any reasonable agency interpretation of the statutory language at issue.

1 The quoted material in this chapter is taken from Chevron U.S.A. Inc. v. NRDC, 467 U.S. 837, 842 (1984).
2 Id. at 842–843.
3 Id. at 843.

In applying the test, the Court concluded that Congress did not identify whether it intended the bubble concept to apply to the permit program, leaving to the Court the question of whether the agency's interpretation of "major stationary sources" was reasonable. This analysis, in turn, required the Court to consider (1) the agency's "great expertise"[4] and Congress's likely determination that such expertise supported its delegation of power to the EPA; and (2) the fact that federal judges are not elected, thereby requiring that they respect "legitimate policy choices" made by those who are accountable to a constituency (in this instance, the chief executive).[5] In the Court's view, deference to the agency was appropriate because "judges are not experts in the field" and because addressing statutory ambiguity and choosing between competing interpretations involves policy decisions better left to the agency charged with making policy than with the courts.[6]

***

Analysis

The Court's decision lends itself to attack on numerous fronts. First, there can be little dispute that the two-step framework affords tremendous power to the agencies, with very little oversight by the judicial branch. Indeed, the Court's determinations that any gap or ambiguity in a statute administered by an agency should be understood as an "implied delegation" by Congress opened the door for agencies to define for themselves congressional intent and to improperly engage in lawmaking. And if that was not bad enough, the Court's decision to defer to any reasonable interpretation or statement of the law essentially eliminated any reasonable understanding that the checks and balances contemplated by the Founders was still in place. Rather than saying what the law is, the Court left that determination to the agencies.

Further, the Court identifies no legal basis to support its conclusion that it properly could defer to an agency's interpretation of a federal statute. The fact that an agency might have superior expertise in a particular area is simply not sufficient to permit a court to abandon its duty to interpret a statute pursuant to its plain language. The fact that "judges are not experts in the field" hardly supports the determination that an agency, and not a court, should engage in the process of saying what the law is.

Additionally, the apparently simple two-part test has proven to be anything but simple. Rather, it has spawned significant confusion and has resulted in inconsistent rulings in the courts. Indeed, it became evident that before a court could even attempt to apply the "test," it first had to determine when the test should be applied. This determination has proven to be a complex one, leading to significant disagreement as to what standard(s) a court should embrace in making an initial ruling as to whether *Chevron* even applies. In this regard, courts ultimately recognized that *Chevron* could not properly be invoked for reviewing all questions of statutory interpretation decided by agencies. Other standards of review, including that articulated in *Skidmore v. Swift & Co.*,

4 Id. at 865.
5 Id.
6 Id. at 866.

were necessary. Other conundrums include how a court is to go about determining congressional intent – that is, what are the appropriate tools of statutory construction that a court may use in engaging in step one of the test? These and other problems have muddied the roles that Congress, the agencies, and the court appropriately may play and have confused how those roles are to be carried out.

What is clear is that how agencies are exercising their power to interpret and implement congressional statutes receives little, if any, true oversight. This undermines the careful system of checks and balances contemplated by the Founders, puts at risk the principle of separation of powers, and weakens our democratic system. *Chevron* should be reexamined to better define and demarcate the interpretive roles to be played by the courts and the agencies.

***

Questions

What role can (should) Congress play in clarifying the role of agencies and combating the reality that agencies by and large are free to police themselves?

When, if ever, is it appropriate for the courts to defer to agency expertise?

What should the scope of judicial review be in this context?

Where is the line between an agency's clarification of statutory language and its rewriting of that language, and why should we care?

6

KOREMATSU V. U.S.

No State shall make or enforce any law which shall abridge the privileges or immunities of citizens of the United States; nor shall any State deprive any person of life, liberty, or property, without due process of law; nor deny to any person within its jurisdiction the equal protection of the laws.

—U.S. Const., Amend. XIV, Cl. 1

Summary

- *Korematsu* stands as a painful reminder of the possible consequences flowing from the Court's blind deference to one or more of the coordinate branches.
- *Korematsu* warns against the Court's willingness to expand the principle of precedent to reach a desired, but insupportable, result.

***

Introduction

In *Korematsu*, the Court was presented with the question of, among other things, the appropriate degree of deference due to the executive branch during a time of war.[1] In February 1942, President Franklin Roosevelt issued an executive order that led to the removal of thousands of Japanese Americans from their homes to internment camps in various states across the West. The order derived from the military's purported belief that persons of Japanese ancestry posed a threat to the nation's security and that their wholesale roundup was necessitated by a supposed inability to identify particular individuals actually posing such a risk. Korematsu, an American-born citizen subject to the order, refused to leave his home and was later convicted for his failure to comply.

1 The quoted material in this chapter is taken from Korematsu v. United States, 323 U.S. 214 (1944).

Korematsu challenged his conviction, arguing that the evacuation order was unconstitutional. In a 6–3 decision, the Court upheld the conviction, finding that the deprivation of Korematsu's rights was justified by the "pressing public necessity" to combat espionage and sabotage. The decision marks a low point in the Court's jurisprudence, as it simultaneously announced that citizens could be deprived of their constitutional rights on the basis of race upon an articulation by the executive branch of a military necessity to do so, as well as that there need be no particularized showing as to that necessity. The Court's willingness to blindly defer to the executive's naked assertion of necessity at the expense of citizens' rights was both at odds with its role as protector of those rights and set a potentially dangerous precedent for how supposed dangers posed to national security by racial or ethnic groups might be handled in the future.

The decision

Clearly concerned that removing citizens from their homes and placing them in the equivalent of prison camps based solely on their ancestry was deeply problematic and that a ruling rejecting Korematsu's constitutional challenge would stray far from well-established precedent, the Court opened its opinion by quickly – if not defensively – noting that "all legal restrictions which curtail the civil rights of a single racial group are immediately suspect" and subject to "the most rigid scrutiny." The rigor of that scrutiny, however, is difficult, if not impossible, to detect. Rather than engage in a careful consideration of the scope of the issue presented and its ramifications for future cases testing the contours of the balance of powers in a time of war, the Court instead very quickly tied its analysis to its prior ruling in *Kiyoshi Hirabayashi v. United States*, a case in which the Court upheld a military order that imposed a curfew on Japanese Americans residing in certain coastal areas of the United States. In *Hirabayashi* the Court found the curfew order at issue to fall within the war powers of the president and Congress, and to be an appropriate, temporary, step in preventing espionage and sabotage. Relying on *Hirabayashi*, Justice Black readily concluded that it likewise was not beyond the war powers of the president and Congress to exclude persons of Japanese descent from the West Coast area to achieve the same purpose. Indeed, the Court quickly noted that, as in *Hirabayashi*, it could not reject claims by the military that there were disloyal members in this group of citizens and that these disloyals could not be separately identified. Eschewing its ability to challenge the legitimacy of the military's claim of necessity, the Court acquiesced to its accuracy and truth. Because Korematsu was excluded as a result of the military's contention that it feared a Japanese invasion and that controlling for actual disloyalty by individual persons of Japanese dissent was not possible, Korematsu's conviction was affirmed.

Korematsu has never been explicitly overruled. However, Korematsu's case was re-opened in the mid-1980s and his conviction was set aside.

***

Analysis

Rather than engage in the kind of "rigid scrutiny" that the Court acknowledged was required, the Court instead blindly deferred to the military's unsubstantiated contention that those of Japanese descent presented, as a whole, a national security threat because of the presence of an "unascertained number of disloyal members of the group." Central to the Court's ruling and its willingness to defer to the executive branch was its insistence on viewing the order at issue as merely articulating a "temporary exclusion" of all persons of Japanese descent from the designated areas. Of course, the issue need not have been so narrowed, as Justice Black noted when he specifically stated the Court was not considering the broader issue of whether placing Japanese citizens in internment camps passed constitutional muster. As Justice Roberts pointed out in the dissent, however, failure to comply with the exclusion order was inexorably linked to the subsequent detention of those subject to that order and, accordingly, not fairly susceptible to the surgical treatment the Court afforded it. The Court's careful, strategic narrowing accomplished two goals, however. First, it permitted the Court to rely on so-called precedent in support of its decision. In this regard, by summoning its prior opinion in *Hirabayashi*, the Court could liken the temporary curfew upheld in that decision as necessary to ensuring the national security to the temporary exclusion at issue in *Korematsu*. In so doing, the Court could create the illusion that it was carefully following a prior ruling from a factually similar case. Despite its acknowledgment that there is a distinction between subjecting a group to a curfew and excluding that group from their homes, the Court concluded that the same need identified by the military in *Hirabayashi* – to protect the public from grave, imminent danger – could likewise appropriately be addressed through a temporary suspension of a group's right to remain in their homes.

As Justice Jackson argued in the dissent, however, the Court's urging that *Hirabayashi* dictated the affirmance of Korematsu's conviction is without support. *Hirabayashi*, as Justice Jackson pointed out, was specifically limited to the issue of whether the curfew order in question, as applied at that time and under the particular circumstances of that case, fell within the war power. The *Hirabayashi* decision did not, in Justice Jackson's view, dictate a similar finding with respect to other orders deemed to be militarily reasonable. Rather, Justice Jackson noted the slippery slope posed by the Court's willingness to identify *Hirabayashi* as precedential and expressed his concern as to "[h]ow far the principle of this case would be extended before plausible reasons would play out."[2] In this regard, instead of being guided by the principle of precedent to protect the rights of a group of citizens from an action that the Court acknowledged as unconstitutional, the *Korematsu* court created precedent where it did not actually exist. Doing so both improperly expanded the degree of deference due to the executive branch and extinguished the liberty rights of citizens as to whom the Court had "no doubt were loyal to this country."[3]

In addition to creating the false imprimatur of precedent, the Court's narrowing of the issue before it and its reliance on *Hirabayashi* permitted it to take at face value the military's claim that, as in *Hirabayashi*, persons of Japanese ancestry as a group posed a threat to the security of the United States and that the exclusion order therefore was

2 Id. at 208.
3 Id. at 195.

necessary. Indeed, the Court expressly stated its inability to do anything but adhere to its prior conclusion to that effect:

> Like curfew, exclusion of those of Japanese origin was deemed necessary because of the presence of an unascertained number of disloyal members of the group, most of whom we have no doubt were loyal to this country. It was because we could not reject the finding of the military authorities that it was impossible to bring about an immediate segregation of the disloyal from the loyal that we sustained the validity of the curfew order as applying to the whole group. In the instant case, temporary exclusion of the entire group was rested by the military on the same ground. The judgment that exclusion of the whole group was for the same reason a military imperative answers the contention that the exclusion was in the nature of group punishment based on antagonism to those of Japanese origin.[4]

Although the Court claimed that the proper analysis to apply when the civil rights of a single racial group are restricted is one of "the most rigid scrutiny,"[5] it engaged in no such scrutiny. Indeed, the only "evidence" referenced by the Court supporting the military's contention that it would not effectively identify those who might actually pose a threat was obtained *after* the exclusions. In this regard, the Court noted that following the exclusions and camp internments, a number of citizens of Japanese ancestry subsequently refused to swear unqualified allegiance to the United States and/or requested repatriation to Japan – consequences arguably more indicative of their poor treatment than evidence of their threat to national security. At bottom, the Court substituted the rigid scrutiny that it contended was required for an amorphous "public necessity" test that essentially permitted to Court to defer completely to the executive's judgment that the exclusions and internments were necessary to ensure national security – all at the expense of the Constitution's promise of equal rights and due process.

***

Questions

Should the Court have considered, as advocated by Justice Roberts, that the exclusion was part of a wider plan to forcibly detain Japanese Americans?

What degree of "evidence" could reasonably support the deprivation of a group's constitutional rights, and who should be making that determination?

Why hasn't the Court explicitly overruled Korematsu? Are there valid reasons for its not having done so?

What are the potential ramifications of the Korematsu decision in a post-9/11 world?

4 Id. at 195.
5 Id. at 194.

PART III

The cases that expanded judicial review at the expense of democratic governance

Judicial abuse occurs when judges substitute their own political views for the law.

—Lamar Smith

7

GRISWOLD V. CONNECTICUT

No State shall make or enforce any law which shall abridge the privileges or immunities of citizens of the United States; nor shall any State deprive any person of life, liberty, or property, without due process of law; nor deny to any person within its jurisdiction the equal protection of the laws.

—U.S. Const., Amend. XIV, Cl. 1

Summary

- In *Griswold*, the Court invented constitutional "penumbras" to expand the judicially created and unenumerated right to privacy. The Court's decision is one of the best examples of a normative, outcome-driven, and undemocratic view of constitutional decision making.
- The Court disregarded the constitutional constraints on its Article III reviewing authority and laid the foundation for the creation of new rights in the future that neither the text nor the purposes of any provision support.

***

Introduction

The Constitution is not a panacea for every blot upon the public welfare. Nor should this Court, ordained as a judicial body, be thought of as a general haven for reform movements.

—John Marshall Harlan

Under Article III of the Constitution, the Court's jurisdiction is limited primarily to interpreting treaties, federal statutes, and constitutional provisions, including the Bill of Rights.[1] When interpreting an article, clause, or amendment in the Constitution, such as

1 The quoted material in this chapter is taken from Griswold v. Connecticut, 381 U.S. 479 (1965).

the Presentment Clause or the Fourteenth Amendment, the Court should first consider the text and ascribe to it a meaning that the words can reasonably support. In addition, the Court considers the original purpose(s) of a particular provision at the time it was drafted to ensure that its decision is consistent with such purpose(s). This may include, for example, an analysis of the historical record in Congress that led to the adoption of the Fourteenth Amendment. Finally, the Court considers prior case law and, pursuant to the doctrine of *stare decisis*, typically adheres to its decisions for the purpose of promoting stability and predictability in the law. All three sources of legal authority – the text, its purpose(s), and precedent – function to constrain the Court from issuing decisions based on the Justices' personal values. In essence, the Court's duty is to say what the law is, not what it should be. When the Court disregards this duty, such as through manipulating the Constitution's text to invalidate a law banning contraception or creating a substantive right to privacy that is not inferable from the text, it abuses its Article III reviewing power and infringes on citizens' right to decide such issues democratically.

In *Griswold* and the cases that follow in this section, the Court did precisely that and developed an unenumerated rights jurisprudence that fundamentally changed American constitutionalism, distorted the doctrine of *stare decisis*, and sanctioned lawmaking from the top down, not the bottom up. The Court's decision in *Griswold* expanded the Court's lawmaking power to unreasonable, unprecedented, and unprincipled proportions and spurned the following developments:

- *Outcome-Based Decision-Making.* In *Griswold*, the Court placed almost exclusive emphasis on the utility of an outcome over the process by which that outcome was reached.
- *Broadly Defining New Rights.* The Court invalidated legislation by relying on an unenumerated, broadly phrased, and impossible-to-define "right to privacy" that no honest construction of the Fourteenth Amendment could support, and that gave the Court nearly unbridled authority to create new "rights" in the future.
- *Distortion of Stare Decisis.* The Court relied on the principle of *stare decisis* to expand extra-constitutional, judicially created rights despite the fact that *stare decisis* is designed to constrain the Court's lawmaking power.

At its heart, *Griswold* undermined the Court's institutional legitimacy because, by manipulating the Constitution's text to achieve a desired outcome, the Court's decision appeared to be motivated by ideology and politics, not law.

***

The decision

In *Griswold*, the Court invalidated a Connecticut law that prohibited citizens from using contraception for the purpose of preventing pregnancy. The law in question stated as follows:

> Any person who uses any drug, medicinal article or instrument for the purpose of preventing conception shall be fined not less than fifty dollars or imprisoned not less than sixty days nor more than one year or be both fined and imprisoned.

The Court's decision, and the reasoning upon which it relied, was deeply troubling. Put bluntly, the outcome was preordained despite the fact that the Constitution "does not speak in so many words of the right of privacy in marriage," and that "no particular provision of the Constitution explicitly forbids the State from disrupting the traditional relation of the family."[2]

These facts presented no obstacle to the majority. Writing for the majority, Justice William O. Douglas began his analysis by citing prior cases in which the Court had invented new "rights" through nothing short of a sheer manipulation of the text. Justice Douglas stated as follows:

> The association of people *is not mentioned in the Constitution* nor in the Bill of Rights. The right to educate a child in a school of the parents' choice – whether public or private or parochial – *is also not mentioned*. Nor is the right to study any particular subject or any foreign language. Yet the First Amendment has been construed [by the Court] to include certain of those rights.[3]

Relying on this precedent, the Court held that a substantive "right to privacy" was *implicit* in various provisions in the Constitution, including the Fourteenth Amendment:

> Various guarantees create *zones of privacy*. The right of association contained in the penumbra of the First Amendment is one, as we have seen. The Third Amendment in its prohibition against the quartering of soldiers 'in any house' in time of peace without the consent of the owner is another facet of that privacy. The Fourth Amendment explicitly affirms the 'right of the people to be secure in their persons, houses, papers, and effects, against unreasonable searches and seizures.' The Fifth Amendment in its Self-Incrimination Clause enables the citizen to create a zone of privacy which government may not force him to surrender to his detriment.[4]

Based on these "zones of privacy," the Court took the unprecedented step of declaring that "specific guarantees in the Bill of Rights have penumbras, *formed by emanations from those guarantees that help give them life and substance*."[5]

Although acknowledging that it has had "many controversies over these penumbral rights of 'privacy and repose'" the Court held that its precedents "bear witness that the right of privacy which presses for recognition here is a legitimate one."[6] In the majority's view, the judicially created right to privacy "was older than the Bill of Rights" and an association "that promotes a way of life, not causes; a harmony in living, not political faiths; a bilateral loyalty, not commercial or social projects."[7] Aside from this

2 Id. at 495 (Goldberg, J., concurring).
3 Id. at 482 (emphasis added).
4 Id. at 484 (emphasis added).
5 Id. (emphasis added).
6 Id. at 485.
7 Id. at 486.

language, what really happened in *Griswold* is that a majority of the Justices sat in the Court's conference room trying to devise a way to invalidate a law that they rightfully deemed unwise. Unfortunately, the solution they came up with had nothing to do with the Constitution, and the majority's reasoning is little more than a sinister attempt to give *Griswold* the appearance of legitimacy. Of course, in matters of constitutional law, the appearance of legitimacy is no substitute for actual legitimacy.

***

Analysis

> *The Court now regularly uses the Due Process Clause to override laws enacted by elected representatives, thereby eliminating various liberties of some people if those liberties conflict with unenumerated "fundamental" rights of other people. The Court accomplishes this deprivation without relying upon any applicable law, except the Due Process Clause itself. This subjectivistic doctrine of due process has turned John Jay's "cornerstone" into wax.*
>
> —Andrew T. Hyman, The Institute for Intermediate Study

In a dissenting opinion, Justice Hugo Black emphasized that, although Connecticut's law was, "every bit as offensive to me as it is my Brethren of the majority," no provision in the Constitution provided the Court with the authority to invalidate the law.[8] This fact required the majority to confront a fundamental question: Should we uphold the law because we have no authority to strike it down, or should we find some way to reach the right result, even if it requires us to disregard the text? This was not a hard question. The Court had a constitutional duty to uphold Connecticut's admittedly unwise ban on contraception and enable citizens to seek a policy change through the democratic process. The majority, sadly, chose the latter option and transformed the Court's role from one of interpreting the Constitution to one of creating new unenumerated rights out of thin air or, in the majority's words, "penumbras." In so doing, the Court laid the foundation for an outcome-focused and constitutionally indefensible unenumerated-rights jurisprudence that undermined democracy, damaged its institutional legitimacy, and disregarded a fundamental tenet of American constitutionalism: the United States is a nation of laws, not men.

Purely outcome-driven decisions are inherently undemocratic, regardless of their utility

> *What is a moderate interpretation of the text? Halfway between what it really means and what you'd like it to mean?*
>
> —Justice Antonin Scalia

The process by which the Court reaches an outcome matters more than the outcome itself. Regardless of how desirable an outcome, when the process of reaching that

8 Id. at 507 (Black, J., dissenting).

outcome is fundamentally flawed, a decision can have grave implications for democracy, liberty, federalism, and the separation of powers.

Judges have the power to say what the law is, not what it should be

Regarding democracy, an outcome-driven approach to constitutional interpretation affords to nine unelected judges the power to ignore the Constitution's text and to declare not only what the law is, but also what it should be. As a practical matter, when the Court manipulates or disregards the text to achieve a desired outcome, there exists no conceivable limit on its lawmaking power and rights can be created based on the Justices' policy predilections, not based on the Constitution, not based on the law, and certainly not based on the choices of citizens acting through their elected representatives.

As stated earlier, a substantial number of individuals would probably agree that the Connecticut legislature's decision to ban contraception was "an uncommonly silly" law.[9] But the question before the Court was whether the law was unconstitutional, and not a single word in the text of the Fourteenth Amendment could be construed as supporting the invalidation of Connecticut's law. After all, Connecticut was not depriving citizens of life, liberty, or property without due process of law. Connecticut's law was passed by a majority vote of legislators who were elected by the people through the democratic process. Faced with such unambiguous language, how did the Court manage to conclude that the word "liberty" encompassed a substantive right to privacy, despite conceding that the Constitution "does not speak in so many words of the right of privacy in marriage"?[10] How did the Court reconcile its holding with the fact that Connecticut's law was "not forbidden by any provision of the Federal Constitution as that Constitution was written."[11] It did not. Instead, the majority discovered invisible "penumbras" that lurked underneath the Fourteenth Amendment and emanated whatever so-called unwritten "right" that would get the majority to a destination that it preferred but that the Constitution's text forbid. The majority's holding can be summarized in one sentence:

> The Fourteenth Amendment does not encompass a right to privacy, but it should encompass this right and therefore it does because we say it does.

The "we" in the Constitution refers to the people, not the Court. The Court, by empowering itself to invent implied rights that no interpretation of the Constitution's text could support, undermined the structural components of governance (e.g., separation of powers, federalism) and placed itself at the forefront of deciding issues that the Constitution entrusts to citizens and their elected representatives. In this regard, the Court signaled a level of confidence, indeed arrogance, by suggesting that it could – and should – usurp powers traditionally left to the electorate on those occasions when the Court, in its view, was in a superior position to "get it right."

9 Id. at 527 (Stewart, J., dissenting).
10 Id. at 495 (Goldberg, J., concurring).
11 Id. at 527 (Black, J., dissenting).

Justice Hugo Black emphasized these points in his dissenting opinion, stating that "I like my privacy as well as the next one, but I am nevertheless compelled to admit that government has a right to invade it unless prohibited by some specific constitutional provision."[12] Justice Black stated as follows:

> I repeat so as not to be misunderstood that this Court does have power, which it should exercise, to hold laws unconstitutional where they are forbidden by the Federal Constitution. My point is that there is no provision of the Constitution which either expressly or impliedly vests power in this Court to sit as a supervisory agency over acts of duly constituted legislative bodies and set aside their laws because of the Court's belief that the legislative policies adopted are unreasonable, unwise, arbitrary, capricious or irrational. The adoption of such a loose, flexible, uncontrolled standard for holding laws unconstitutional, if ever it is finally achieved, will amount to a great unconstitutional shift of power to the courts which I believe and am constrained to say will be bad for the courts and worse for the country. Subjecting federal and state laws to such an unrestrained and unrestrainable judicial control as to the wisdom of legislative enactments would, I fear, jeopardize the separation of governmental powers that the Framers set up and at the same time threaten to take away much of the power of States to govern themselves which the Constitution plainly intended them to have.[13]

In addition, Justice Goldberg implicitly criticized living constitutionalism, arguing that it compromised the fundamental values upon which the Constitution was based:

> I realize that many good and able men have eloquently spoken and written, sometimes in rhapsodical strains, about the duty of this Court to keep the Constitution in tune with the times. The idea is that the Constitution must be changed from time to time and that this Court is charged with a duty to make those changes. For myself, I must with all deference reject that philosophy. The Constitution makers knew the need for change and provided for it. Amendments suggested by the people's elected representatives can be submitted to the people or their selected agents for ratification. That method of change was good for our Fathers, and being somewhat old fashioned I must add it is good enough for me.[14]

As Justice Stewart recognized, it is the "essence of judicial duty to subordinate our own personal views, our own ideas of what legislation is wise and what is not," and if "the law . . . [in question] does not reflect the standards of the people of Connecticut, the people of Connecticut can freely exercise their true Ninth and Tenth Amendment

12 Id. at 510.
13 Id. at 520–521.
14 Id. at 522 (Goldberg, J., concurring).

rights to persuade their elected representatives to repeal it."[15] Such a process is "the constitutional way to take this law off the books."[16]

Justice John Marshall Harlan underscored these sentiments in his concurring opinion, and although agreeing that the law infringed on a right that was "implicit in the concept of ordered liberty," Harlan understood that the majority's sweeping opinion gave the Court nearly unfettered authority to invalidate laws based on subjective values:

> [B]y limiting the content of the Due Process Clause of the Fourteenth Amendment to the protection of rights which can be found elsewhere in the Constitution, in this instance in the Bill of Rights, judges will thus be confined to "interpretation" of specific constitutional provisions, and will thereby be restrained from introducing their own notions of constitutional right and wrong into the "vague contours of the Due Process Clause."[17]

Also, Justice Harlan correctly observed that judicial restraint can be achieved "only by continual insistence upon respect for the teachings of history, solid recognition of the basic values that underlie our society, and wise appreciation of the great roles that the doctrines of federalism and separation of powers have played in establishing and preserving American freedoms."[18] In *Griswold*, the majority showed animosity toward, not appreciation for, these principles.

As discussed later, the implications of *Griswold* are still being felt today. For example, the Court has embraced *Griswold*'s ethereal penumbras to create a collection of "rights," including the right "to define one's own concept of existence . . . and the mystery of human life," and a right "within a lawful realm, to define and express [one's] identity."[19] What's more, by defining these "rights" in such broad terms, the Court has given itself the power to recognize additional rights in future – and unforeseeable – contexts. That is a prescription for judicial review of the most undemocratic kind.

Judges act in a legal, not political (or lawmaking) or ideological, capacity

Decisions such as *Griswold* are based on normative, not legal, considerations and severely damage the Court's institutional legitimacy because the Justices are acting in a political, not legal and constitutional, capacity. After all, many divisive policy issues, such as whether to allow contraception, whether women have a right to terminate

15 Id. at 531–523 (Stewart, J., dissenting).
16 Id. at 531.
17 Id. at 500–501 (Harlan, J., concurring) (quoting Rochin v. People of the State of California, 342 U.S. 165, 170 (1952)).
18 Id. at 501.
19 Planned Parenthood of Southeastern Pennsylvania v. Casey, 505 U.S. 833, 851 (1992); Obergefell v. Hodges, 135 S. Ct. 2584, 2593 (2015).

a pregnancy, or whether individuals have a right to assisted suicide, are mentioned nowhere in the Constitution, and not even the most ambiguous clauses in the Constitution provide a basis to recognize these rights. As a result, there exists no credible source of legal authority to justify the creation or expansion of such a right. Think about it: Why did the majority in *Griswold* believe it necessary to create constitutional penumbras, and why in *Planned Parenthood of Southeastern Pennsylvania v. Casey* did the Court base its decision to reaffirm *Roe* on a judicial right to "define one's own concept of existence, and of the mystery of human life"?[20] Because these "rights" do not exist in the Constitution, but rather in the deep recesses of the Justices' minds where subjectivity reigns supreme.

At bottom, issues such as whether to permit first-trimester abortions implicate deeply moral, not legal, judgments, and one's view regarding abortion cannot be characterized as objectively "right" or "wrong." The basic purpose of the Constitution – and of basing decisions on a reasonable interpretation of its language – is to prevent unelected judges from imposing their moral views upon an entire country. That is precisely why the process of legal decision making is so vital – it prevents the judiciary from removing policy-based decisions from the democratic process and substituting its moral judgments for those of citizens. When the Court disregards this principle and, as in *Griswold*, reaches outcomes despite the lack of any legitimate source of legal authority, a perception is created that subjective values, not objective legal analysis, drive the Court's decisions. For this reason, the Court should not reach any outcome, regardless of how desirable, unless the Constitution provides a credible path by which that outcome can be legally justified.

In *Griswold*, the Court disregarded any constraints on its Article III power and instead gave itself the authority "to determine what is or is not constitutional on the basis of their own appraisal of what laws are unwise or unnecessary."[21] For that reason, *Griswold* should be seen for what it truly represents, rather than celebrated for the result it reached. The same holds true for the cases that followed in *Griswold*'s wake. As discussed in the chapters on *Planned Parenthood*, *Lawrence*, and *Obergefell*, the Court manipulated the Fourteenth Amendment's Due Process Clause and invented unenumerated rights based on imprecise and impossible-to-define standards. For example, in *Planned Parenthood*, the Court reaffirmed *Roe v. Wade* based on the right to "define the mystery of human life"; in *Lawrence* on "liberty in its spatial and more transcendent dimensions" and on the judge-made notion that "history and tradition are the starting but not in all cases the ending point" in constitutional interpretation; and in *Obergefell* on the Court's "new insights" and "reasoned judgment" regarding the definition of liberty.[22] In all of these cases – *each of which was decided by a 5–4 margin* – the majority all but ignored the Fourteenth Amendment's text and substituted its subjective preferences for those of democratically elected institutions. Under what accepted principle of constitutional law can these decisions be justified? None – unless a desired outcome is all that matters.

20 Id.

21 Griswold, 381 U.S. at 511–512 (Black, J., dissenting).

22 Lawrence, 539 U.S. at 572 (quoting County of Sacramento v. Lewis, 523 U.S. 833, 857 (1998) (Kennedy, J., concurring).

What happened to the Ninth Amendment as a source of unenumerated rights?

Perhaps the most perplexing aspect of cases such as *Griswold* is that the Ninth Amendment provided the Court with at least an arguable textual basis upon which to invalidate Connecticut's law. The amendment states as follows (emphasis added):

> The enumeration in the Constitution, of certain rights, shall not be construed to deny or disparage others *retained* by the people.[23]

In his concurring opinion in *Griswold*, Justice Goldberg argued that the Ninth Amendment was the appropriate textual basis for invalidating the law. Justice Goldberg explained that the "language and history of the Ninth Amendment reveal that the Framers of the Constitution believed that there are additional fundamental rights, protected from governmental infringement, which exist alongside those fundamental rights specifically mentioned in the first eight constitutional amendments."[24] For Justice Goldberg, "the right of privacy in the marital relation is fundamental and basic – a personal right 'retained by the people' within the meaning of the Ninth Amendment."[25] As a result, Connecticut could not "constitutionally abridge this fundamental right."[26] The Court's decision in *Griswold* would have been grounded more firmly in the Constitution's text – and more legitimate – if it had accepted Justice Goldberg's position. In fact, Justice Goldberg's dissent underscores the proposition that honest decision-making processes and desirable outcomes are not mutually exclusive concepts.

The Court's refusal to base its decision on the Ninth Amendment suggests that the majority intended *Griswold* to have an impact that extended far beyond the issue of whether Connecticut's ban on contraception violated the Constitution. The Court may have envisioned *Griswold* serving as the foundation for the creation of unenumerated rights in future cases, either under the nebulous "right to privacy" or pursuant to the doctrine known as "substantive due process," which states that the Fourteenth Amendment has a substantive "sphere of liberty" that encompasses unenumerated rights. The Court's decisions in *Roe*, *Planned Parenthood*, and *Obergefell* confirm this proposition.

Of course, such an interpretation of the Fourteenth Amendment both ignores the clause's plain language and empowers the Court to invent new rights based on a word – liberty – that is as broad in its possible manifestations as it is limitless in its possible applications. After all, "liberty" is not a legal term of art in any meaningful sense, and given one's policy preferences, can arguably support the creation of nearly any "right" that the human imagination can conceive. Moreover, why should nine life-tenured, unelected judges have the authority to determine the meaning of liberty? It seems that if liberty is to mean anything at all, it should give citizens autonomy to determine through the democratic process whether the Constitution's penumbras give

23 U.S. Const., Amend. IX.
24 381 U.S. at 488 (Goldberg, J., concurring).
25 Id. at 499.
26 Id.

"life and substance" to unenumerated rights that the liberty protects "in its spatial and more transcendent dimensions."[27]

The flaws in *Griswold* are most troubling when one considers the Court's decisions in *Citizens United* and *Clinton*. In *Citizens United*, the First Amendment provided no guidance concerning whether corporations were "speakers" under the First Amendment and whether money was "speech." In *Clinton*, the Presentment Clause's text was ambiguous concerning whether the line item veto impermissibly vested law-making authority in the executive branch. If the Court was focused on the utility of the outcome in *Citizens United* and *Clinton* – as it certainly was in *Griswold* – the Court would have upheld both statutes, thus permitting Congress to restrict corporate expenditures for the purpose of safeguarding the integrity of elections and deferring to the judgment of the legislative and executive branches on how to enhance fiscal accountability. Instead, the Court relied on the Constitution's text, despite its ambiguous language, to invalidate legislation that made democracy and the government function more effectively. On the other hand, in *Griswold*, the text was discarded in favor of an outcome born from invisible emanations that rose from the Constitution like steam from a freshly baked potato.

To be clear, this is not to say that the Court should always defer to the coordinate branches when the text is ambiguous or when alternative constructions of a provision are possible. Excessive deference to the coordinate branches is, in some cases, inconsistent with the Court's duty to interpret the Constitution, prevent the coordinate branches from exceeding their enumerated powers, protect politically powerless groups, and provide a remedy in situations where the legislature is unable or unwilling to remedy constitutional harms. On the other hand, the Court should not interpret ambiguous constitutional provisions to invalidate laws that ensure fairness in elections and accountability in government, both of which constitute bedrock values upon which a healthy democracy depends. In addition, the Court should not, as it did in *Griswold*, invent rights by construing a particular provision, such as the Fourteenth Amendment, in an intellectually dishonest manner. When the Court reaches an admittedly desirable outcome through an irretrievably tainted decision-making process, neither democracy nor the rule of law is vindicated. Instead, the law is imposed upon citizens through sheer will – and shallow reasoning.

Ill-conceived precedent distorts the doctrine of *stare decisis*

In *Griswold*, the Court cited precedent, holding that, among other things, the First Amendment protects an unenumerated right to association and the Fourteenth Amendment protects the right to raise a family and educate one's child. Without analyzing the merits of those cases, it suffices to say that the Court's reliance on rights that were *inferred* from other constitutional provisions distorts the doctrine of *stare decisis*, which is designed to *constrain*, not *expand*, the Court's decision-making authority. After all, when the Court infers rights from previously inferred rights, there exist virtually no constraints on its lawmaking power.

27 Lawrence, 539 U.S. at 562.

To make matters worse, the inferred rights upon which the Court relied were created in entirely different contexts. The right to association under the First Amendment, for example, is arguably a logical outgrowth of the right to free speech itself because, if individuals could not associate to collectively express their opinions, they would have little, if any, opportunity to meaningfully contribute to public debate. Furthermore, the unenumerated right to privacy under the Fourth Amendment logically flows from its purposes: to protect citizens from unwarranted searches of their homes, papers, and effects. Conversely, no construction of the Fourteenth Amendment's Due Process Clause even remotely supports an inference that it protects a substantive right to privacy. That, in a nutshell, is the difference between reasonable and unreasonable interpretations of the Constitution.

Pragmatism still matters: linking procedures to outcomes through reasonable interpretations of the text

This discussion is not meant to suggest that the Court should *never* consider the utility of a particular outcome. As discussed in Part VII, the Court should consider, but not disproportionately weigh, the pragmatic implications of a particular decision and consider the utility of an outcome if it is predicated on a reasonable construction of the text. After all, the Supreme Court's decision is the last word on the issue. Accordingly, the Court should strive to create workable rules, guide lower courts, legislatures, and litigants, examine whether redress through the legislative process is available, and decide only the issues presented by a case. The Court should also consider the fairness of a particular outcome because the Court's decisions often affect the lives and liberties of millions of citizens.

However, the fact that the Court should consider whether a particular decision leads to a desirable outcome does not mean that the Court should disregard the process by which it reaches that outcome. The question is: How can the Court arrive at desirable outcomes while simultaneously ensuring that its decisions are rooted in the text and thus respect the structural constraints on its reviewing authority? *Griswold* provided a very unsatisfactory answer to this question.

Concededly, when addressing this question, basic interpretive principles, such as relying strictly on text of the Constitution, examining the Founders' intent when drafting a particular provision, or deferring to the coordinate branches, may in some instances provide insufficient guidance. The landmark case of *Plessy v. Ferguson*, which upheld the segregation of African American and Caucasian students provided that both races were provided with equal facilities (the separate but equal doctrine), was arguably correct under a strict or originalist reading of the Equal Protection Clause because the law on its face did not subject either race to unequal treatment of the law. Notwithstanding, the purpose of "separate but equal" was intolerable racial prejudice toward African Americans, rendering them unequal in the eyes of the law. In *Brown v. Board of Education*, the Court correctly invalidated the separate but equal doctrine, summarily declaring the doctrine to be "inherently unequal."[28]

28 347 U.S. 483, 495 (1954).

Citizens of all political persuasions rightfully celebrate *Brown* as a landmark decision strengthening civil rights. Similarly, in *Loving v. Virginia*, the Court rightfully invalidated a law prohibiting interracial marriage. Although the law applied equally to Caucasians and African Americans, it simultaneously denied African American and Caucasian citizens the right to marry the person of their choice and therefore impermissibly treated interracial couples differently than same-race couples. Although the text and original purpose of the Due Process and Equal Protection Clauses did not necessarily support these outcomes, the clauses could be reasonably interpreted to support such a result because the motive undergirding this was animus (and therefore discrimination) toward a particular group. In *Griswold*, the opposite was true.

These decisions stand for the proposition that, at least in some cases, the Court should intervene and embrace an expanded, yet tenable, interpretation of the Constitution to achieve a just result. In doing so, the Court strengthens democracy because it empowers politically and socially marginalized groups and gives them a voice in the democratic process while simultaneously respecting the limits on its reviewing power. But this fact does not justify decisions such as *Griswold*, where no conceivable interpretation of the Fourteenth Amendment supported the invalidation of Connecticut's law; where, as in *Citizens United*, the text was indeterminate; or, where, as in *Clinton*, the text is susceptible to reasonably alternative interpretations and would have enhanced fiscal accountability in government.

Griswold in the broader societal and cultural context

The sociocultural climate within which *Griswold* was decided underscores the proposition that the decision was politically motivated. In 1965, the United States was in the midst of a cultural revolution, with the civil rights, feminist, antiwar, and liberal movements galvanizing citizens across the country and contributing to antigovernment sentiment. In particular, the feminist movement and a fairly pervasive societal attitude toward sexual liberation reflected a rejection of traditional moral values, including a largely patriarchal social order. Consequently, the Court's decision appeared to represent a reaction to, even an affirmation of, the cultural climate of the 1960s and implicitly a repudiation of traditional moral values. In this way, the Court's decision suggests that the changing political landscape, not rigorous legal reasoning and honest constitutional interpretation, influenced the majority. Indeed, the majority's invention of constitutional "penumbras" reflected a tacit acknowledgement that the Constitution's text could not possibly support the decision to invalidate Connecticut's contraception ban. Ultimately, the Court's decision raises a basic question that the Court, in *Griswold* and the cases in its wake, refused to answer. Why should the zeitgeist of the 1960s, and the vagaries of public opinion generally, have such a profound influence on the Court and constitutional meaning? After all, when a jurist is influenced by such factors, the Constitution's meaning becomes as flimsy as the majority's penumbras are fictitious, and judicial decision making becomes as subjective as *Griswold*'s reasoning was spurious.

***

Questions

If not to lay the foundation for creating rights in future cases, what motivated the Court to create constitutional "penumbras" when it could have relied on the Ninth Amendment?

Is the Court ever justified in disregarding the Constitution to reach a desirable outcome?

Is there a tenable distinction between unconstitutional and "uncommonly silly" laws?

8

ROE V. WADE

No State shall make or enforce any law which shall abridge the privileges or immunities of citizens of the United States; nor shall any State deprive any person of life, liberty, or property, without due process of law; nor deny to any person within its jurisdiction the equal protection of the laws.

—U.S. Const., Amend. XIV, Cl. 1

Summary

- *Roe v. Wade* was a logical outgrowth of *Griswold*'s constitutional penumbras, and the Court's decision fundamentally changed the balance of power between the federal and state governments.
- The *Roe* Court embraced an expansive form of judicial power – living constitutionalism – and gave itself the power to change constitutional meaning.
- *Roe* damaged the Court's institutional legitimacy and politicized both the judiciary and the nomination process.
- *Roe* sparked a backlash in the states that continues to undermine the abortion right.
- *Roe* empowered the Court in future cases to ignore the Constitution's text to achieve predetermined outcomes.

***

Introduction

Words have meaning. And their meaning doesn't change.

—Justice Antonin Scalia

Citizens obviously are sharply divided concerning whether women should have the right to terminate a pregnancy.[1] Some citizens believe that abortion should be legal only

1 The quoted material in this chapter is taken from Roe v. Wade, 410 U.S. 113 (1973).

in certain circumstances, such as in the first trimester of pregnancy. Others believe that abortion should be legal only in cases of rape or incest, whereas others would permit abortions at nearly any stage to protect the health of the mother. But few, if any, debates focus on the process by which abortion became a fundamental constitutional right and on whether and how that process has had effects well beyond the issue of abortion itself. Stated another way, little consideration has been given to either how abortion came to be a fundamental right or why the process that identified it as such should be of significant concern and is worthy of inquiry – and perhaps a healthy amount of skepticism.

The inquiry should begin at the beginning – with the language of the Constitution. Whether you are a lawyer or layperson, ask yourself whether a reasonable interpretation of this language supports creating a right to terminate a pregnancy at any stage. Before answering that question, consider what the Supreme Court said in *Roe v. Wade*.

***

The decision

In *Roe*, the plaintiff challenged a Texas law that prohibited abortions except to save the life of the mother. Texas's asserted interest was to protect the life of the unborn fetus. In a 7–2 decision, the Court held that the Fourteenth Amendment to the United States Constitution protects a woman's right to terminate a pregnancy prior to viability, which equates to approximately the first twenty-two weeks of a pregnancy.

How did the Court arrive at this conclusion? Through a decision-making process that reflects perhaps the most unprecedented example of judicial overreaching. The Court began, as it did in *Griswold*, by conceding that "the Constitution does not explicitly mention any right of privacy."[2] Nonetheless, the majority inexplicably concluded that "the Court has recognized that a right of personal privacy, or a guarantee of certain areas or zones of privacy, does exist under the Constitution" in "the penumbras of the Bill of Rights" and in "the concept of liberty guaranteed by the first section of the Fourteenth Amendment."[3] Without explaining the textual or historical basis for arriving at these conclusions, the Court proceeded to infer a right to abortion from the implied right to privacy:

> This right of privacy, whether it be founded in the Fourteenth Amendment's concept of personal liberty and restrictions upon state action, *as we feel it is*, or, as the District Court determined, in the Ninth Amendment's reservation of rights to the people, *is broad enough to encompass a woman's decision whether or not to terminate her pregnancy*.[4]

That passage, in a nutshell, summarizes *Roe v. Wade*. The Court held that the *unenumerated* right to privacy was part of the substantive liberty protected by the Fourteenth Amendment, and, like other rights relating to family, child rearing, personal relationships, and intimacy, encompassed a woman's right to terminate a pregnancy.

2 Id. at 152.
3 Id.
4 Id. at 153 (emphasis added).

Additionally, the Court relied on opinions from medical experts to establish a trimester abortion framework. Under this approach, women had a nearly unfettered right to abortion in the first trimester. In the second and third trimesters, states had a stronger interest in protecting human life and could regulate the abortion procedure. Although many people viewed *Roe* as a landmark decision protecting women's privacy and autonomy, *Roe* proved to be anything but that. It was, and continues to be, the height of judicial arrogance.

The startling aspect of *Roe* is that the Court was so unapologetic about its unadulterated abuse of judicial power. This should not be surprising. The Justices are not elected and they have tenure for life. How did the Court manage to infer an abortion right out of a constitutional provision that prohibits the states from depriving persons of "life, liberty, or property *without due process of law*"?[5] It did something quite extraordinary. The Court acknowledged that it was not relying on the Constitution itself. Instead, it looked to *Griswold*'s invisible penumbras to create from thin air what it could not interpret from constitutional text.

At its basis, *Roe*, like *Griswold*, was the catalyst for the Court's contemporary, outcome-based jurisprudence.

***

Analysis

> *One of the most curious things about Roe is that, behind its own verbal smokescreen, the substantive judgment on which it rests is nowhere to be found.*
>
> —Lawrence Tribe, Professor of Law, Harvard University

Only two Justices dissented in *Roe*. Their reasoning was simple: the Fourteenth Amendment simply does not protect a substantive right to privacy. As then–Associate Justice William Rehnquist noted, to find a right to abortion in the Constitution, the "Court necessarily has had to find within the Scope of the Fourteenth Amendment a right that was apparently completely unknown to the drafters of the Amendment."[6] In all likelihood, the Court believed that it was reaching a fair and just outcome. Unfortunately, that belief, which is rooted in subjective values, is never a reason to reach an outcome that few would characterize as legitimate. As in *Griswold*, by focusing on the utility of the outcome, the Court disregarded the constitutional processes that are designed to check the Court's power and promote a participatory democracy. In doing so, the Court (1) politicized the judiciary; (2) expanded the scope of implied and unenumerated rights; and (3) upset the careful balance between the state and federal government.

The backlash – federalism undermined

Roe disrupted the delicate balance between the state and federal governments because the Court appeared to be impermissibly overreaching by deciding matters that were

5 U.S. Const., Amend. XIV, Cl. 1 (emphasis added).
6 Roe, 410 U.S. at 174 (Rehnquist, J., dissenting).

within the state's powers to regulate. As a result, there was a backlash against *Roe* that endangered the very right that *Roe* created. Over the years, states have launched indirect attacks on *Roe* by enacting legislation that, among other things, required women to obtain the consent of their husband before having an abortion and, most recently, required abortion providers to obtain hospital-admitting privileges. These attacks continue to this day and are motivated by the belief that the Court overstepped its constitutional authority. As a result, the Court has revisited the abortion issue several times and issued decisions that provide little guidance regarding the permissible scope of abortion restrictions. All of this could have been avoided by interpreting the text to encompass all rights that it could reasonably support and to exclude those that it cannot.

To the surprise of some, Justice Ruth Bader Ginsburg, a staunch supporter of abortion rights, has criticized *Roe*'s broad language, stating that "[h]eavy-handed judicial intervention (in the context of *Roe*) was difficult to justify and appears to have provoked, not resolved, conflict."[7] Justice Ginsburg prudently argued in favor of an incremental approach that would allow the Court to "put its stamp of approval on the side of change and let that change develop in the political process."[8]

The politicization of the judiciary

When the Rule of Law disappears, we are ruled by the whims of men.
—Tiffany Madison, Journalist and Author

The Court's decision in *Roe* did tremendous damage to the Court's institutional legitimacy. The *Roe* Court almost unapologetically reached its decision based solely on the outcome it deemed most desirable without regard for ensuring a faithful interpretation of either the text or history, and certainly with little concern for the purpose of the Fourteenth Amendment or the importance of resolving such issues through the democratic process. As a result, the Court not only invented a right in *Roe*; it created the very real perception that decisions by nine unelected judges were motivated by outcomes and ideology, not process and reason.

Given decisions such as *Roe*, it should come as no surprise that the federal judiciary has become increasingly politicized. For example, the process of nominating judges to the federal bench, particularly the Supreme Court, has become contentious, if not toxic. In 1986, Robert Bork's nomination was derailed – and his reputation severely damaged – after senators in the Democratic Party all but accused Bork of being a member of the Ku Klux Klan. At Bork's nomination hearing, former Senator Edward Kennedy stated as follows:

> Robert Bork's America is a land in which women would be forced into back-alley abortions, blacks would sit at segregated lunch counters, rogue police could

7 Timothy B. Carney, Honest Pro-Choicers Admit Roe v. Wade Was a Horrible Decision (Jan. 22, 2011), available at: http://www.sfexaminer.com/honest-pro-choicers-admit-roe-v-wade-was-a-horrible-decision/.

8 Sarah Muller, Liberal Justice Ruth Bader Ginsburg Says Roe v. Wade Went Too Far (May 13, 2013), available at: http://www.msnbc.com/the-last-word/liberal-justice-ruth-bader-ginsburg-says-roe.

> break down citizens' doors in midnight raids, schoolchildren could not be taught about evolution, writers and artists could be censored at the whim of the Government, and the doors of the Federal courts would be shut on the fingers of millions of citizen.[9]

Bork was defeated by a vote of 58–42.[10] Four years later, President George H. W. Bush nominated Clarence Thomas to the Supreme Court, and the confirmation fight that ensued was nothing short of despicable. The Senate attacked Thomas with unproven allegations of sexual harassment and shared the lurid details of this alleged harassment before a nationally televised audience. In fact, the nomination process was filled with such vitriol that Thomas angrily declared the process to be little more than the "high tech lynching for uppity blacks who in any way deign to think for themselves."[11] Could this possibly be the type of democracy that the Founders envisioned?

There is a reason that the nomination process has become so contentious, and that reason can be traced to *Griswold* and *Roe*: once the Court got into the business of deciding cases based primarily upon the desirability of an outcome, elected representatives perceived, rightfully or not, that ideology and subjectivity would dictate a Justice's approach to constitutional interpretation. To an extent, this perception reflects reality. After all, one can likely predict how the Court will rule based on the ideology of the presidents who appointed the Justices. That should make citizens of all political persuasions uneasy.

In fact, perception met reality in *Bush v. Gore*, when former Justice John Paul Stevens issued a stinging dissent criticizing the Court decisions to end the 2000 election between George W. Bush and Al Gore:

> The endorsement of that position by the majority of this Court can only lend credence to the most cynical appraisal of the work of judges throughout the land. It is confidence in the men and women who administer the judicial system that is the true backbone of the rule of law. Time will one day heal the wound to that confidence that will be inflicted by today's decision. One thing, however, is certain. Although we may never know with complete certainty the identity of the winner of this year's Presidential election, the identity of the loser is perfectly clear. *It is the Nation's confidence in the judge as an impartial guardian of the rule of law.*[12]

Justice Stevens's words clearly frame the issue: the process by which we reach a result is necessarily as important as the result itself. Regarding that process, the Court should not, as it did in *Griswold* and *Roe*, decide questions that properly belong to the people and their elected representatives. This result harms all citizens. In *Bush v. Gore*, conservatives cheered the Court's decision, and in *Roe v. Wade*, progressives

9 James Reston, Washington; Kennedy and Bork (July 5, 1987), available at: http://www.nytimes.com/1987/07/05/opinion/washington-kennedy-and-bork.html.

10 Linda Greenhouse, Bork's Nomination Is Rejected; Reagan 'Saddened' (Oct. 24, 1987), available at: http://www.nytimes.com/1987/10/24/politics/24REAG.html?pagewanted=all.

11 Emma Coleman Jordan, For Clarence Thomas, Lying Is Personal Only (Oct. 14, 2007), available at: http://www.washingtonpost.com/wp-dyn/content/article/2007/10/12/AR2007101201883.html.

12 531 U.S. 98, 128–129 (Stevens, J., dissenting) (emphasis added).

celebrated. That, in a nutshell, is the point – and the problem. When one's opinion of a decision is based on agreement with the result, regardless of the process by which that result was achieved, the Court ceases to be relevant.

The "implied rights" problem

Beginning with *Griswold* and continuing with *Roe*, the Court created an "implied rights" problem. Specifically, when courts create fundamental constitutional rights by inferring those rights from the text rather than from a reasonable interpretation of its words, they lay a new, shifting foundation upon which additional phantom rights can be inferred from yet other "implied rights." This *ad hoc* approach to judicial decision making divorces the Court from the constraints on its reviewing authority and gives them the power to independently invent rights by sheer will. Justice Potter Stewart emphasized this point in *Griswold*:

> What provision of the Constitution, then, does make this state law invalid? The Court says it is the right of privacy 'created by several fundamental constitutional guarantees.' With all deference, I can find no such general right of privacy in the Bill of Rights, in any other part of the Constitution, or in any case ever before decided by this Court.[13]

Consider the text of the Fourteenth Amendment and the rights that were inferred from that language:

> No state shall deprive any person of life, liberty, or property, without due process of law; nor deny to any person within its jurisdiction the equal protection of the laws.

Case	*The Right Established*
Griswold v. Connecticut	Privacy
Roe v. Wade	Abortion (implied from privacy)
Planned Parenthood of Southeastern Pennsylvania v Casey	Reaffirming abortion based on the right "to define one's own concept of existence . . . and the mystery of human life") (implied from privacy)
Lawrence v. Texas	Right to engage in private sexual activity (implied from privacy)
United States v. Windsor	Right to equal dignity (implied from privacy)
Obergefell v. Hodges	Right to define and express one's identity (implied from privacy)

To be clear, it does not matter whether one thinks that citizens *should* have these rights. The question is whether *the Court* should be deciding whether these rights exist. If an asserted right can be grounded in the text and is consistent with its purposes, the answer is yes. If the asserted right cannot be so supported, the answer is no. In *Roe*, the Court roundly ignored these principles, and since that time – and in direct response – many states have sought to eviscerate a woman's right to abortion.

13 381 U.S. at 530 (Stewart, J., dissenting).

In the final analysis, one must ask, was it all worth it? Would the abortion right have been more secure, and the Court's institutional legitimacy maintained, if the abortion right had been created from the bottom up and through democratic discourse? As discussed in Chapter 9, after *Planned Parenthood v. Casey*, there can be little doubt that the answer to this question is yes.

***

Questions

Could the Court have grounded Roe in the Constitution's text, such as the Ninth Amendment, Privileges and Immunities, or Equal Protection Clause? If so, write the opinion.

Is there a basis to argue that the Due Process Clause of the Fourteenth Amendment is ambiguous?

9

PLANNED PARENTHOOD OF SOUTHEASTERN PENNSYLVANIA V. CASEY

> *No State shall make or enforce any law which shall abridge the privileges or immunities of citizens of the United States; nor shall any State deprive any person of life, liberty, or property, without due process of law; nor deny to any person within its jurisdiction the equal protection of the laws.*
>
> —U.S. Const., Amend. XIV, Cl. 1

Summary

- In *Planned Parenthood*, the Court created new "rights" to both reaffirm *Roe v. Wade* and lay the groundwork for recognizing future unenumerated rights.
- The Court expanded *Griswold*'s penumbras and adopted an extremely broad and untenable conception of "liberty" under the Fourteenth Amendment.
- The Court invented a difficult-to-define and unworkable "undue burden" test to evaluate the constitutionality of abortion restrictions, which led to contentious abortion-related disputes at the state and federal level that continue to this day.
- The Court applied principles of *stare decisis* selectively to simultaneously uphold and overrule portions of *Roe*.

***

Introduction

In *Planned Parenthood*, the Court damaged its institutional legitimacy to an extent that rivaled the backlash *Roe* engendered.[1] The fatal defect in the Court's reasoning was its reliance on an expansion of substantive "liberty" under the Due Process

1 The quoted material in this chapter is taken from Planned Parenthood of Southeastern Pennsylvania v. Casey, 505 U.S. 833 (1992).

Clause, both to reaffirm *Roe* and to invent an entirely new standard to govern the constitutionality of abortion restrictions. The application of what the Court titled "*Griswold*-liberty" ushered in an era of unprecedented raw judicial power in which the Court's "reasoned judgment" was employed to define "the liberty of all" and to self-servingly rely on the doctrine of *stare decisis* to, ironically, overrule a portion of *Roe*.[2] As a result, the Court's decision in *Planned Parenthood* weakened the liberty of *all* citizens by undermining their voice in the democratic process and infringing on citizens' right to determine for themselves, through the democratic process, what right "liberty" ought to encompass.

***

The decision

In *Planned Parenthood*, the Court decided the constitutionality of several provisions in the Pennsylvania Abortion Control Act, which contained the following provisions:

- A woman seeking an abortion must give informed consent prior to the abortion procedure and be provided with certain information at least 24 hours before the abortion is performed.
- Minors seeking to obtain an abortion must obtain the informed consent of one of their parents, although a judicial bypass option is available if the minor does not wish to or cannot obtain a parent's consent.
- A married woman seeking an abortion must, subject to certain exceptions, sign a statement indicating that she has notified her husband of her intended abortion.

The Court began its analysis by stating that "although a literal reading of the [Due Process] Clause might suggest that it governs only the procedures by which a State may deprive persons of liberty, for at least 105 years," it "has been understood to contain a substantive component as well, one 'barring certain government actions regardless of the fairness of the procedures used to implement them.'"[3] As a result, "*all fundamental rights comprised within the term liberty* are protected by the Federal Constitution from invasion by the States."[4]

The Court noted as follows: "It is tempting, as a means of curbing the discretion of federal judges, to suppose that liberty encompasses no more than those rights already guaranteed to the individual against federal interference by the express provisions of the first eight Amendments to the Constitution."[5]

The Court also acknowledged that it was "tempting, for the same reason, to suppose that the Due Process Clause protects only those practices, defined at the most specific level, that were protected against government interference by other rules of

2 Id. at 849.
3 Id. at 846 (emphasis added) (brackets added).
4 Id. at 847 (emphasis added) (quoting Whitney v. California, 274 U.S. 357, 373 (1927)).
5 Id.

law when the Fourteenth Amendment was ratified."[6] Notwithstanding, the Court stated that it has "never accepted that view," which would be "inconsistent with *our* law."[7] Rather than adhere to the Fourteenth Amendment's plain language, the Court held that the "controlling word in the cases before us is 'liberty'"[8] without regard for the context in which "liberty" appears in the Due Process Clause. In support of this proposition, the Court stated that "[m]arriage is mentioned nowhere in the Bill of Rights . . . but the Court was no doubt correct in finding it to be an aspect of liberty protected against state interference by the substantive component of the Due Process Clause."[9] As a result, "neither the Bill of Rights nor the specific practices of States at the time of the adoption of the Fourteenth Amendment marks the outer limits of the *substantive sphere of liberty* which the Fourteenth Amendment protects."[10] Rather, there is a "realm of personal liberty within which the government may not enter" and which the Court is empowered to define:[11]

> The inescapable fact is that adjudication of substantive due process claims may call upon the Court in interpreting the Constitution to exercise that same capacity which by tradition courts always have exercised: reasoned judgment. Its boundaries are not susceptible of expression as a simple rule.[12]

With this language, the Court declared that "[o]ur obligation is to *define the* liberty *of all*" under the Fourteenth Amendment, the meaning of which *evolves* over time:

> Due process has not been reduced to any formula; its content cannot be determined by reference to any code. The best that can be said is that through the course of this Court's decisions it has represented the balance which our Nation, built upon postulates of respect for the liberty of the individual, has struck between that liberty and the demands of organized society . . . The balance of which I speak is the balance struck by this country, having regard to what history teaches are the traditions from which it developed as well as the traditions from which it broke. *That tradition is a living thing.*[13]

Despite this obvious yet unsuccessful attempt to justify its decision, the majority implicitly acknowledged that its decision was at odds with not only the Constitution, but also with "conventional constitutional doctrine that where reasonable people disagree the government can adopt one position or the other."[14] This doctrine should have been applied because, as the Court acknowledged, "[m]en and women of good conscience can disagree, and we suppose some always shall disagree, about the profound

6 Id.
7 Id. (emphasis added).
8 Id. at 846.
9 Id. at 847–848.
10 Id. at 848.
11 Id. at 847.
12 Id. at 849.
13 Id. at 849–850 (quoting Poe v. Ullman, 367 U.S. 497, 542 (1961) (emphasis added).
14 Id. at 851.

moral and spiritual implications of terminating a pregnancy, even in its earliest stage."[15] Notwithstanding, the Court held that this doctrine "assumes a state of affairs in which the choice does not intrude upon a protected liberty, as defined by nine unelected, life-tenured judges."[16]

For the majority, matters relating to marriage and procreation implicated "liberty" because they involved "the most intimate and personal choices a person may make in a lifetime, choices central to personal dignity and autonomy, [and] central to the liberty protected by the Fourteenth Amendment."[17] The Court stated as follows:

> The mother who carries a child to full term is subject to anxieties, to physical constraints, to pain that only she must bear. That these sacrifices have from the beginning of the human race been endured by woman with a pride that ennobles her in the eyes of others and gives to the infant a bond of love cannot alone be grounds for the State to insist she make the sacrifice. Her suffering is too intimate and personal for the State to insist, without more, upon its own vision of the woman's role, however dominant that vision has been in the course of our history and our culture. The destiny of the woman must be shaped to a large extent on her own conception of her spiritual imperatives and her place in society.[18]

The Court, per Justice Kennedy, also explained that "[a]t the heart of liberty is the right to define one's own concept of existence, of meaning, of the universe, and of the mystery of human life."[19] Relying on *Griswold*, the Court held that "in some critical respects the abortion decision is of the same character as the decision to use contraception" because they "involve personal decisions concerning not only the meaning of procreation but . . . human responsibility and respect for it."[20] To be sure, "it was this dimension of personal liberty that *Roe* sought to protect, and its holding invoked the reasoning and the tradition of the precedents . . . granting protection to substantive liberties of the person."[21] For the majority, *Roe* was properly characterized "not only as an exemplar of *Griswold*-liberty but as a rule (whether or not mistaken) of personal autonomy and bodily integrity."[22]

For these reasons, the Court reaffirmed the "essential" holding in *Roe*, noting that "the reservations any of us may have in reaffirming the central holding of *Roe* are outweighed by the explication of individual liberty we have given combined with the force of *stare decisis*."[23] In applying *stare decisis* to uphold *Roe*, the Court explained as follows:

> [T]he rule of stare decisis is customarily informed by a series of prudential and pragmatic considerations designed to test the consistency of overruling a prior

15 Id. at 850.
16 Id. at 851.
17 Id. (brackets added).
18 Id. at 852.
19 Id. at 851.
20 Id. at 852.
21 Id. at 853.
22 Id. at 857.
23 Id. at 853.

decision with the ideal of the rule of law, and to gauge the respective costs of reaffirming and overruling a prior case.[24]

These considerations included the following:

> [W]hether the rule has proven to be intolerable simply in defying practical workability, . . . whether the rule is subject to a kind of reliance that would lend a special hardship to the consequences of overruling and add inequity to the cost of repudiation . . . or whether facts have so changed, or come to be seen so differently, as to have robbed the old rule of significant application or justification.[25]

Against this backdrop, the Court held that *Roe* had not proven unworkable, that "[t]he ability of women to participate equally in the economic and social life of the Nation has been facilitated by their ability to control their reproductive lives," and that "[n]o development of constitutional law since the case was decided has implicitly or explicitly left *Roe* behind as a mere survivor of obsolete constitutional thinking."[26] Consequently, "overruling *Roe*'s central holding would . . . seriously weaken the Court's capacity to exercise *the judicial power* and to function as the Supreme Court of a Nation dedicated to the rule of law."[27]

Ironically, the Court simultaneously overruled a substantial portion of *Roe*, holding that "the rule of *stare decisis* is not an 'inexorable command,' and certainly it is not such in every constitutional case."[28] Specifically, the Court rejected the trimester framework that the *Roe* Court established, stating that "[a] framework of this rigidity was unnecessary and in its later interpretation sometimes contradicted the State's permissible exercise of its powers," including the interest in protecting human life.[29] For example, the state may enact some laws prior to viability that would withstand constitutional scrutiny:

> [E]ven in the earliest stages of pregnancy, the State may enact rules and regulations designed to encourage her to know that there are philosophic and social arguments of great weight that can be brought to bear in favor of continuing the pregnancy to full term and that there are procedures and institutions to allow adoption of unwanted children as well as a certain degree of state assistance if the mother chooses to raise the child herself.[30]

Nevertheless, the Court held that, before viability, "[l]iberty must not be extinguished for want of a line that is clear" and endeavored to replace the trimester framework with a new standard, despite acknowledging that "any judicial act of line-drawing may seem somewhat arbitrary."[31] This standard, which the Court titled the "undue

24 Id. at 854.
25 Id. at 854–855.
26 Id. at 856–857.
27 Id. at 865 (emphasis added).
28 Id. at 854 (internal citation omitted).
29 Id. at 872.
30 Id.
31 Id. at 870.

burden" test, prohibited states, prior to viability, from placing substantial obstacles in the path of a woman seeking an abortion. The Court explained that "[o]nly where state regulation imposes an undue burden on a woman's ability to make this decision does the power of the State reach into the heart of the liberty protected by the Due Process Clause."[32] Put differently, "[a] finding of an undue burden is a shorthand for the conclusion that a state regulation has the purpose or effect of placing a substantial obstacle in the path of a woman seeking an abortion of a nonviable."[33] Under this standard, "[t]he fact that a law which serves a valid purpose, one not designed to strike at the right itself, has the incidental effect of making it more difficult or more expensive to procure an abortion cannot be enough to invalidate it."[34]

Applying this new framework, the Court held that Pennsylvania's informed consent requirement did not impose a substantial burden on a woman, explaining that "[W]e see no reason why the State may not require doctors to inform a woman seeking an abortion of the availability of materials relating to the consequences to the fetus, even when those consequences have no direct relation to her health."[35]

The Court also upheld the requirement that women wait twenty-four hours before terminating a pregnancy, but invalidated the portion of Pennsylvania's law requiring married women to obtain the written consent of their husband prior to obtaining an abortion.

***

Analysis

Dictatorship naturally arises out of democracy, and the most aggravated form of tyranny and slavery out of the most extreme liberty.

—Plato

The Court had an opportunity in *Casey* to acknowledge that *Roe* was constitutionally indefensible and should therefore be overruled. If it had done so, the Court would have begun to repair the damage that *Roe* did to its institutional legitimacy and placed the divisive issue of abortion rights in the hands of citizens across the country, not nine unelected judges on the federal bench. Instead, the Court compounded the injury *Roe* inflicted on democracy and exacerbated the backlash by states that perceived the Court's decision as an impermissible encroachment on their lawmaking authority. The majority's breathtakingly broad decision was equally as indefensible as *Roe*, and equally as deleterious to democracy.

The Court's decision: (1) relied on the amorphous concept of "*Griswold*-liberty" to reaffirm the abortion right; (2) created an unworkable standard to govern the

32 Id. at 874.
33 Id. at 877.
34 Id. at 874.
35 Id. at 882.

permissibility of abortion restrictions; and (3) selectively relied on the doctrine of *stare decisis*. At bottom, the Court's decision was a textbook example of manipulating the Constitution's text to achieve a desired outcome – one that continues to spurn contentious abortion-related litigation throughout the federal courts and legislation at the state level that seeks to eviscerate a woman's right to abortion.

Griswold-liberty, the rise of arbitrariness, and the collapse of structural constraints

Like *Griswold* and *Roe*, the Court erred by holding that there is "substantive sphere of liberty" that the Due Process Clause protects because the word liberty is qualified by the language "without due process of law." There is simply no method by which to construe liberty as encompassing substantive, unenumerated constitutional rights and no source of legal authority, apart from indefensible decisions such as *Roe* and *Griswold*, that could support such a construction.

To be sure, the Court's assertion that the Due Process Clause, including the term "liberty," can be invoked to invalidate arbitrary legislation ignores the fact that the Court's reliance on "*Griswold*-liberty" is itself arbitrary. The term "*Griswold*-liberty" is neither a legal term of art nor a prescription for liberty in a true sense, but rather a license for the Court to justify the invention of constitutional "rights" by impermissibly intervening in the democratic process at the state and federal level. In short, liberty is a prescription for arbitrariness of the most unconstitutional kind and judicial power of the most undemocratic – and unaccountable – kind.

As a result, when the Court has a monopoly on the definition of "liberty," citizens lose their grasp on autonomy. After *Planned Parenthood*, the citizens of every state were prohibited from deciding through the democratic process whether abortion should be a constitutional right. This fact underscores the problem with the Court's *Griswold*-based jurisprudence: it undermines the Constitution's structural components, which strive to create a decentralized form of governance that gives the national government authority only in areas expressly enumerated in the Constitution, that envisions citizen participation in the democratic process, and that promotes lawmaking from the bottom up, not the top down.

The Court's reliance on "*Griswold*-liberty" has undermined, if not entirely subverted, these structural constraints because it centralizes power at the Court, reduces citizens' voice in governance, and imposes law from the top down. This approach transforms democracy into a quasi-oligarchy and cripples a vital component of democracy: the right of the people of each state to decide the laws under which they will be governed. A healthy democracy includes the right of states to disagree on whether to permit abortion rights, the right of citizens to lobby the legislature to change the law, and the right of state supreme courts to interpret the law based on the history, traditions, and values of each state. A democracy that promotes governance from the bottom up facilitates a system where elected officials are accountable to their constituents, where government is transparent, and where citizens possess autonomy and self-determination – the truest expression of liberty.

The "undue burden" standard imposes an undue burden on the rule of law – and democracy

The Court's decision to adopt the "undue burden" standard ensured that the scope of the abortion right, and the permissibility of state laws regulating abortion, would remain unclear. Like the word "liberty," the undue burden standard can be interpreted and defined in a variety of ways and cause confusion among lower courts and legislatures, thus resulting in conflicting decisions at the federal and state level. In other words, the Court's decision failed to bring clarity and predictability to the law, which in turn enabled states to easily test the limits of the "undue burden" standard by enacting legislation that made it difficult to obtain abortions and therefore threatened to weaken the abortion right itself. In Texas and Mississippi, for example, the legislatures passed laws requiring abortion providers to obtain hospital-admitting privileges, which led to the closure of many abortion clinics and made it nearly impossible for poor women to access abortion services. For these women, abortion became a right that existed only in the abstract.

Undoubtedly, the Court adopted this standard to balance a woman's interest in terminating a pregnancy against the competing interests of the state in protecting human life. The problem with a "balancing of interest" framework is that it results in ad hoc, case-by-case decision making in which the Court, over decades, will invariably expand or limit the abortion right based in substantial part on the ideological leanings of the Justices. Simply put, the undue burden standard, like the invocation of liberty, leads to the politicization of the Court, uncertainty in the law, and leads to predictability of the worst kind: the knowledge of how a Justice will likely rule based on the president responsible for his or her appointment.

Judicial power corrupts the judiciary

The majority emphasized that "the root of American governmental power is revealed most clearly in the instance of the power conferred by the Constitution upon the Judiciary of the United States and specifically upon this Court."[36] The Court further noted that "the Court's power lies, rather, in its legitimacy, a product of substance and perception that shows itself in *the people's acceptance of the Judiciary as fit to determine what the Nation's law means and to declare what it demands.*"[37] That acceptance, the majority concluded in *Planned Parenthood*, must be of the Court's "reasoned judgment" on matters of social policy and of its desire to define "the liberty of all" regarding issues on which the Constitution is silent.

The problem is that "reasoned judgment" is only valid if the judgment to which the majority referred was legal, not moral, and based on an interpretation, not manipulation, of the Constitution's text. Put differently, if the Court's decision is rooted in a plausible interpretation of the text, it is inherently the product of reasoned judgment. In this sense, the concept of exercising "reasoned judgment" is redundant *unless* the Court is relying on this term to reach an outcome that the Constitution's text cannot support. This is exactly what happened in *Griswold*, *Roe*, and *Planned Parenthood*; these decisions

36 Id. at 865.
37 Id. (emphasis added).

resulted from the exercise of arbitrary, not reasoned, judgment, and embraced a chilling view of judicial power that no citizen, regardless of viewpoint or ideology, should accept.

Stare decisis becomes *stare indecisis*

The Court's invocation of *stare decisis* was, at best, self-serving and, at worst, disingenuous. The majority's opinion began by affirming *Roe*'s "essential holding," which recognized "the right of the woman to choose to have an abortion before viability and to obtain it without undue interference from the State" and of the State's right "to restrict abortions after fetal viability, if the law contains exceptions for pregnancies which endanger the woman's life or health."[38] In upholding this portion of *Roe*, the Court relied heavily on the principles underlying *stare decisis*, such as the interest in creating workable rules and protecting citizens' reliance on a prior ruling.

Amazingly, however, the principles the Court invoked in one breath were abandoned in the next when it overruled the trimester framework in favor of a standard prohibiting the state from placing an undue burden on a woman's right to obtain an abortion. If, as the Court stated, the objectives of retaining workable rules and protecting citizens' reliance interests supported reaffirming *Roe*, they likewise counseled in favor of retaining the trimester framework because the undue burden standard lacked sufficient specificity to guide courts regarding the scope of the state's power to restrict abortion. After all, what types of laws constitute an "undue burden" on the abortion right, and what factors should the courts consider when making this determination? The undue burden standard fails to answer any of these questions, and predictably has resulted in a muddled jurisprudence that, over forty years after *Roe*, continues to lack clarity or cohesion. One commentator opined as follows:

> The Casey authors . . . appealed chiefly to *stare decisis* rather than arguing that Roe itself was a sound decision. [Justice Antonin] Scalia points out, however, that they really did not preserve Roe itself: they essentially made up a whole new opinion with an entirely new standard at its heart: the amorphous 'undue burden' standard. This was not only an implicit rejection of Roe but contradicted numerous other Court abortion precedents. The plurality's reliance on *stare decisis* was thus 'contrived,' a 'keep-what-you-want-and-throw-away-the-rest' version that really was at odds with the whole point of *stare decisis*.[39]

Accordingly, apart from the fact that the undue burden standard is inherently unworkable, the Court's self-serving reliance on *stare decisis* served to weaken its doctrinal underpinnings and cast doubt upon its application to future cases. To be clear, the purposes of doctrines such as *stare decisis* can only be furthered if those responsible for its application do so in a consistent and justifiable manner. In *Planned Parenthood*, the Court's reliance on *stare decisis* was inconsistent – affirming *Roe* but rejecting the trimester framework – and unjustifiable because of the undue burden standard's vagueness.

38 Id. at 846.
39 505 U.S. 993.

Why not rely on the Equal Protection Clause?

One question that arises in *Planned Parenthood*'s wake is why the Court refused to rely on either the Ninth Amendment to hold that the liberty interest at issue was a right *retained* by citizens, or that the law violated the Equal Protection Clause by disparately impacting women, who are forced to bear the social, financial, and psychological costs of an unwanted pregnancy. The Court appeared to consider the Equal Protection Clause as the basis for its decision when it explained that "[t]he ability of women to participate equally in the economic and social life of the Nation has been facilitated by their ability to control their reproductive lives."[40] This statement is certainly true, and it provided the Court with a solid foundation upon which to hold that prohibitions on abortion (and unreasonable restrictions) disparately impact women and therefore violate their right to equal protection under the law. The Court's likely reason for rejecting this reasoning is simple: it wanted to broaden, not constrain, its power to create new rights in future cases. That is why "liberty in its spatial and in its more transcendent dimensions" is so appealing. It gives judges the power to do whatever they want – for whatever reason they want.

Ultimately, the criticisms of *Griswold* in Chapter 7, *Lawrence* in Chapter 10, and *Obergefell* in Chapter 11, should not be construed to suggest support for contraception laws or opposition to abortion or same-sex marriage. As a policy matter, permitting women to access abortion services and extending the right to marry to same-sex couples enables a greater number of citizens to enjoy liberty equally under the law and be protected from legislation motivated by prejudice and animus. The point is merely that the Court should not have decided these questions because they lacked the constitutional authority to do so. Had the Court reached contrary results in these cases, citizens would have had the opportunity to advocate for policy changes through the legislature, to participate in a constructive dialogue on the merits of their positions, and to ensure that elected officials responded to the concerns voiced by their constituents. These and other elements are necessary to foster a robust democracy and decentralized governance structure. Unfortunately, by removing this issue from the democratic process, the Court undermined the liberty and autonomy of all citizens.

***

Questions

Should the Court simply have ruled that women have a categorical right to first-trimester abortions and that no state interests can override this right?

Is there a benefit to adopting categorical rather than indeterminate rules that courts must apply in future cases? If so, what are the benefits and drawbacks?

Instead of basing its decision on the right to "to define one's own concept of existence, of meaning, of the universe, and of the mystery of human life," should the Court have relied on the Equal Protection Clause to reaffirm the abortion right?

Should prospective fathers have a voice in a woman's decision to terminate a pregnancy? If so, to what extent?

40 Planned Parenthood, 505 U.S. at 856.

10

LAWRENCE V. TEXAS

> *No State shall make or enforce any law which shall abridge the privileges or immunities of citizens of the United States; nor shall any State deprive any person of life, liberty, or property, without due process of law; nor deny to any person within its jurisdiction the equal protection of the laws.*
>
> —U.S. Const., Amend. XIV, Cl. 1

Summary

- In *Lawrence*, on behalf of a 5–4 majority, Justice Kennedy invalidated a Texas law banning sodomy between same-sex couples by creating a new penumbra-like right to liberty "in its spatial and in its more transcendent dimensions." In doing so, Justice Kennedy overruled the Court's prior decision in *Bowers v. Hardwick* where the Court upheld a sodomy ban against same *and* opposite-sex couples.
- Justice Sandra Day O'Connor wrote a concurring opinion and correctly relied on the Equal Protection Clause to hold that the law impermissibly discriminated against same-sex couples.
- Justice Kennedy relied on foreign law from the European Court of Human Rights to interpret the *US* Constitution.

***

Introduction

The Court's opinion in *Lawrence* is the modern-day equivalent of *Griswold*, as Justice Kennedy relied on an ambiguous, penumbra-like exposition regarding liberty to invalidate a law banning sodomy between same-sex couples.[1] Although the Court reached the

1 The quoted material in this chapter is taken from Lawrence v. Texas, 539 U.S. 558 (2003).

right outcome, the reasoning unnecessarily expanded the Court's already-unworkable unenumerated rights jurisprudence with language that was far broader than necessary to invalidate the statute, and with dicta that eschewed even the pretense of judicial restraint.

***

The decision

Writing for the majority, Justice Kennedy began by stating that the case involved liberty "in its spatial and in its more transcendent dimensions."[2] Not surprisingly, Justice Kennedy concluded that the constitutionality of the sodomy ban "should be resolved by determining whether the petitioners were free as adults to engage in the private conduct in the exercise of their liberty under the Due Process Clause of the Fourteenth Amendment to the Constitution."[3] Although acknowledging that sodomy was looked upon with disfavor throughout the country's history, Justice Kennedy declared that "[h]istory and tradition are the starting point but not in all cases the ending point of the substantive due process inquiry."[4]

With the latter statement, Justice Kennedy eschewed the traditional tests governing the recognition of a new constitutional right and shifted the focus entirely to whether the law infringed on same-sex couples' liberty. Justice Kennedy stated as follows:

> It suffices for us to acknowledge that adults may choose to enter upon this [same-sex] relationship in the confines of their homes and their own private lives and still retain their dignity as free persons. *When sexuality finds overt expression in intimate conduct with another person, the conduct can be but one element in a personal bond that is more enduring. The liberty protected by the Constitution allows homosexual persons the right to make this choice.*[5]

Justice Kennedy also emphasized that "the stigma this criminal statute imposes . . . is not trivial," because it demeaned same-sex couples:

> The case does involve two adults who, with full and mutual consent from each other, engaged in sexual practices common to a homosexual lifestyle. The petitioners are entitled to respect for their private lives. The State cannot *demean their existence or control their destiny by making their private sexual conduct a crime. Their right to liberty under the Due Process Clause gives them the full right to engage in their conduct without intervention of the government.*[6]

Additionally, Justice Kennedy relied on the following passage from *Planned Parenthood v. Casey*, where the Court reaffirmed the central holding in *Roe v. Wade*:

> These matters, involving the most intimate and personal choices a person may make in a lifetime, choices central to personal dignity and autonomy, are central

2 Id. at 562.
3 Id. at 564.
4 Id. at 572 (quoting County of Sacramento v. Lewis, 523 U.S. 833, 857 (1998)) (Kennedy, J., concurring).
5 Id. at 567 (emphasis added).
6 Id. at 578 (emphasis added).

> to the liberty protected by the Fourteenth Amendment. *At the heart of liberty is the right to define one's own concept of existence, of meaning, of the universe, and of the mystery of human life.* Beliefs about these matters could not define the attributes of personhood were they formed under compulsion of the State.[7]

In so holding, Justice Kennedy overruled *Bowers v. Hardwick*, even though the sodomy ban in *Bowers* applied to same *and* opposite-sex couples. Justice Kennedy asserted that the Court in *Bowers* "misapprehended the claim of liberty there presented to it" by focusing on whether there was a constitutional right to sodomy, rather than on whether the law infringed on an individual's liberty.[8] What's more, Justice Kennedy cited a decision from a *foreign* court (the European Court of Human Rights) that had invalidated a sodomy ban.

Lastly, Justice Kennedy held that *the Court* had the authority to recognize new rights that the Founders did not foresee.:

> Had those who drew and ratified the Due Process Clauses of the Fifth Amendment or the Fourteenth Amendment known the components of liberty in its manifold possibilities, they might have been more specific. They did not presume to have this insight. They knew times can blind us to certain truths and later generations can see that laws once thought necessary and proper in fact serve only to oppress.[9]

Finally, in a not-so-subtle nod to living constitutionalism, Justice Kennedy pronounced that "[a]s the Constitution endures, persons in every generation can invoke its principles in their own search for greater freedom."[10]

***

Analysis

> *At the end of its opinion . . . the Court says that the present case "does not involve whether the government must give formal recognition to any relationship that homosexual persons seek to enter." Do not believe it.*
>
> —Justice Antonin Scalia (dissenting opinion in *Lawrence* – twelve years before the Court recognized a right to same-sex marriage in *Obergefell v. Hodges*)

Justice Kennedy's opinion in *Lawrence* was the twenty-first century's version of *Griswold*, reflecting a vision of judicial power that was nothing short of staggering. Specifically, the Court: (1) singlehandedly rejected the standard that it had established for recognizing new constitutional rights, in favor of a right to "liberty . . . in its spatial and in its more transcendent dimensions"; (2) refused to base its decision on the Fourteenth Amendment's Equal Protection Clause, which would have firmly rooted

7 Id. at 574 (internal citation omitted) (emphasis added).
8 Id. at 567.
9 Id. at 578–579.
10 Id. at 579.

the decision in the Constitution and promoted judicial restraint; and (3) laid the foundation for the creation of a right to same-sex marriage, while simultaneously – and disingenuously – disavowing such an intent.

The seductive trappings of liberty – and the living constitution

> *If you think aficionados of a living constitution want to bring you flexibility, think again. You think the death penalty is a good idea. Persuade your fellow citizens to adopt it. You want a right to abortion? Persuade your fellow citizens and enact it. That's flexibility.*
>
> —Justice Antonin Scalia

In his majority opinion, Justice Kennedy flatly rejected the Court's well-settled standards governing the recognition of new rights, the purpose of which was to ensure that judges did not feel "free to roam where unguided speculation might take them."[11] In *Washington v. Glucksberg*, the Court held that an asserted right will only be considered fundamental if it is "so rooted in the traditions and conscience of our people as to be ranked as fundamental" and "implicit in the concept of ordered liberty," such that "neither liberty nor justice would exist if they were sacrificed."[12] In *Glucksberg*, the Court required "a 'careful description' of the asserted fundamental liberty interest" and emphasized that judges must "exercise the utmost care whenever we are asked to break new ground in this field, lest the liberty protected by the Due Process Clause be subtly transformed into the policy preferences of the Members of this Court."[13] This approach reflects the Court's reluctance "to expand the concept of substantive due process because guideposts for responsible decision-making in this unchartered area are scarce and open-ended," and also a recognition that "by extending constitutional protection to an asserted right or liberty interest, we [the Court], to a great extent, place the matter outside the arena of public debate and legislative action."[14]

Justice Kennedy ignored these prophylactic rules in his opinion, stating that "history and tradition are the beginning but not the end of the substantive due process inquiry."[15] The reason for doing so was obvious: under the Court's precedent, the answer to the question of whether sodomy was a fundamental right would have been *no*. For this reason, Justice Kennedy needed an alternative path by which to invalidate the statute, and "liberty" was waiting with open arms.

For the majority, relying on liberty was all but irresistible because virtually *any* right can be considered an expression of "liberty" and worthy of constitutional protection. For example, one can argue that polygamists should have the "liberty" to marry twenty wives, that citizens should have the "liberty" to snort cocaine or inject heroine, or that states should have the "liberty" to segregate their schools. It is precisely for this reason that *Glucksberg* relied on history and tradition, and required a "careful description" of

11 Planned Parenthood, 505 U.S. at 850 (internal citation omitted).
12 521 U.S. 702, 721 (1997) (internal citations omitted).
13 Id. (internal citations omitted).
14 Id. at 720 (internal citations omitted) (brackets added).
15 Lawrence, 539 U.S. at 572 (quoting County of Sacramento v. Lewis, 523 U.S. 833, 857 (1998)).

an asserted fundamental right: these factors constrain the Court by preventing the Justices from imposing subjective values on an entire nation, from encroaching on democratic choice, and from rendering decisions that extend far beyond the issues presented in a given case. The Court's decision in *Lawrence* brushed aside these concerns, and in so doing incentivized citizens to seek political change through the judiciary, rather than through the legislature.

What's worse, the tenor of Justice Kennedy's opinion suggests that he believes judges are "free to roam where unguided speculation might take them" and empowered to "*define the liberty of all.*"[16] In *Obergefell v. Hodges*, Justice Kennedy reinforced this perception, reasoning as follows:

> *The dynamic of our constitutional system is that individuals need not await legislative action before asserting a fundamental right.* The Nation's courts are open to injured individuals who come to them to vindicate their own direct, personal stake in our basic charter. An individual can invoke a right to constitutional protection when he or she is harmed, even if the broader public disagrees and even if the legislature refuses to act. The idea of the Constitution 'was to withdraw certain subjects from the vicissitudes of political controversy, to place them beyond the reach of majorities and officials and to establish them as legal principles to be applied by the courts.'[17]

The problem with this passage is that the Constitution only allows the Court "to withdraw certain subjects from the vicissitudes of political controversy" if the state enacts an unconstitutional law.[18] On the other hand, unwise laws, such as the contraception ban in *Griswold*, may be "uncommonly silly," but they are not necessarily unconstitutional.

If a law is not unconstitutional, citizens have the right to lobby their elected representatives and "await legislative action" through democratic debate. That is the essence of democracy. Of course, in *Lawrence*, the Equal Protection Clause provided a textual basis to invalidate Texas's statute. The fact that Justice Kennedy chose instead to rely on "liberty in its spatial and in its more transcendent dimensions" should serve as a reminder that absolute power corrupts absolutely.

Where have you gone, Justice O'Connor? The equal protection rationale

Justice Day O'Connor concurred in the judgment, drafting an opinion that was both principled and pragmatic. O'Connor disagreed with Justice Kennedy's reasoning, stating that "[r]ather than relying on the substantive component of the Fourteenth Amendment's Due Process Clause, as the Court does, I base my conclusion on the Fourteenth Amendment's Equal Protection Clause."[19]

16 Planned Parenthood, 505 U.S. at 850 (emphasis added).
17 Obergefell v. Hodges, 135 S. Ct. 2584, 2605 (2015) (emphasis added).
18 West Virginia Board of Education v. Barnette, 319 U.S. 624, 638 (1943).
19 Lawrence, 539 U.S. at 579.

In support of this position, Justice O'Connor noted that "legislation is presumed to be valid and will be sustained if the classification drawn by the statute is rationally related to a legitimate state interest."[20] Conversely, where "the challenged legislation inhibits personal relationships," there is an increased likelihood that the legislation will not withstand constitutional scrutiny.[21]

For Justice O'Connor, the critical factor supporting invalidation of the law was that it treated same- and opposite-sex couples differently. O'Connor emphasized that "[s]odomy between opposite-sex partners . . . is not a crime in Texas," revealing that "Texas treats the same conduct differently based solely on the participants."[22] As a result, Texas "makes homosexuals unequal in the eyes of the law by making particular conduct – and only that conduct – subject to criminal sanction."[23] Also, the asserted interest in enacting the law – promotion of morality – was not a legitimate basis upon which to discriminate against a particular group. As Justice O'Connor stated, "[m]oral disapproval of this group, like a bare desire to harm the group, is an interest that is insufficient to satisfy rational basis review under the Equal Protection Clause."[24]

Given that there existed a textual basis for invalidating the law, one must ask why Justice Kennedy made little mention of the Equal Protection Clause in his majority opinion. The answer, as Justice Scalia noted in his dissent, is that Kennedy was laying the foundation for the eventual recognition by the Court of a right to same-sex marriage:

> At the end of its opinion . . . the Court says that the present case 'does not involve whether the government must give formal recognition to any relationship that homosexual persons seek to enter.' Do not believe it . . . Today's opinion dismantles the structure of constitutional law that has permitted a distinction to be made between heterosexual and homosexual unions, insofar as formal recognition in marriage is concerned. If moral disapprobation of homosexual conduct is 'no legitimate state interest' for purposes of proscribing that conduct; and if, as the Court coos (casting aside all pretense of neutrality), '[w]hen sexuality finds overt expression in intimate conduct with another person, the conduct can be but one element in a personal bond that is more enduring', . . . what justification could there possibly be for denying the benefits of marriage to homosexual couples exercising '[t]he liberty protected by the Constitution,' [s]urely not the encouragement of procreation, since the sterile and the elderly are allowed to marry. This case 'does not involve' the issue of homosexual marriage only if one entertains the belief that principle and logic have nothing to do with the decisions of this Court. Many will hope that, as the Court comfortingly assures us, this is so.[25]

Justice Scalia's prediction proved correct. As discussed in Chapter 11, in *Obergefell v. Hodges*, twelve years after *Lawrence* was decided, the Court created a right to

20 Id. (quoting Cleburne v. Cleburne Living Center, Inc., 473 U.S. 432, 439 (1985)).
21 Id. at 580.
22 Id. at 581.
23 Id.
24 Id. at 583 (internal citations omitted).
25 Id. at 604–605 (Scalia, J., dissenting).

same-sex marriage. Writing for a bare 5–4 majority, Justice Kennedy relied not only on an all-encompassing definition of "liberty," but also on a right to equal dignity that is found nowhere in the Constitution. Perhaps equal dignity was lurking in those invisible "penumbras," just waiting to be discovered.

Why was it necessary to overrule *Bowers*?

Another troubling aspect of Justice Kennedy's opinion in *Lawrence* was that there was no need to overrule *Bowers*, where the Court upheld a law banning sodomy against same- and opposite-sex couples. Admittedly, the law at issue in *Bowers*, like the contraception ban in *Griswold*, was "uncommonly silly."[26] But the law was not unconstitutional because it did not offend any provision of the Constitution, and unlike the ban on interracial marriage that was invalidated in *Loving v. Virginia*, the law in *Bowers* involved moral disapproval of a specific behavior, not the codification of animus toward a particular group. In *Lawrence*, as Justice O'Connor correctly held, the state's sodomy ban extended only to same-sex couples, and therefore intentionally singled out same-sex couples for discriminatory treatment in violation of the Equal Protection Clause.

Admittedly, Justice Kennedy did make reference to the Equal Protection Clause in his opinion, but he refused to apply any of the legal standards that are used in equal protection cases. Under the Court's well-settled precedent, a law that classifies groups on the basis of among other things, race, ethnicity, or national origin, or that infringes on an established fundamental right, is subject to strict scrutiny. This standard requires the state to show that the law in question furthers a compelling governmental interest and is narrowly tailored to achieve that interest. Laws discriminating on the basis of gender are subject to intermediate scrutiny, requiring the state to show that such laws are substantially related to the achievement of legitimate governmental objectives. If a law does not implicate race, ethnicity, national origin, or gender, the Court applies the "rational basis" test, which requires the state to demonstrate that the law is rationally related to the achievement of legitimate governmental objectives.

Justice Kennedy applied none of these standards. Instead, he described equality in broad and prosaic terms, much in the same way as liberty was described in *Planned Parenthood*. Why did he do so? Like the Court in *Griswold*, Justice Kennedy was laying the groundwork for the future recognition of same-sex marriage, all while assuring readers that *Lawrence* (and later, *U.S. v. Windsor*) would have no effect on the states' authority to define the marriage relationship. After *Obergefell*, we know that none of this was true – then or now.

To make matters worse, Justice Kennedy rejected the Court's well-settled standards governing the creation of new rights under the substantive due process doctrine (i.e., whether the asserted right is "deeply rooted in the Nation's history and tradition") and reformulated the legal question to ask not whether the Constitution protected sodomy (which it does not), but instead whether the law infringed on same-sex couples' liberty interest. Put differently, to reach the desired outcome in *Lawrence*, Justice Kennedy manipulated the process by which the outcome was reached by overruling settled precedent, throwing the Court's equal protection and substantive due process decisions

26 381 U.S. at 527 (Stewart, J., dissenting).

into chaos with a newer and impossible-to-apply standard and making *stare decisis* seem like a doctrine that may be discarded when inconvenient. When one thinks of how far Justice Kennedy traveled to reach an obviously preordained outcome, it becomes difficult to dispute that his view of judicial power knows no boundaries.

Ironically, several years before *Lawrence* was decided, Justice Kennedy stated as follows:

> Any society that relies on nine unelected judges to resolve the most serious issues of the day is not a functioning democracy. I just don't think that a democracy is responsible if it doesn't have a political, rational, respectful, decent discourse so it can solve these problems before they come to the Court.[27]

Sadly, Justice Kennedy's statement does not match his jurisprudence – or make democracy work for the people.

***

Questions

Justice Kennedy and Justice O'Connor reached the same result but through different reasoning. Which reasoning was more persuasive and why?

If the Texas law had only prohibited sodomy among male same-sex couples and the state asserted that the interest was to reduce the spread of HIV, would the law have been constitutional?

Should the Court rely on foreign sources of law in its opinions? If not, what are the differences between the United States and foreign legal systems that counsel against such reliance? If so, to what extent and in what types of cases?

27 Brian Resnick, Anthony Kennedy: The U.S. 'Is Not a Functioning Democracy,' (Oct. 4, 2013), available at: http://www.theatlantic.com/politics/archive/2013/10/anthony-kennedy-the-us-is-not-a-functioning-democracy/454092/.

11

OBERGEFELL V. HODGES

> *No State shall make or enforce any law which shall abridge the privileges or immunities of citizens of the United States; nor shall any State deprive any person of life, liberty, or property, without due process of law; nor deny to any person within its jurisdiction the equal protection of the laws.*
>
> —U.S. Const., Amend. XIV, Cl. 1

Summary

- In *Obergefell*, Justice Kennedy authored an opinion for a 5–4 majority recognizing a right to same-sex marriage – the result Justice Scalia predicted twelve years earlier in *Lawrence* – based on legal fictions and dishonest reasoning.
- Justice Kennedy expanded the meaning of "liberty" to encompass a right to equal dignity under the law. Justice Kennedy effectively overruled the Court's decision in *Washington v. Glucksberg* and emphasized that the Court had an obligation to exercise "reasoned judgment" when "new insights" develop regarding the scope of individual liberty.
- The Court reached the correct outcome, but should have relied on the Equal Protection Clause, not vague promulgations of "liberty."

***

Introduction

In *Obergefell*, "*Griswold* liberty" was elevated to a new level when a bare majority of the Court invented a fundamental right to same-sex marriage – the result Justice Scalia predicted twelve years earlier in his *Lawrence* dissent.[1] Writing for a 5–4 majority,

1 The quoted material in this chapter is taken from Obergefell v. Hodges, 576 U.S., 135 S. Ct. 2584 (2015).

Justice Kennedy intentionally – and inexplicably – broadened the substantive due process doctrine (i.e., liberty) by holding that "liberty" encompassed, among other things, a right to intimate association, which the Court had previously inferred from the First, not Fourteenth, Amendment and a right to "equal dignity" under the law. As Justice Thomas recognized in his dissent, "the concept of 'liberty' it [the majority] conjures up bears no resemblance to any plausible meaning of that word as it is used in the Due Process Clauses."[2]

Moreover, as in *Lawrence*, Justice Kennedy refused to base the Court's decision on the Equal Protection Clause, which lower federal courts, such as the Seventh Circuit in *Baskin v. Bogan*, had relied on to invalidate same-sex marriage bans.[3] Instead, Justice Kennedy conflated "liberty" with the equal protection guarantee, stating that "the interlocking nature of these constitutional safeguards" and "synergy between the two protections . . . leads to a stronger understanding of the other."[4] Those wondering why Justice Kennedy went to such great lengths to invalidate same-sex marriage bans when a straightforward application of the Equal Protection Clause would have led to the same outcome need only recall *Griswold* and *Lawrence* to obtain the answer.

Ultimately, under the umbrella of substantive due process, *Obergefell* all but severed the constitutional constraints on the Court's lawmaking power. Justice Thomas emphasized this point, stating that "[b]y straying from the text of the Constitution, substantive due process exalts judges at the expense of the People from whom they derive their authority."[5] The Court's decision ensures that other groups, including polygamists, will allege that the ever-expanding sphere of liberty and equal dignity supports recognizing their chosen form of intimate association as a fundamental right. Such a result underscores "the dangerous fiction of treating the Due Process Clause as a font of substantive rights" because "it invites judges to do exactly what the majority has done here – 'roa[m] at large in the constitutional field guided only by their personal views as to the fundamental rights protected by that doctrine.' "[6]

***

The decision

In *Obergefell*, the Court invalidated state laws banning same-sex marriage, a decision that came two years after *Windsor*, where the Court, again by a 5–4 majority, invalidated Section Two of the Defense of Marriage Act, which had defined marriage as a union between opposite-sex couples. In *Windsor*, Justice Kennedy emphasized same-sex couples' "right" to equal dignity under the law, a term found nowhere in the Constitution and scarcely mentioned in prior decisions. Yet, as in *Lawrence*, Justice Kennedy assured readers that the decision would not impinge on the traditional authority of the states to define marriage. In his stinging dissent, Justice Scalia again

2 Id. at 2632 (Thomas, J., dissenting) (brackets added).
3 766 F.3d 648 (7th Cir. 2014).
4 135 S. Ct. at 2590.
5 Id. at 2631 (Thomas, J., dissenting).
6 Id.

predicted that, like *Lawrence*, Justice Kennedy's words could not be trusted and that Kennedy was laying the foundation for the recognition of a fundamental right to same-sex marriage. Once again, Justice Scalia was correct.

Again writing for a 5–4 majority, Justice Kennedy's decision was premised on four grounds. First, individuals have a right to intimate association. Second, marriage is part of an "enduring bond" that supports a two-person union more than any other institution.[7] Third, marriage protects children and therefore is related to the fundamental (and judicially created) right to child rearing, procreation, and education. Fourth, marriage is embedded in our country's history and tradition, and denying same-sex couples membership in this institution offends their right to liberty and equal dignity under the law.

Individuals have a constitutional right to intimate association

Justice Kennedy began his opinion with the prophetic statement that "the Constitution extends liberty to all within its reach."[8] Within the Constitution's "reach" were the right to privacy and the right to make intimate choices concerning sexual and personal relationships. Justice Kennedy explained that "like choices about marriage shape an individual's destiny," and "choices concerning contraception, family relationships, procreation, and childrearing, all of which are protected by the Constitution, decisions concerning marriage are among the most intimate that an individual can make."[9] Justice Kennedy stated as follows:

> The nature of marriage is that, through its enduring bond, two persons together can find other freedoms, such as expression, intimacy, and spirituality. This is true for all persons, whatever their sexual orientation . . . There is dignity in the bond between two men or two women who seek to marry and in their autonomy to make such profound choices.[10]

In Justice Kennedy's view, "[i]t would be contradictory to recognize a right of privacy with respect to other matters of family life and not with respect to the decision to enter the relationship that is the foundation of the family in our society."[11] Indeed, "[m]arriage responds to the *universal fear that a lonely person might call out only to find no one there*," and "offers the hope of companionship and understanding and assurance that while both still live there will be someone to care for the other."[12] Put differently, the right to marry dignifies couples who "wish to define themselves by their commitment to each other."[13]

7 Id. at 2599.
8 Id. at 2593.
9 Id. at 2599.
10 Id.
11 Id. (internal citation omitted).
12 Id. at 2600 (emphasis added).
13 Id. (internal citation omitted).

Marriage supports a two-person union like no other and is part of a personal bond that is more enduring

Justice Kennedy emphasized that marriage is a sacred and enduring bond between *two* individuals. This begs the question of why, under the broad reach of liberty, marriage must be confined to only two individuals. Chief Justice Robert raised this point in his dissent:

> If '[t]here is dignity in the bond between two men or two women who seek to marry and in their autonomy to make such profound choices,' why would there be any less dignity in the bond between three people who, in exercising their autonomy, seek to make the profound choice to marry? If a same-sex couple has the constitutional right to marry because their children would otherwise 'suffer the stigma of knowing their families are somehow lesser,' why wouldn't the same reasoning apply to a family of three or more persons raising children? If not having the opportunity to marry 'serves to disrespect and subordinate' gay and lesbian couples, why wouldn't the same 'imposition of this disability,' serve to disrespect and subordinate people who find fulfillment in polyamorous relationships?[14]

Justice Kennedy provided no answer to this question, likely because the insertion of "two" was as arbitrary as the decision to create a fundamental right to same-sex marriage.

Marriage safeguards children and draws meaning from related rights of child rearing, procreation, and education

Justice Kennedy also concluded that same-sex marriage bans stigmatize, harm, and humiliate the children of same-sex marriage:

> Without the recognition, stability, and predictability marriage offers, their children suffer the stigma of knowing their families are somehow lesser. They . . . suffer the significant material costs of being raised by unmarried parents, relegated through no fault of their own to a more difficult and uncertain family life. The marriage laws at issue here thus harm and humiliate the children of same-sex couples.[15]

As such, granting same-sex couples the right to marry allows children "to understand the integrity and closeness of their own family and its concord with other families in their community and in their daily lives."[16] Also, "[m]arriage . . . affords the permanency and stability important to children's best interests."[17]

14 Id. at 2621–2622 (Roberts, C. J., dissenting).
15 Id. at 2600–2601.
16 Id. at 2600 (internal citation omitted).
17 Id.

Marriage is embedded in the nation's history, and denying same-sex couples the right to marriage infringes upon their right to equal dignity under the law

Justice Kennedy relied heavily on marriage's historical importance as a bedrock cultural institution despite the fact that, throughout history, marriage has been defined and understood as the union of opposite-sex couples. Like his opinion in *Lawrence*, Justice Kennedy brushed aside over 200 years of history by stating that "rights come not from ancient sources alone," but "from a *better informed understanding* of how constitutional imperatives define a liberty that remains urgent in our own era."[18] Accordingly, although the "limitation of marriage to opposite-sex couples may long have seemed natural and just," the justification for extending the marriage right "is now manifest."[19] These statements beg two questions: From where does this new insight manifest itself, and what are these other "sources" of rights? In *Obergefell*, the answer was certainly not the United States Constitution, but rather the living Constitution, which apparently guides our understanding of liberty in the "heady days of the here and now."[20]

Unmoved by these concerns Justice Kennedy applied his "new insights" to hold that same-sex marriage bans relegate same-sex couples "to an instability many opposite-sex couples would deem intolerable in their own lives."[21] Also, "exclusion from that status has the effect of teaching that gays and lesbians are unequal in important respects."[22] Consequently, although "many who deem same-sex marriage to be wrong reach that conclusion based on decent and honorable religious or philosophical premises," such beliefs offend the Constitution when memorialized into law, as these beliefs place "the imprimatur of the State itself on an exclusion that soon demeans or stigmatizes those whose own liberty is then denied."[23] Justice Kennedy stated as follows:

> In forming a marital union, two people become something greater than once they were. As some of the petitioners in these cases demonstrate, marriage embodies a love that may endure even past death. It would misunderstand these men and women to say they disrespect the idea of marriage. Their plea is that they do respect it, respect it so deeply that they seek to find its fulfillment for themselves. Their hope is not to be condemned to live in loneliness, excluded from one of civilization's oldest institutions. *They ask for equal dignity in the eyes of the law. The Constitution grants them that right.*[24]

18 Id. at 2602 (emphasis added).
19 Id.
20 Id. at 2623 (Roberts, C. J., dissenting).
21 Id. at 2601.
22 Id. at 2602.
23 Id.
24 Id. at 2608 (emphasis added).

For these reasons, Justice Kennedy held that denying same-sex couples the right to marry "would disparage their choices and diminish their personhood," as marriage "embodies the highest ideals of love, fidelity, devotion, sacrifice, and family."[25]

***

Analysis

> *We might have covered ourselves with honor today, by promising all sides of this debate that it was theirs to settle and that we would respect their resolution. We might have let the People decide. But that the majority will not do. Some will rejoice in today's decision, and some will despair at it; that is the nature of a controversy that matters so much to so many. But the Court has cheated both sides, robbing the winners of an honest victory, and the losers of the peace that comes from a fair defeat. We owed both of them better.*
>
> —Justice Antonin Scalia (dissenting in *United States v. Windsor*)

Justice Kennedy's majority opinion in *Obergefell* was based on "the mystical aphorisms of a fortune cookie."[26] In the opinion, Kennedy (1) relied on a burgeoning concept – equal dignity – that is not mentioned anywhere in the Constitution, and that is potentially broader than *Griswold* liberty; and (2) drafted an opinion that represents the height of judicial arrogance, and is a classic example of how the exercise of "raw judicial power" can undermine participatory democracy.

Liberty is ushered into a new (transcendent) dimension

> *If, even as the price to be paid for a fifth vote, I ever joined an opinion for the Court that began: "The Constitution promises liberty to all within its reach, a liberty that includes certain specific rights that allow persons, within a lawful realm, to define and express their identity," I would hide my head in a bag.*
>
> —Justice Antonin Scalia (dissenting in *Obergefell v. Hodges*)

In *Obergefell*, Justice Kennedy expanded the definition of liberty *and* equality by effectively championing a new right to "equal dignity," a concept he championed in *Windsor*, rather than merely relying on liberty "in its spatial and in its more transcendent dimensions," or on same-sex couples' right to "define the mysteries of human life."[27] To accomplish this feat, Justice Kennedy conflated the Fourteenth Amendment's "substantive sphere of liberty" with the guarantee of equal protection of the law, holding that liberty and equality, although embodied in separate clauses, were interrelated. Citing *Lawrence*, Justice Kennedy stated as follows:

> In *Lawrence* the Court acknowledged the interlocking nature of these constitutional safeguards [liberty and equality] in the context of the legal treatment of

25 Id.
26 Id. at 2630, fn. 22 (Scalia, J., dissenting).
27 Lawrence, 539 U.S. at 562, 574.

> gays and lesbians . . . Although *Lawrence* elaborated its holding under the Due Process Clause, it acknowledged, and sought to remedy, the continuing inequality that resulted from laws making intimacy in the lives of gays and lesbians a crime against the State. *Lawrence* therefore drew upon principles of liberty and equality to define and protect the rights of gays and lesbians, holding the State 'cannot demean their existence or control their destiny by making their private sexual conduct a crime.'[28]

The problem with this analysis is that the concept of, or the right to, equal dignity is not, as Chief Justice Roberts stated in his compelling dissent, an "*enumerated* constitutional right."[29] As Chief Justice Roberts noted, "[t]here is . . . no 'Companionship and Understanding' or 'Nobility and Dignity' Clause in the Constitution."[30] Nor does the right to equal dignity comport with *any* reasonable interpretation of the Fourteenth Amendment, which prevents the government from depriving "any person of life, liberty, or property, *without due process of law*," *or* from denying "*to* any person within its jurisdiction *the equal protection of the laws*."[31] Implying a right to "equal dignity" from these words is nothing short of an exercise in legal gymnastics.

Chief Justice Roberts emphasized that the reasoning upon which the Court relied enabled judges to expand or create rights based solely on personal values:

> Expanding a right suddenly and dramatically is likely to require tearing it up from its roots. Even a sincere profession of 'discipline' does not provide a meaningful constraint on a judge, for 'what he is really likely to be 'discovering,' whether or not he is fully aware of it, are his own values.' The only way to ensure restraint in this delicate enterprise is 'continual insistence upon respect for the teachings of history, solid recognition of the basic values that underlie our society, and wise appreciation of the great roles [of] the doctrines of federalism and separation of powers.'[32]

In support of this proposition, Chief Justice Roberts relied on *Washington v. Glucksberg*, where the Court emphasized that "[a]llowing unelected federal judges to select which unenumerated rights rank as 'fundamental' – and to strike down state laws on the basis of that determination – raises obvious concerns about the judicial role."[33] Not surprisingly, Justice Kennedy ignored these principles. As Chief Justice Roberts stated, "[p]erhaps recognizing how little support it can derive from precedent, the majority goes out of its way to jettison the 'careful' approach to implied fundamental rights taken by this Court in *Glucksberg*."[34]

28 Obergefell, 135 S. Ct. at 2604 (internal citation omitted) (brackets added).
29 Id. at 2616 (Roberts, C. J., dissenting) (emphasis in original).
30 Id.
31 U.S. Const., Amend. XIV, Cl. 1 (emphasis added).
32 Obergefell, 135 S. Ct. at 2618. (internal citations omitted).
33 Id. at 2616.
34 Id. at 2620–2621.

Justice Kennedy did not "exercise the utmost care" and appeared indifferent to the danger that the "liberty protected by the Due Process Clause [was being] subtly transformed into the policy preferences of the Members of [the] Court."[35] As Chief Justice Roberts asserted, "nobody could rightly accuse the majority of taking a careful approach."[36] Instead, and just as in *Lawrence*, when he summarily overruled *Bowers*, Kennedy effectively overruled *Glucksberg*, ignoring both *stare decisis* and the legal standards governing the creation of fundamental constitutional rights. When the Court must go to such great lengths – overruling precedent, ignoring the text, and inventing new rights – to reach an outcome that its "reasoned judgment" deems desirable, it should be no surprise that the result is "an opinion lacking even a thin veneer of law," and a Court more powerful than the people.[37] Justice Scalia explained as follows:

> But what really astounds is the hubris reflected in today's judicial Putsch. The five Justices who compose today's majority are entirely comfortable concluding that every State violated the Constitution for all of the 135 years between the Fourteenth Amendment's ratification and Massachusetts' permitting of same-sex marriages in 2003. They have discovered in the Fourteenth Amendment a 'fundamental right' overlooked by every person alive at the time of ratification, and almost everyone else in the time since. They see what lesser legal minds – minds like Thomas Cooley, John Marshall Harlan, Oliver Wendell Holmes, Jr., Learned Hand, Louis Brandeis, William Howard Taft, Benjamin Cardozo, Hugo Black, Felix Frankfurter, Robert Jackson, and Henry Friendly – could not. They are certain that the People ratified the Fourteenth Amendment to bestow on them the power to remove questions from the democratic process when that is called for by their 'reasoned judgment.'[38]

In his dissenting opinion, Justice Samuel Alito summarized the defects – and dangers – in the Court's decision:

> Today's decision will . . . have a fundamental effect on this Court and its ability to uphold the rule of law. If a bare majority of Justices can invent a new right and impose that right on the rest of the country, the only real limit on what future majorities will be able to do is their own sense of what those with political power and cultural influence are willing to tolerate. Even enthusiastic supporters of same-sex marriage should worry about the scope of the power that today's majority claims. Today's decision shows that decades of attempts to restrain this Court's abuse of its authority have failed. A lesson that some will take from today's decision is that preaching about the proper method of interpreting the Constitution or the virtues of judicial self-restraint and humility cannot compete with the temptation to achieve what is viewed as a noble end by any practicable

35 Id. at 2616 (internal citation omitted).
36 Id. at 2621.
37 Id. at 2628 (Scalia, J., dissenting).
38 Id. at 2629–2630.

> means. I do not doubt that my colleagues in the majority sincerely see in the Constitution a vision of liberty that happens to coincide with their own. But this sincerity is cause for concern, not comfort. What it evidences is the deep and perhaps irremediable corruption of our legal culture's conception of constitutional interpretation.[39]

After *Obergefell*, the Court will undoubtedly feel free to create whatever future rights it desires under the self-serving blanket of liberty and equal dignity, or whatever catchphrase is fashionable in the "heady days of the here and now."[40] Equal dignity is now the sword that slashes whatever constraints remained on the Court's lawmaking power after *Griswold*, and the Court's "new insight" is the constitutional shield against judicial accountability.

A better informed understanding – known as "reasoned judgment"

At bottom, the right to equal dignity was predicated in large part on Justice Kennedy's belief that "new insights" provided a "better informed understanding" of the meaning of liberty and equality. Justice Kennedy stated that these insights, along with "societal understandings," can reveal "unjustified inequality within our most fundamental institutions that once passed unnoticed and unchallenged."[41] Unfortunately, although predictably, Justice Kennedy did not identify the source of these insights or societal understandings, or explain why five Justices had the authority to impose such insights on all fifty states. And even if "new insights" do emerge, they provide the Court with no authority to create fundamental rights, and therefore have no constitutional significance unless they are based on a reasonable interpretation of the Constitution's text. *Griswold*-liberty and equal dignity have no such foundation and epitomize the types of "insights" that do not originate from a legitimate source of legal authority, but rather from a majority of the Justices' subjective views regarding "liberty in its spatial and in its more transcendent dimensions" and the particular rights that emanate from *Griswold*'s invisible "penumbras."

In his dissent, Chief Justice Roberts noted that this approach to constitutional interpretation "omits even a pretense of humility, openly relying on its desire to remake society according to its own 'new insight' into the 'nature of injustice.'"[42] This prompted Chief Justice Roberts, perhaps out of sheer exasperation, to write, *"Just who do we think we are?"*[43]

Instead of allowing citizens to resolve this issue democratically, the Court decided "for itself a question the Constitution leaves to the people, at a time when the people are engaged in a vibrant debate on that question," and it "answers that question based

39 Id. at 2643 (Alito, J., dissenting).
40 Id. at 2623 (Roberts, C. J., dissenting).
41 Id. at 2603.
42 Id. at 2612 (Roberts, C. J., dissenting) (internal citation omitted).
43 Id. (emphasis added).

not on neutral principles of constitutional law, but on its own 'understanding of what freedom is and must become.' "[44] Chief Justice Roberts stated as follows:

> [F]or those who believe in a government of laws, not of men, the majority's approach is deeply disheartening. Supporters of same-sex marriage have achieved considerable success persuading their fellow citizens – through the democratic process – to adopt their view. That ends today. Five lawyers have closed the debate and enacted their own vision of marriage as a matter of constitutional law. Stealing this issue from the people will for many casts a cloud over same-sex marriage, making a dramatic social change that much more difficult to accept.[45]

What's worse, the Court's decision in *Obergefell* was issued just as "the winds of [democratic] change were freshening at their [same-sex couples'] backs."[46] Justice Roberts explained the consequences of the Court's decision on democracy:

> When decisions are reached through democratic means, some people will inevitably be disappointed with the results. But those whose views do not prevail at least know that they have had their say, and accordingly are – in the tradition of our political culture – reconciled to the result of a fair and honest debate. In addition, they can gear up to raise the issue later, hoping to persuade enough on the winning side to think again. 'That is exactly how our system of government is supposed to work.'[47]

Conversely, democracy does not function properly when the Court has "no basis for striking down a practice that is not expressly prohibited by the Fourteenth Amendment's text," with an opinion "lacking even a thin veneer of law" and riddled with "mummeries and straining-to-be-memorable passages."[48] Justice Thomas echoed this sentiment, stating as follows:

> Petitioners argue that by enshrining the traditional definition of marriage in their State Constitutions through voter-approved amendments, the States have put the issue 'beyond the reach of the normal democratic process.' But the result petitioners seek is far less democratic. They ask nine judges on this Court to enshrine their definition of marriage in the Federal Constitution and . . . put it beyond the reach of the normal democratic process for the entire Nation. That a 'bare majority' of this Court is able to grant this wish, wiping out with a stroke of the keyboard the results of the political process in over 30 States, based on a provision that guarantees only 'due process' is but further evidence of the danger of substantive due process.[49]

44 Id.
45 Id. at 2611.
46 Id. at 2625 (brackets added).
47 Id.
48 Id. at 2628 (Scalia, J., dissenting).
49 Id. at 2631–2632 (Thomas, J., dissenting).

In essence, the *Obergefell* majority "discovered in the Fourteenth Amendment a 'fundamental right' overlooked by every person alive at the time of ratification, and almost everyone else in the time since."[50] It did not matter to Justice Kennedy that change was occurring democratically – as it should when the Constitution is silent on an issue such as same-sex marriage. Nor was Justice Kennedy moved by the fact that when a decision by nine unelected and life-tenured judges "from the People a question properly left to them," the Justices are "reminded of [their] impotence," and the "Court's reputation for clear thinking and sober analysis" diminishes.[51] Most importantly, "a system of government that makes the People subordinate to a committee of nine unelected lawyers does not deserve to be called a democracy."[52] Put bluntly, in *Obergefell*, democracy yielded to oligarchy, just as in *Citizens United*, where democracy surrendered to plutocracy.

Justice Kennedy's opinion may remind some readers of a passage in *Lawrence* when he assured the country that the Court's decision would not lead to a judicially created right to same-sex marriage. Twelve years later, in a judicial sleight of hand, Justice Kennedy gave the Court power to say not only what the law *is*, but also what it *should be*. Perhaps this fact is what caused Justice Scalia to state "if even as the price to be paid for a fifth vote, I ever joined an opinion for the Court that began: 'The Constitution promises liberty to all within its reach, a liberty that includes certain specific rights that allow persons, within a lawful realm, to define and express their identity,' I would hide my head in a bag."[53]

The Court's purple prose damages its institutional legitimacy

> *The world does not expect logic and precision in poetry or inspirational pop philosophy; it demands them in the law. The stuff contained in today's opinion has to diminish this Court's reputation for clear thinking and sober analysis.*
>
> —Justice Antonin Scalia (dissenting in *Obergefell v. Hodges*)

In *Obergefell*, Justice Kennedy brushed aside the admonition that the Court is "most vulnerable and comes nearest to illegitimacy when it deals with judge-made constitutional law having little or no cognizable roots in the language or even the design of the Constitution."[54] After *Obergefell*, there can be little question that the distinction between legal and political questions has all but vanished and that the difference between law and politics has collapsed.

Justice Kennedy's opinion was littered with flowery rhetoric regarding liberty and dignity, but it completely disregarded the historical definition of marriage, obscured the meaning of the Fourteenth Amendment, and showed no respect for the democratic

50 Id. at 2629 (Scalia, J., dissenting).
51 Id. at 2630.
52 Id. at 2629.
53 Id. at 2643, fn. 22.
54 Id. at 2618 (internal citation omitted).

process. In short, the opinion was an embarrassing moment for the Court and the rule of law. As Justice Scalia stated in his dissent, "[t]he opinion is couched in a style that is as pretentious as its content is egotistic. It is one thing for separate concurring or dissenting opinions to contain extravagances, even silly extravagances, of thought and expression; it is something else for the official opinion of the Court to do so."[55]

Decisions resting on such reasoning result in the perception that the "Supreme Court of the United States has descended from the disciplined legal reasoning of John Marshall and Joseph Story to the mystical aphorisms of the fortune cookie," with an opinion that was filled with "showy profundities [that] are often profoundly incoherent."[56]

Chief Justice Roberts echoed this sentiment, stating that, "[s]tripped of its shiny rhetorical gloss, the majority's argument is that the Due Process Clause gives same-sex couples a fundamental right to marry because it will be good for them and for society."[57] Unfortunately, no amount of rhetorical gloss could alter the fact that the Court's opinion was "indefensible as a matter of constitutional law."[58] Chief Justice Roberts stated as follows:

> If you are among the many Americans – of whatever sexual orientation – who favor expanding same-sex marriage, by all means celebrate today's decision. Celebrate the achievement of a desired goal. Celebrate the opportunity for a new expression of commitment to a partner. Celebrate the availability of new benefits. *But do not celebrate the Constitution. It had nothing to do with it.*[59]

Justice Roberts was correct – the Constitution, and any conceivable constraint on the Court's power, was a mere afterthought.

At bottom, Justice Kennedy's opinion contributed to the perception, and perhaps confirmed a reality, that the outcome of a case depends in substantial part on the ideological composition of the Court, not the Constitution's language. Like its decisions in *Griswold*, *Roe*, *Planned Parenthood*, and *Lawrence*, *Obergefell* exacted grave injury on the rule of law and on the relationship between citizens and government. As Justice Thomas emphasized, "this distortion of our Constitution not only ignores the text, it inverts the relationship between the individual and the state in our Republic."[60] To appreciate the extent to which the Court's jurisprudence has strayed from the Fourteenth Amendment's text, consider the following summary of the Court's recent expressions of Griswold-liberty:

Griswold v. Connecticut

The Constitution contains penumbras, "formed by emanations, which help give them [the Bill of Rights] life and substance."

55 Id. at 2630.
56 Id. (brackets added).
57 Id. at 2616.
58 Id.
59 Id. at 2626 (emphasis added).
60 Id. at 2631 (Scalia, J., dissenting).

Planned Parenthood v. Casey

Citizens have the right to "define one's own concept of existence, of meaning, of the universe, and of the mystery of human life."

Lawrence v. Texas

The Constitution protects liberty in "its more spatial and transcendent dimensions."

Obergefell v. Hodges

"Marriage responds to the universal fear that a lonely person might call out only to find no one there."

As Justice Scalia stated, these statements would more likely be found in a fortune cookie than a decision of the United States Supreme Court. In fact, they are both indefensible as a matter of constitutional law and inimical to a healthy conception of democracy. After *Obergefell*, there is a little to stop the Court from manipulating the Constitution to achieve desired outcomes and subjective policy preferences – without any accountability whatsoever to citizens or fidelity to the law itself.

To be clear, this discussion is not meant to suggest that same-sex couples should not have the right to marry or that same-sex marriage would not constitute good public policy. It is simply to say that citizens, not the Court, should have decided this issue democratically or, at the very least, that the Court in *Obergefell* should have relied on the Equal Protection Clause, which provides a stronger textual basis upon which to invalidate same-sex marriage bans.

A view of liberty that is anything but libertarian

Justice Kennedy's opinion in *Obergefell* revealed that power, not liberty, was the driving force undergirding his constitutional philosophy, and that principles of federalism can be discarded whenever a majority of the Court believes that the "convenience of the moment" transcends the commitment to honest decision making.[61] Justice Alito stated as follows:

> The system of federalism established by our Constitution provides a way for people with different beliefs to live together in a single nation. If the issue of same-sex marriage had been left to the people of the States, it is likely that some States would recognize same-sex marriage and others would not. It is also possible that some States would tie recognition to protection for conscience rights. The majority today makes that impossible. By imposing its own views on the entire country, the majority facilitates the marginalization of the many Americans who have traditional ideas. Recalling the harsh treatment of gays and lesbians in the past, some may think that turnabout is fair play. But if that sentiment prevails, the Nation will experience bitter and lasting wounds.[62]

In fact, Justice Kennedy's judicial philosophy belies any contention that he truly believes in liberty and repudiates any notion of judicial restraint. In *Citizens United*,

61 Clinton, 525 U.S. at 449.
62 Obergefell, 135 S. Ct. at 2643 (Alito, J., dissenting).

Justice Kennedy drafted the majority opinion prohibiting Congress from addressing the noxious effects of corporate expenditures on the integrity of the electoral process. One must wonder how ordinary citizens can experience liberty in a meaningful sense when wealthy corporations donate large amounts of money to influence elected officials, marginalize the voices of millions of citizens, and compromise the fairness of our political system.

Similarly, in *Clinton*, Justice Kennedy relied heavily on the text of the Constitution (the Presentment Clause) to invalidate the Line Item Veto Act and therefore prevent Congress from experimenting with a solution that would have reduced wasteful government spending. Justice Kennedy reasoned that "[c]oncentration of power in the hands of a single branch is a threat to "liberty," including the "political liberty of our citizens."[63] Despite acknowledging that a "Nation cannot plunder its own treasury without putting its Constitution and its survival in peril, and that the Line Item Veto will tend to restrain persistent excessive spending," Justice Kennedy wrote that the Constitution's "structure requires a stability which transcends the convenience of the moment."[64] One must wonder how a solution that reduces wasteful spending undermines liberty. Additionally, in cases such as *Planned Parenthood* and *Lawrence*, Justice Kennedy ignored the text and relied on "reasoned judgment" that only five members of the Court could divine. The inherent contradictions in Justice Kennedy's jurisprudence suggest that liberty in its most abstract sense is the vehicle by which Justice Kennedy engages in the "exercise of raw judicial power."[65]

In the final analysis, Justice Kennedy's opinion and reasoning turn the Constitution's vision for American democracy on its head. Instead of decentralization and bottom-up lawmaking, *Obergefell* embraces centralization and top-down decision making by unelected judges. Instead of democracy, *Obergefell* sanctions oligarchy. Instead of restraint and humility, *Obergefell* represents activism and hubris. The fact that this occurs under the guise of "liberty" is perhaps the best evidence that "liberty" furthers purposes that are anything but libertarian, much in the same way that "penumbras" can give "life and substance" to a constitutional vision that is anything but egalitarian. The Court's decision in *Obergefell* should alarm citizens of all political persuasions and should offend anyone who believes that the individual, not the Court, has the right to "define one's own concept of existence, of meaning, of the universe, and of the mystery of human life."[66] American constitutional law now allows the judges to do and say whatever they want – with impunity. As Justice Alito stated in his dissenting opinion, "[m]ost Americans – understandably – will cheer or lament today's decision because of their views on the issue of same-sex marriage," although "all Americans, whatever their thinking on that issue, should worry about what the majority's claim of power portends."[67]

63 Clinton, 524 U.S. at 452.
64 Id. at 449.
65 Roe, 410 U.S. at 222 (White, J., dissenting).
66 Planned Parenthood, 833 U.S. at 851.
67 Obergefell, 135 S. Ct. at 2643 (Alito, J., dissenting).

Obergefell in the broader societal and cultural context

Like *Griswold*, the Court's decision in *Obergefell* appeared to be a response to the changing cultural and social climate in the United States. In the mid to late 1990s, lower federal and state courts, as well as legislatures in some states, created "civil unions" that provide same-sex couples with benefits similar to those afforded opposite-sex couples. Additionally, in the first decade of the twentieth century, a small number of lower federal and state courts, relying in substantial part on *Lawrence*, began to invalidate same-sex marriage bans, holding that such bans violated the Due Process and Equal Protection Clauses of the Fourteenth Amendment. In 2013, arguably in response to the changing public attitudes toward same-sex unions, the Court decided *Windsor*, in which it invalidated a provision of the federal Defense of Marriage Act that restricted the definition of "marriage" to opposite-sex couples. In *Windsor*'s aftermath, the judiciary's and public's support for same-sex marriage strengthened, as several federal courts of appeal invalidated bans on same-sex marriage and opinion polls showed that a slight majority of Americans supported extending the right to marry to same-sex couples. Three years later in *Obergefell*, the Court struck down same-sex marriage bans in every state, holding that they violated the judicially created right to "equal dignity" under the Fourteenth Amendment. Both *Windsor* and *Obergefell* underscore how the Court's interpretation of the Constitution – and the protections it afforded to same-sex couples – increased at a rate that corresponded to contemporary societal attitudes and public opinion polls. In other words, constitutional meaning has nothing to do with the Constitution.

After all, on what basis did the Court suddenly "discover" a right to same-sex marriage in the Due Process Clause, particularly after *Baker v. Carr*, where five decades earlier it refused to hear a case challenging bans on same-sex marriage? The only possible basis was the subjective value judgments of five Justices who relied on changing societal attitudes to render a decision that in appearance, and perhaps in actuality, was unquestionably – and unapologetically – political. One might wonder if the *Obergefell* majority would rely on public opinion if such polls showed that a majority of Americans favored segregation in public schools. The answer, of course, is no. The majority would willingly hold that segregation violated the Constitution and eschew the legitimacy of basing constitutional interpretation on contemporary values. That, in a nutshell, is the height of hypocrisy and the hallmark of a heavy-handed jurist.

Ultimately, the Court's decision damaged its institutional legitimacy and deprived same-sex marriage couples of the validation that comes when rights are created democratically. Chief Justice Roberts stated as follows:

> However heartened the proponents of same-sex marriage might be on this day, it is worth acknowledging what they have lost, and lost forever: the opportunity to win the true acceptance that comes from persuading their fellow citizens of the justice of their cause. And they lose this just when the winds of change were freshening at their backs.[68]

68 Id. at 2625.

Put simply, the majority's opinion was "an act of will, not legal judgment."[69]

***

Questions

Should the Court's decision have applied to states that already recognized civil unions and therefore accorded the same rights and privileges to same-sex couples?

After Obergefell, can bans on polygamy withstand constitutional scrutiny?

If history and tradition are the starting, but not ending, point in due process cases, what constraints remain to prevent the Court from abusing its Article III power?

Should the Court have invalidated same-sex marriage bans based on the Equal Protection Clause?

69 Id. at 2612 (Roberts, C. J., dissenting).

PART IV

The cases that weakened individual rights and promoted inequality

The disposition to admire, and almost to worship, the rich and the powerful, and to despise, or, at least, to neglect persons of poor and mean condition is the great and most universal cause of the corruption of our moral sentiments.

—Adam Smith

12

THE SLAUGHTERHOUSE CASES

No State shall make or enforce any law which shall abridge the privileges or immunities of citizens of the United States.

—U.S. Const., Amend. XIV, Cl. 1

Summary

- In *The Slaughterhouse Cases*, the Court held that the Privileges and Immunities Clause of the Fourteenth Amendment only includes the rights expressly enumerated in the United States Constitution and that the states have the sole authority to create unenumerated rights.
- The Court construed the phrase "Citizens of the United States" to mean citizens of the federal government, and in so doing distinguished federal from state citizenship. This interpretation left citizens vulnerable to the arbitrary exercise of the states' police powers.
- The Court should have construed the Privileges and Immunities Clause together with the Ninth Amendment to hold that the clause protects unenumerated rights that are retained by the people. The Court's decision indirectly led it to later manipulate the Due Process Clause to create a substantive right to liberty.

***

Introduction

In *The Slaughterhouse Cases*, the Court interpreted the Fourteenth Amendment's Privileges and Immunities Clause to only protect rights expressly enumerated in the Constitution and held that the states have the sole authority to create unenumerated rights.[1] The Court's narrow interpretation of the clause, along with its unworkable distinction between federal and state citizenship, rendered individuals, in their capacity as state citizens, vulnerable to arbitrary state legislation. Additionally, the Court's decision ignored the plain language of the Ninth Amendment, which states that the rights enumerated in the Constitution shall not be construed to "deny or disparage" other rights retained by the people.[2] In so doing, the Court missed an opportunity to strengthen judicial review in a manner that would be consistent with the Constitution's text and indirectly led to the creation of heavily criticized doctrines such as substantive due process.

***

The decision

In *The Slaughterhouse Cases*, the state of Louisiana enacted a law that granted exclusive rights to a specific corporation to, among other things, "establish and erect within certain territorial limits . . . one or more stock-yards, stock-landings, and slaughter-houses, and imposes upon it the duty of erecting, on or before the first day of June, 1869, one grand slaughter-house of sufficient capacity for slaughtering five hundred animals per day."[3] The designated corporation had "the sole and exclusive privilege of conducting and carrying on the live-stock landing and slaughter-house business within the limits and privilege granted by the act, and that all such animals shall be landed at the stock-landings and slaughtered at the slaughter-houses of the company, and nowhere else."[4]

The petitioners, a group of butchers doing business in Louisiana, challenged the statute's constitutionality, arguing that the law violated the Privileges and Immunities Clause of the Fourteenth Amendment. The Court summarized their arguments as follows:

> This statute is denounced [by the butchers] not only as creating a monopoly and conferring odious and exclusive privileges upon a small number of persons at the expense of the great body of the community of New Orleans, but it is asserted that it deprives a large and meritorious class of citizens – the whole of the butchers of the city – of the right to exercise their trade, the business to which they have been trained and on which they depend for the support of themselves and their families, and that the unrestricted exercise of the business of butchering is necessary to the daily subsistence of the population of the city.[5]

In a 5–4 decision, the Court rejected the butchers' claim, holding that the Privileges and Immunities Clause only protects fundamental rights that are expressly enumerated

1 The quoted material in this chapter is taken from The Slaughterhouse Cases, 83 U.S. 36 (1873).
2 U.S. Const., Amend. IX.
3 Id. at 59.
4 Id.
5 Id. at 60 (brackets added).

in the Constitution. Writing for the majority, Chief Justice Samuel Freeman Miller held that the Privileges and Immunities Clause only protects individuals in their capacity as citizens of the federal government, meaning that the clause only prohibits states from infringing on federal enumerated rights.

Accordingly, to the extent that fundamental rights exist independently of the federal constitution, the states, not the federal government, had *sole* authority to create such rights. Chief Justice Miller held that the "privileges and immunities secured to citizens of each State in the several States, by the provision in question, are those privileges and immunities which are common to the citizens in the latter States *under their constitution and laws by virtue of their being citizens* [of the states]."[6] As a result, the Privileges and Immunities Clause does not "control the power of the State governments over the rights of its own citizens," and its sole purpose was the following:

> [T]o declare to the several States, that whatever those rights, as you grant or establish them to your own citizens, or as you limit or qualify, or impose restrictions on their exercise . . . shall be the measure of the rights of citizens of other States within your jurisdiction.[7]

For this reason, "the entire domain of the privileges and immunities of citizens of the States . . . lay within the constitutional and legislative power of the States, and without that of the Federal government."[8] The majority held that this interpretation was consistent with principles of federalism and decentralization:

> [W]hen, as in the case before us, these consequences are so serious, so far-reaching and pervading, so great a departure from the structure and spirit of our institutions; when the effect is to fetter and degrade the State governments by subjecting them to the control of Congress, in the exercise of powers heretofore universally conceded to them of the most ordinary and fundamental character; when in fact it radically changes the whole theory of the relations of the State and Federal governments to each other and of both these governments to the people; the argument has a force that is irresistible, in the absence of language which expresses such a purpose too clearly to admit of doubt.[9]

Therefore, the Privileges and Immunities Clause only includes "privileges and immunities" that "belong to citizens of the States as such, and . . . *are left to the State governments for security and protection*, and not by this article placed under the special care of the Federal government."[10]

Under this interpretation, the monopoly created by statute constituted a lawful and traditional exercise of Louisiana's police power, which "in its essential nature, [is] one

6 Id. at 76–77 (emphasis added). (internal citation omitted) (brackets added).
7 Id. at 77.
8 Id.
9 Id. at 78.
10 Id. (emphasis added).

which has been, up to the present period in the constitutional history of this country, always conceded to belong to the States."[11] Justice Miller stated as follows:

> This power is, and must be from its very nature, incapable of any very exact definition or limitation. Upon it depends the security of social order, the life and health of the citizen, the comfort of an existence in a thickly populated community, the enjoyment of private and social life, and the beneficial use of property. 'It extends . . . to the protection of the lives, limbs, health, comfort, and quiet of all persons, and the protection of all property within the State; . . . and persons and property are subject to all kinds of restraints and burdens in order to secure the general comfort, health, and prosperity of the State. Of the perfect right of the legislature to do this no question ever was, or, upon acknowledged general principles, ever can be made, so far as natural persons are concerned.'[12]

Based on this rationale, the Court rejected the butchers' claim and reserved for the states the sole authority to create unenumerated fundamental rights.

***

Analysis

The Slaughterhouse Cases was wrongly decided and should be overruled. The majority's decision: (1) construed the words "privileges and immunities" far too narrowly and permanently changed the trajectory of the Court's Fourteenth Amendment jurisprudence; (2) indirectly spurned the eventual rise of doctrines such as substantive due process, including the creation of a substantive component to liberty and a right to "equal dignity" under the law; and (3) neglected the fact that the Privileges and Immunities Clause is the only legitimate basis in the Fourteenth Amendment upon which to recognize fundamental unenumerated rights, especially when construed in conjunction with the Ninth Amendment.

"Citizens of the United States" should include state citizenship

The Court's interpretation of the phrase "Citizens of the United States" was far too narrow and enabled state governments to subject citizens to basic violations of their civil rights and liberties. By permitting the state of Louisiana to create a monopoly, the Court sanctioned anticapitalist legislation that undermined the free market economy and left butchers (and citizens in future cases) without any legal or legislative remedy whatsoever unless the state provided such a remedy. In this way, the Court's interpretation of "Citizens of the United States" severely limited the scope of judicial review and ignored the text of the Ninth Amendment, which states that "[t]he enumeration in the Constitution, of certain rights, shall not be construed to deny or disparage other rights *retained* by the people."[13]

11 Id. at 62 (brackets added).
12 Id. (internal citation omitted).
13 U.S. Const., Amend. IX (emphasis added).

The Court's decision also insulated the states from federal judicial oversight over legislation, such as the Louisiana statute creating a monopoly, that would compromise citizens' economic and social liberty. If a state decided to sterilize intellectually disabled individuals, what provision of the federal Constitution would prevent the state from doing so? Certainly not the Fourteenth Amendment, which the Court construed as protecting no substantive rights whatsoever. Likewise, if a state decided to compel all citizens to participate in controlled medical experiments, what federal constitutional provision could citizens rely on to challenge the law? None. This approach endorsed an expansive view of state power that was just as injurious to citizens as *Griswold*-liberty.

The Privileges and Immunities Clause can be a source of substantive constitutional rights when construed in conjunction with the Ninth Amendment

The Court's decision indirectly led to the eventual development of substantive due process, constitutional penumbras, and a right to "equal dignity" under the law. Why? The Court interpreted the Privileges and Immunities Clause in a manner that foreclosed any possibility that it could be a source of fundamental unenumerated rights and ignored the text of the Ninth Amendment.

The Privileges and Immunities Clause prohibits states from enforcing "any law which shall abridge the privileges or immunities of citizens of the United States," and the Ninth Amendment provides that the "enumeration in the Constitution, of certain rights, shall not be construed to deny or disparage others retained by the people."[14] As a practical matter, this means that other fundamental rights exist apart from those enumerated in the federal constitution.

The Court could – and should – have held that the Fourteenth Amendment's "privileges and immunities" include rights retained by the people under the Ninth Amendment, which would have provided a textual basis for the creation of unenumerated rights in appropriate cases. As Justice Goldberg stated in his *Griswold* concurrence, the "language and history of the Ninth Amendment reveal that the Framers of the Constitution believed that there are additional fundamental rights, protected from governmental infringement, which exist alongside those fundamental rights specifically mentioned in the first eight constitutional amendments."[15]

Admittedly, some may disagree with this interpretation of the Ninth Amendment and Privileges and Immunities Clause, but that is not the point. The fact that this interpretation may be debatable does not mean that it is unreasonable, in part because the language in both provisions is ambiguous. In addition, the Privileges and Immunities Clause and Ninth Amendment would enable the Court to recognize new rights based on the Constitution's text, rather than by inventing "penumbras" or by discovering "liberty in its spacial and in its more transcendent dimensions."[16] As a result, the Court would preserve its institutional legitimacy, have sufficient flexibility to invalidate

14 U.S. Const., Amend. XIV, Cl. 1; U.S. Const., Amend. IX.
15 Griswold, 381 U.S. at 488 (Goldberg, J., concurring).
16 Lawrence, 539 U.S. at 562.

arbitrary state legislation, and respect the boundaries of its Article III reviewing authority.

It can be argued that this approach is a distinction without a difference because the Court would merely rely on the Privileges and Immunities Clause and Ninth Amendment to create a right to abortion and same-sex marriage. This argument disregards the fact that the Court would be required to develop workable standards to determine whether an asserted right is a "privilege and immunity." In fact, the Court has already created those standards: in *Glucksberg*, the Court held that fundamental rights must be "deeply rooted in the Nation's history and traditions" and "implicit in the concept of ordered liberty."[17] Thus, abortion and same-sex marriage would not likely be considered "privileges and immunities." In *Lawrence* and *Obergefell*, however, the Court eliminated these standards – and any pretense of judicial restraint – by inventing rights out of thin air and enabling the Court, in future cases, to create whatever rights it deemed fundamental.

At its core, the Court's reasoning essentially reads the Ninth Amendment out of the Constitution. If a state refuses to recognize any rights independent of those enumerated in the federal constitution, then citizens have no retained rights whatsoever and have relatively few grounds on which to challenge the constitutionality of state legislation. To make matters worse, the decision eventually led the Court to manipulate the language of the Due Process Clause – and alter constitutional meaning – to achieve outcomes that the text could not support. This led to the perception that the Court's decisions were motivated by ideology, which compromised its institutional legitimacy and undermined the rule of law.

***

Questions

Is "arbitrariness" a workable standard, or does it enable the Court to disregard the constraints on its reviewing power?

How could the Court have interpreted the Privileges and Immunities Clause and Ninth Amendment to enable the creation of unenumerated rights without giving the Court the power to create any right whatsoever? What standards would you use to constrain the Court?

How much deference should the Court give to state laws that do not violate an express provision in the Constitution, yet can be arbitrary in their application?

Why has the Court been reluctant to rely on the Ninth Amendment as a source of substantive rights?

17 Id. at 500 (internal citation omitted).

13

MILLIKEN V. BRADLEY

> *No State shall make or enforce any law which shall abridge the privileges or immunities of citizens of the United States; nor shall any State deprive any person of life, liberty, or property, without due process of law; nor deny to any person within its jurisdiction the equal protection of the laws.*
>
> —U.S. Const., Amend. XIV, Cl. 1

Summary

- *Milliken* is a results-directed decision that blatantly disregarded the Court's prior precedent and directives regarding school segregation.
- The decision improperly wrested control of developing effective remedies to school segregation from the judiciary in favor of leaving that power with the entities responsible for spawning it.
- *Milliken* effectively closed the door on attempts to eliminate segregation by removing the ability for courts to order interdistrict relief.
- The Court signaled an alarming retreat from *Brown*'s denouncement of the "separate but equal" doctrine.

***

Introduction

On April 7, 1970, the Detroit Board of Education adopted a voluntary desegregation plan to address the increasing racial polarization of the Detroit city schools. The state legislature responded by passing Public Act 48, a statute that placed school districts under the local control of neighborhoods, thereby preventing implementation of the April 7 plan. The Detroit Branch of the National Association for the Advancement of Colored People (NAACP) brought suit, asserting that Public Act 48 unconstitutionally interfered with the previously adopted desegregation plan and contending that the

Detroit Public School System was racially segregated due to official actions on both the state and federal levels. After considering evidence showing such actions and their links to Detroit's segregated school system, the district court determined that the only way to effectively address what indisputably was a constitutional violation was to reach outside of the city of Detroit itself and into the neighboring districts to unify the schools. In this regard, the district court concluded that anything but an interdistrict approach would result in an all-black school system. The Sixth Circuit agreed. Writing for the majority, Chief Justice Burger similarly upheld the finding of discrimination in Detroit, but disagreed that the courts could appropriately institute an interdistrict desegregation plan to address that problem absent an interdistrict violation of the U.S. Constitution. Because there allegedly had been no showing that the suburban districts had engaged in actions intended to segregate the Detroit city schools, the Court concluded that the multidistrict remedy proposed by the district court was impermissible. The result of the Court's ruling was that the Detroit city schools, and others throughout the nation, would remain segregated.

***

The decision

In a 5–4 ruling, the *Milliken* Court concluded that the only effective remedy to curing what was concededly a segregated school system could not be implemented because the Constitution forbade such a solution. In reaching this conclusion the Court did not dispute that the Detroit City School District was segregated. Indeed, it specifically acknowledged that the district court correctly had identified this segregation as the "condition" offending the Constitution.[1] Rather, the Court took issue with the multidistrict remedy proposed by the district court.

First, the Court took aim at the district court's understanding of what constituted desegregation. Specifically, it questioned what, in its view, was an unwarranted attempt by the district court to produce what it believed to be a desirable racial balance.[2] In weighing the merits of the Detroit-only plans versus a multidistrict approach, the District Court concluded that the former would not accomplish desegregation because under such a regime the racial composition of each school would not substantially reflect the racial composition of the population of the metropolitan area as a whole.[3] Relying on *Swann v. Charlotte-Mecklenburg Board of Education* the Court stated that, in the context of addressing a segregated school system, desegregation "does not require any particular racial balance in each school, grade or classroom" as suggested by the district court.[4]

The Court also disputed the district court's conclusion that an interdistrict solution was possible because the school district boundary lines "are simply matters of political convenience and may not be used to deny constitutional rights."[5] Rather, the majority found that the district court's willingness to rearrange school district lines to achieve

1 The quoted material in this chapter is taken from Milliken v. Bradley, 418 U.S. 717, 738 (1978).
2 Id. at 740.
3 Id.
4 Id. at 740–741.
5 Id. at 739.

an appropriate racial composition improperly impinged on the "tradition" that the educational process falls under the ambit of local control.[6] In this regard, the Court identified a series of perceived logistical problems that would be posed through an interdistrict approach and that embracing such an approach would require judges to take on tasks for which they are not qualified and would "deprive the people of control of schools through their elected representatives."[7]

Finally, invoking the principle announced in *Swann* that it is the "nature of the violation that determines the scope of the remedy,"[8] the Court stated that in devising a solution, lower courts are limited to tailoring a remedy to fit the precise parameters of the constitutional violation. Hence, because the identified condition of segregation was limited to Detroit, the district court could not properly seek to include in its solution suburban districts, which in the Court's reading of the evidence, had not been shown to commit any constitutional violation.[9] Specifically, the Court concluded that "without an interdistrict violation and interdistrict effect, there is no constitutional wrong calling for an interdistrict remedy."[10]

***

Analysis

> *The organizers and perpetuators of segregation are as much the enemy of America as any foreign invader.*
>
> —Bayard Rustin

Milliken provided the Court an opportunity to address the growing national scourge of segregation and to clearly underscore the judiciary's vital role in crafting workable solutions to eliminate it. The Court's conclusion that the multidistrict solution advanced by the district court and embraced by the Sixth Circuit was inappropriate because there had been no constitutional wrong calling for such a remedy rejected that opportunity and essentially closed the door on courts' ability to fashion effective remedies to end segregation. The Court's unwillingness to do this is built on a flimsy, if not wholly flawed, logic that begins with its treatment of the evidence developed in the District Court. Despite the fact that the record evidence showed a comprehensive, systematic attempt by the Detroit Board of Education and the state to create a segregated school system, and despite the fact that the District Court carefully demonstrated how a multidistrict approach was the only effective remedy to address that segregation, the Court ignored that evidence. By doing so, the Court was able to suggest that the multidistrict remedy was improper because there was nothing showing any violation by the outlying school districts and no evidence of any interdistrict violation or effect.[11]

6 Id. at 742.
7 Id. at 743–744.
8 Id. (quoting Swann at Swann, 402 U.S. at 15).
9 Id. at 745.
10 Id.
11 Id.

Of course, this crimped view was completely contrary to the Court's prior position that the courts should have considerable flexibility in crafting desegregation plans. Indeed, as Justice White pointed out in dissent, the majority's ruling instead signaled that the prime concern in assessing a proposed remedy is whether it would impose "undue administrative inconvenience to the State."[12] For the majority, supposed logistical problems attendant to the district court's multidistrict plan made it impractical for courts to administer and weighed in favor of leaving control of the schools in the hands of elected representatives.[13] The Court's decision crippled the ability of lower courts to devise solutions based on their familiarity with the facts, the local community, and the problems facing that community – leaving resolution of the problem with the entities that created those problems. At its heart, the Court's ruling effectively condoned the segregation of the Detroit school system and signaled that the "separate but equal" principle denounced by *Brown* was alive and well.

***

Questions

Why did the Court impose such a narrow reading of what constituted a violation?
What economic motives might have driven the Court's decision?
How did Milliken affect the Court's jurisprudence going forward?

12 Id. at 763.
13 Id. at 743.

14

SAN ANTONIO INDEPENDENT SCHOOL DISTRICT V. RODRIGUEZ

No State shall make or enforce any law which shall abridge the privileges or immunities of citizens of the United States; nor shall any State deprive any person of life, liberty, or property, without due process of law; nor deny to any person within its jurisdiction the equal protection of the laws.

—U.S. Const., Amend. XIV, Cl. 1

Summary

- *Rodriquez* provided the Court an opportunity to solidify the promise of *Brown* by ensuring equal educational opportunities to all – an opportunity the majority chose to forego.
- The Court improperly deferred to state and local governments' economic interests rather than address the wealth-based discrimination those interests were spawning.
- The decision weakened the democratic process and undermined the ability of all citizens to engage in the political process fully and fairly.

***

Introduction

In *Rodriguez* the Court considered whether significant differences in funding between Texas public school districts violated the Equal Protection Clause of the Fourteenth Amendment. Specifically, the Court addressed the issue of whether education is a fundamental right that must be provided equally to all students, regardless of a school district's economic health. In a 5–4 decision, the majority held that education is not a fundamental right and that wealth is not a suspect class requiring the Court to scrutinize a state's educational funding scheme. In so ruling, the Court failed to recognize the direct relationship between funding and the quality of education received, and thereby gave the green light to local and state governments to provide lesser educations to students located in poorer school districts. The Court's decision is regrettable, as it significantly narrowed the Court's commitment in *Brown* to ensuring equal educational opportunities to all and weakened the democratic process by compromising one of its most important tools – a well-informed, fully engaged electorate. Rather than intervene to protect the right that *Brown* recognized as one that must be made available to all on equal terms, the Court improperly deferred to the economic interests of local and state governments.

***

The decision

In *Rodriguez*, the Court considered the constitutionality of Texas's public school funding scheme. The funding program operated by receiving contributions from both state and local contributions, as well as from the federal government. Individual school districts were responsible for providing a percentage of the necessary resources for the program, and those resources were derived from property taxes on citizens living within the various school districts. The lower the amount generated by property taxes, the lower the amount of funding available to a district's schools. Parents of children attending the Edgewood School District brought suit on behalf of themselves and their children, as well as all children in Texas residing in school districts with low property valuations, contending that the funding scheme violated the plaintiffs' equal protection rights under the Fourteenth Amendment. At the heart of the action were the plaintiffs' dual contentions that education is a fundamental right and that wealth should be treated as a suspect class. Either premise, if accepted by the Court, would require a strict scrutiny review and a showing by the state that it had chosen the least restrictive means for achieving its interest. Although the district court for the Western District of Texas agreed with the plaintiffs, the Court squarely rejected both theories. As to the first, the majority concluded that the Constitution neither explicitly nor implicitly guarantees a right to education.[1] As to the second, the Court declined to recognize wealth as a suspect classification under the circumstances. Concluding that Texas's funding system therefore was not subject to strict scrutiny but instead to a rational basis review, the Court subsequently determined that the scheme easily satisfied that standard and that the plaintiffs' equal protection claim accordingly failed.[2]

The Court analyzed each constitutional theory in turn. With respect to the contention that wealth should be treated as a suspect classification requiring strict scrutiny, Justice Powell began by noting what he believed to be a threshold problem – the perceived inability to properly identify or define the "poor" who allegedly made up the class.[3] In this regard, he observed that the claim of discrimination advanced against the Texas system could be described in several ways – none of which fell neatly into any customary equal protection analysis.[4] In particular, he identified one potentially disadvantaged class as definably "poor persons" as measured by some identifiable level

1 The quoted material in this chapter is taken from *San Antonio Independent School District v. Rodriguez*, 411 U.S. 1, 34–35 (1973).
2 Id. at 55.
3 Id. at 19.
4 Id. at 19–20.

of poverty.[5] A second potential class could be those "who are relatively poorer."[6] A third could consist of those, regardless of income, who happen to live in relatively poorer school districts.[7] For the majority, the task then became determining whether the Texas financing system did, in fact, discriminate on any of these possible bases and, if so, whether the classifications could properly be understood as suspect.

The Court premised its analysis on prior case law, stating that under prior Court precedents, classifications based on wealth were limited to: (1) those instances in which an individual's financial status left that person "completely unable to pay for some desired benefit"; and (2) as a result, the person "sustained an absolute deprivation of a meaningful opportunity to enjoy that benefit."[8] The Court determined that these characteristics were not present in any of the three potentially defined groups. Specifically, the Court concluded that there were insufficient facts to support the claim that the poorest people were concentrated in the poorest districts, and that there was no evidence showing that the system absolutely deprived "poor" people of an education. Rather, as to the latter, because the Texas system guaranteed "at least an adequate program of education"[9] and because "the Equal Protection Clause does not require absolute equality or precisely equal advantages,"[10] the Court concluded that the Texas system did not operate to the peculiar disadvantage of any suspect class.[11]

As to the plaintiffs' contention that education is a fundamental right subject to strict scrutiny, the Court began with a nod toward *Brown v. Board of Education* and the Court's unanimous recognition in that case that "education is perhaps the most important function of state and local governments."[12] Despite that acknowledgement, Justice Powell quickly clarified that "the importance of a service performed by the State does not determine whether it must be regarded as fundamental for purposes of examination under the Equal Protection Clause."[13] Rather, to avoid the Court becoming a "super legislature" by identifying for itself the importance of any particular issue, Justice Powell cautioned, "[I]t is not the province of this Court to create substantive constitutional rights in the name of guaranteeing equal protection of the laws."[14] Instead, the Court is bound to assess "whether there is a right to education explicitly or implicitly guaranteed by the Constitution."[15] The Court quickly noted that education is not explicitly provided protection under the Constitution.[16] The Court likewise eschewed the argument that, because education bears a close relationship to a person's ability to effectively exercise explicitly guaranteed rights (e.g., rights afforded by the First Amendment and the right to vote), that the Court should recognize education as a fundamental personal right.

5 Id.
6 Id.
7 Id.
8 Id. at 20–21.
9 Id. at 24.
10 Id. at 24.
11 Id. at 29.
12 Id. at 29 (citing Brown, 347 U.S. at 493).
13 Id. at 30.
14 Id. at 33.
15 Id. at 33–34.
16 Id. at 35.

The Court articulated two reasons for doing so. First, the Court noted that the Constitution does not guarantee citizens "the most effective speech or the most informed electoral choice."[17] Accordingly, in the Court's view, even assuming that some minimum level of education is a constitutionally protected prerequisite to exercising these enumerated rights, the Texas financing system did precisely that by offering its students "an opportunity to acquire the basic minimal skills necessary for the enjoyment of the rights of speech and of full participation in the political process."[18] The Court also noted that it could identify no reasonable distinction between education and other significant personal interests, such as access to appropriate food and clothing. In the Court's view, recognizing all of these interests as fundamental under the Constitution and imposing a strict scrutiny review to a state's actions with respect to the same would improperly inject the judiciary into areas best left to local governance and state legislative efforts.[19]

Because the Court embraced neither of the plaintiffs' constitutional challenges and requests for strict scrutiny, Justice Powell concluded that there only need be a showing that the state's system bore "some rational relationship to legitimate state purposes."[20] Finding that the Texas system concerned the state's raising and disbursement of local tax revenue – an area in which the Court historically has deferred to state legislatures – and that it implicated complex questions of educational policy of which the Court lacked "specialized knowledge and experience,"[21] Justice Powell stated that the Court should "refrain from imposing on the States inflexible constitutional restraints that could circumscribe or handicap the continued research and experimentation so vital to finding even partial solutions to educational problems and to keeping abreast of ever-changing conditions."[22] Because the Texas system's reliance on both state and local revenue was similar to that employed in other states, and because the system sought to achieve a balance between the dual goals of providing an education to every child with parents' desire to provide the best education to their own children, the Court concluded that the funding disparities between the school districts did not evidence invidious discrimination, but instead indicated a rational attempt by the state to further a legitimate state interest.[23]

* * *

Analysis

Although couched in terms of a neutral constitutional analysis, and despite the majority's claim that nothing in its holding "detracts from our historic dedication to public education,"[24] the decision suffers from a lack of analytical integrity and veers far from the vision of educational opportunity envisioned by *Brown*. More to the point, the Court

17 Id. at 36.
18 Id. at 37.
19 Id. at 36–37.
20 Id. at 40.
21 Id. at 40–42.
22 Id. at 43.
23 Id. at 55.
24 Id. at 30.

failed to step in when it should have to address and cure a demonstrably discriminatory scheme that favored the wealthy, denied educational opportunities based on that classification, and weakened the poor's ability to fully and fairly participate in the democratic process and to enjoy their rights of free speech and association.

With respect to the Court's analysis, as the dissent correctly pointed out, the majority misconstrued evidence gathered in the district court demonstrating that the funding scheme had a significant disparate impact on the poorer school districts and that the state's attempts to lessen the gap between the districts were either nonexistent or insufficient. The dissent likewise pointed out the "absurdity" of the majority's argument that the difference between per-pupil spending among the school districts had no discriminatory consequences vis-a-vis the educational opportunities available to Texas students.[25]

As to the Court's determination that it could not, and should not, involve itself in issues of school funding, the Court excused itself from addressing a fundamental reality – that unequal resources in the schools means unequal educational opportunities, and unequal educational opportunities means unequal participation in the democratic process. The system sanctioned by the Court as appropriately leaving to local control the issue of student funding has resulted in perpetuating inequality and announcing that *Brown*'s vision of extending the opportunity of education "to all on equal terms" was a narrow one indeed. Given the importance of the obvious link between education and its role in "shaping the lives of citizens" and in permitting full participation in the political process, the Court was under an obligation, as Justice Marshall argued in the dissent, to view the demonstrated inequalities spawned by the Texas system with a skeptical eye. Its failure to do so, and its willingness to count on state legislatures to address this entrenched discrimination, marks a failure by the Court to perform an essential role of the judiciary: to protect a politically powerless group and to provide a remedy where the legislature is unable or unwilling to remedy a constitutional harm.

***

Questions

Could the Court have opted to invoke the Ninth Amendment and found a constitutional right to education outside the scope of the Fourteenth Amendment?

The Court suggested a constitutional challenge might be based on a state's failure to provide an adequate education for all children. What might such a challenge look like, and how likely would it be to succeed?

In what ways might the Court's decision to leave issues of school funding to state and local government be justified? Were the Court's concerns about federalism arguably legitimate?

What impact do you think this case subsequently had on state legislative initiatives regarding public education?

25 Id. at 83–84.

15

MCCLESKEY V. KEMP

Excessive bail shall not be required, nor excessive fines imposed, nor cruel and unusual punishments inflicted.

—U.S. Const., Amend. VIII

Summary

- In *McCleskey v. Kemp* the Court essentially closed the door on racial challenges to convictions and sentencing, thereby fostering continued racial disparity in the criminal justice system.
- Although presented with the opportunity to address and correct the racially biased manner in which death sentences are meted out, the Court failed to intervene to protect minority rights, opting instead to defer to a failed state legislative process.

***

Introduction

In the spring of 1978 Warren McCleskey was convicted of armed robbery and murder in the Superior Court of Fulton County, Georgia. The convictions arose out of a furniture store robbery that McCleskey, an African American man, admitted having participated in and the contemporaneous shooting of a white police officer. McCleskey denied that he had shot the officer, but he later was convicted of murder and sentenced to death. McCleskey appealed his conviction and sentence, contending that the Georgia capital sentencing process was administered in a racially discriminatory manner in violation of his rights under both the Eighth and Fourteenth Amendments of the Constitution. Specifically, McCleskey came forward with statistical evidence demonstrating that race played a critical role in who was sentenced to death in Georgia. The report, a detailed study by Professor David Baldus, showed that African Americans were significantly more likely to receive a death sentence in

Georgia than white defendants, and that African Americans who killed whites likewise were more likely to be sentenced to death than were whites who killed African Americans. Despite this evidence – evidence that the Court assumed to be valid – in a 5–4 decision, the Court rejected both of McCleskey's constitutional claims. As to his equal protection claim, the Court ruled that the statistical evidence offered by McCleskey failed to prove that his own conviction and sentence were the result of racial prejudice. As to his claim under the Eight Amendment, the Court concluded that the procedural safeguards governing Georgia's sentencing procedures eliminated any "constitutionally significant" risk that McCleskey's death sentence was indiscriminately imposed. In rejecting McCleskey's constitutional challenges, the Court improperly turned a blind eye to what was clear evidence of racial discrimination and sanctioned a failed legislative attempt to ensure fairness in capital sentencing. The Court's ruling in *McCleskey* effectively ended any meaningful challenges to the death penalty in the United States.

***

The decision

The issue before the *McCleskey* Court was whether statistical evidence that indicated that race was a substantial factor in determining whether a defendant received the death penalty could support a constitutional challenge under either the Fourteenth or Eighth Amendment.

McCleskey argued that the Baldus analysis, a sophisticated statistical study that the Court was willing to assume was accurate, demonstrated discriminatory intent by Georgia in its imposition of the death penalty, thereby violating his equal protection rights under the Fourteenth Amendment. He also asserted that the study showed that his sentence was disproportionate to similarly situated defendants in violation of his rights under the Eighth Amendment. The Court rejected both contentions. In doing so, the Court relied on three principal arguments. First, it asserted that McCleskey's position threatened the ability of decision makers in the criminal justice process to properly exercise their discretion.[1] Second, the Court understood that the statutory protections instituted by Georgia in the wake of the Court's decision in *Gregg v. Georgia* acted as sufficient safeguards against the risk that a defendant's death sentence might be tied to race. Finally, the Court stated its belief that issues regarding sentencing were best left to the state legislative process.

As to McCleskey's Fourteenth Amendment claim, the Court began its analysis noting that a defendant asserting such a claim must prove purposeful discrimination, which in turn requires a showing that the purposeful discrimination had a discriminatory effect on that defendant.[2] Thus, in the Court's view, to support his equal protection claim, McCleskey was required to "prove that the decision-makers in *his* case acted with discriminatory purpose."[3] McCleskey urged that the Baldus study compelled an

1 The quoted material in this chapter is taken from McCleskey v. Kemp, 481 U.S. 293, 297 (1987).
2 Id. at 292.
3 Id. (emphasis in original).

inference that his sentence was the result of purposeful discrimination.[4] Although the Court acknowledged that in the areas of venire selection and Title VII cases it had permitted the use of statistical evidence to support a claim of constitutional violation, the Court found McCleskey's attempted use of such evidence in a capital case to be "fundamentally different."[5] In this regard, the Court expressed its concern that the discretion exercised in the criminal justice system – a component of the system that the Court believed to be "essential" – would be threatened by the use of such evidence. Specifically, the Court stated:

> McCleskey challenges decisions at the heart of the State's criminal justice system. . . . Implementation of these laws necessarily requires discretionary judgments. Because discretion is essential to the criminal justice process, we would demand exceptionally clear proof before we would infer that the discretion has been abused. The unique nature of the decisions at issue in this case also counsels against adopting such an inference from the disparities indicated by the Baldus study.[6]

Accordingly, the Court rejected McCleskey's disparate impact claim.

With respect to McCleskey's Eighth Amendment claim, the Court engaged in a detailed discussion of its prior ruling in *Gregg v. Georgia*, a case in which the Court ruled that imposition of the death penalty would not constitute cruel and unusual punishment if its imposition was the result of a careful assessment of the specific characteristics of the case and of the defendant.[7] In particular, the Court noted in *Gregg* that Georgia had implemented a statutory system that safeguarded against arbitrary and capricious death sentences – the same system in effect when McCleskey was sentenced.[8] Because McCleskey's sentence was imposed under procedures specifically designed to guard against capricious, discriminatory sentencing, the Court concluded that McCleskey's death sentence was not "wantonly and freakishly" imposed, and accordingly rejected his claim that the sentence was disproportionate within the meaning of the Eighth Amendment.[9] In so doing, the Court recognized that although there might be a risk that a defendant's sentence could be correlated with race, the safeguards designed to eliminate such bias, coupled with the benefits that discretion provides to defendants in the criminal justice system, outweighed such a risk.[10] Specifically, the Court concluded that the Baldus study did not "demonstrate a constitutionally significant risk of racial bias affecting the Georgia capital sentencing process."[11]

4 Id. at 293.
5 Id. at 294.
6 Id. at 297.
7 Id. at 302, 308.
8 Id. at 302–303.
9 Id. at 308.
10 Id. at 313.
11 Id.

Finally, the Court opined that McCleskey's arguments were "best presented to the legislative bodies."[12] Indeed, the Court specifically stated:

> It is not the responsibility – or indeed even the right – of this Court to determine the appropriate punishment for particular crimes. It is the legislatures, the elected representatives of the people, that are "constituted to respond to the will and consequently the moral values of the people."[13]

Viewing McCleskey's challenge as one seeking to invalidate capital punishment rather than as a specific challenge regarding whether the law of Georgia – as enacted by its legislature – was correctly applied, the Court rejected that challenge and concluded, as had the district court and the Eleventh Circuit, that the law had been carefully and correctly applied in McCleskey's case.[14]

Justices Brennan and Marshall dissented, arguing that the death penalty is in all circumstances cruel and unusual punishment prohibited by the Eighth Amendment.[15] Joined by Justices Blackmun and Stevens, Justice Brennan pointed out that under the Court's prior jurisprudence there was no requirement that McCleskey prove that race influenced his sentencing decision. Rather, under the Eighth Amendment, the Court consistently had ruled that a defendant need only show that the circumstances under which a death sentence was imposed created an unacceptable risk that the sentence was influenced by impermissible considerations.[16] Because of the obviously high stakes involved in a capital case, and because the Baldus study identified that it was more likely than not that race influenced McCleskey's sentence, the dissent argued that McCleskey's constitutional challenges should not have been dismissed.

***

Analysis

The Court's unwillingness to find that the Baldus study demonstrated a constitutionally significant risk that racial bias informed the imposition of McCleskey's death sentence is troubling on multiple levels. First, the Court's rigid adherence to the premise that the guidelines it sanctioned in *Gregg* were sufficient to safeguard against racial bias in sentencing cannot be squared with the simple fact that the Baldus study showed otherwise. Quite clearly, the study indicated that, despite those safeguards, the Georgia criminal justice system was meting out death sentences to African Americans at a rate four times greater than the same sentence was being given to whites. The McCleskey case offered the Court an opportunity to assess the validity of its assumption that the *Gregg* safeguards could, in fact, sufficiently police against racially motivated sentencing. The numerical disparities identified by the Baldus report showed that it was more

12 Id. at 319.
13 Id. (quoting Furman v. Georgia (1972)).
14 Id. at 319.
15 Id. at 320.
16 Id. at 322.

likely than not that race played a role in the imposition of McCleskey's death sentence. That fact alone should have suggested to the Court that the procedures that presumably were protecting McCleskey and others in capital cases were not providing much protection at all. The Court's refusal to acknowledge this, presumably because to do so would have required a potential overhaul of its prior capital punishment jurisprudence, cannot be justified. The Court could have, and should have, prevented the wrong that this case brought into sharp focus.

Indeed, the McCleskey case is a prime example of where the Court should have given McCleskey's constitutional claims wide berth. There can be little dispute that his claims under both the Fourteenth and Eighth Amendments were plausible and could find support in both a reading of the text as well as in the Court's prior case law. Accordingly, the Court should have embraced a reading of both amendments that would have avoided the injustice that the Baldus report clearly was highlighting and that would have protected the rights of McCleskey and other marginalized defendants. The Court should have intervened because it was evident that the legislative process that the Court so fondly embraced was failing African Americans. The Court's refusal to do so essentially closed the door on any future challenges to the grave disparities in sentencing that the Baldus report exposed, and certainly ended any meaningful challenges to the death penalty itself.

***

Questions

What justifications might the Court have for deferring to the legislative process?

What is a "constitutionally significant risk" under McCleskey?

Can McCleskey be squared with the Court's prior equal protection jurisprudence?

16

GENERAL ELECTRIC CO. V. GILBERT

Gender equality is more than a goal in itself. It is a precondition for meeting the challenge of reducing poverty, promoting sustainable development and building good governance.
—Kofi Annan

Summary

- The Court's decision in *Gilbert* was based on an erroneous understanding of the protections provided by Title VII.
- The decision articulated and embraced a cramped and illogical definition of what constitutes sex discrimination.
- The Court's determination that distinctions based on gender-based characteristics do not give rise to claims of discrimination under Title VII perpetuated workplace inequality and opened the door for employers to engage in discriminatory conduct with impunity.

***

Introduction

In *Gilbert*, a class of women employed by General Electric brought a Title VII claim against the company on the ground that the comprehensive disability plan offered by General Electric excluded coverage for pregnancy-related disabilities. The Court rejected the women's claim of discrimination, finding that Title VII does not encompass pregnant women because the act only protected against discrimination based on sex. Because the plan's pregnancy exclusion was based on the distinction between pregnant and nonpregnant persons and not on a distinction between women and men, the exclusion was not discriminatory. As the dissent correctly recognized, the Court's refusal to acknowledge that pregnancy-based discrimination is, in fact, sex-based discrimination was both illogical and flew in the face of evidence substantiating that the denial of pregnancy-based benefits had significantly and negatively affected women's employment opportunities and financial status. The Court's determination that Title VII required only that the sexes be treated equally, rather than that they both receive the same opportunities, smacks of the same misguided thinking that resulted in *Plessy v. Ferguson*. In ruling as it did, the Court relinquished its obligation to protect individual rights and to promote equality in favor of advancing stereotypes and deep-seated prejudices against women.

***

The decision

In *General Electric Co. v. Gilbert*, the Court considered the constitutionality of a provision in General Electric's employee disability plan that excluded from coverage disabilities arising from pregnancy. Women challenging the exclusion argued that it constituted sex discrimination in violation of Title VII of the Civil Rights Act of 1964. Both the district court for the Eastern District of Virginia and the Fourth Circuit Court of Appeals agreed. In a 6–3 decision, the Court reversed, holding that employers could legally exclude conditions related to pregnancy from comprehensive employee benefits plans in the absence of a showing that such an exclusion was a pretext for discriminating against women.

In so ruling, the Court analogized to the Equal Protection Clause of the Fourteenth Amendment and determined that pregnancy benefits would be protected under Title VII only if their exclusion was to effect an invidious discrimination.[1] Relying on its decision in *Geduldig v. Aiello*, which held that a similar insurance plan did not exclude on the basis of gender, but instead merely removed a risk from coverage based on the distinction between pregnant and nonpregnant persons,[2] the Court similarly found General Electric's plan nondiscriminatory because "there is no risk from which men are protected and women are not."[3] In sum, the Court concluded that the exclusion of a benefit is not problematic under Title VII so long as the benefits that are provided are provided to both sexes.

***

Analysis

In ruling as it did, the Court essentially held that pregnancy-based discrimination does not constitute gender discrimination. In this regard, the Court assigned a particularly pinched definition to sex discrimination under Title VII, limiting it to those instances in which men are treated more favorably than women. Such a crimped reading, of course, eliminated any claim of discrimination based on distinctions linked to characteristics that are uniquely female.

1 The quoted material in this chapter is taken from General Electric Co. v. Gilbert, 429 U.S. 125, 136 (1976).
2 Id. at 134–35.
3 Id. at 138 (quoting 417 U.S. 484, 496–97 (1974)).

As the dissent pointed out, the framework chosen by the Court (that exclusion of the pregnancy benefit was a gender-neutral risk assignment) was flawed on multiple levels. First, as Justices Brennan and Marshall correctly pointed out, the majority's underlying assumption that the pregnancy exclusion was the product of a gender-free risk-assignment process could not be squared with record evidence showing that General Electric had long engaged in practices that "served to undercut the employment opportunities to women" who became pregnant.[4] For example, the dissent noted, among other things, that women were offered no benefit plan at all until the 1930s and 1940s because General Electric believed that women's presence in the workplace was both minor and temporary,[5] and that the company's recent policies required pregnant women to take leave three months prior to birth and precluded their return until six weeks after birth.[6] Likewise, the majority ignored the district court's conclusion that the pregnancy exclusion was motivated by discriminatory intent.[7]

The dissent also correctly took aim at the logic underpinning its contention that the pregnancy exclusion was neutral in nature. In particular, the dissent pointed out that the Court's suggestion that the voluntary nature of pregnancy set it apart from other disabilities could not explain why other "voluntary" disabilities such as, for example, sports injuries and cosmetic surgery were not excluded.[8] Similarly, the majority's assertion that pregnancy could not properly be labeled a disease ignored the fact that General Electric precluded coverage in a meaningful percentage of pregnancies that in fact involved or were complicated by disease.[9] Finally, the dissent accurately identified that the plan could not accurately be understood as facially neutral in light of the fact that no male-specific disabilities (e.g., vasectomies, circumcisions, and prostatectomies) were excluded.[10]

In addition to the factual and logical fallacies behind the majority's assumption that General Electric's plan was facially neutral, the dissent correctly noted that the majority erred in not fairly considering whether General Electric's plan nonetheless had the effect of discriminating against women. In this regard, the dissent pointed out that the majority opinion improperly disregarded Equal Employment Opportunity Commission (EEOC) guidelines that expressly recognized pregnancy as a disability subject to coverage[11] and ignored the reality that "pregnancy exclusions built into disability programs both financially burden women workers and act to break down the continuity of the employment relationship, thereby exacerbating women's comparatively transient role in the labor force."[12]

The Court's error in holding that the exclusion of pregnancy benefits was not sex based was subsequently addressed through passage of the Pregnancy Discrimination

4 Id. at 149.
5 Id. at 150.
6 Id.
7 Id.
8 Id. at 151.
9 Id.
10 Id. at 152.
11 Id. at 156.
12 Id. at 158.

Act in 1978, an amendment to Title VII. Despite its passage, however, the door remained open for courts to construe the act as carving out only a narrow exception to the *Gilbert* majority's equal protection analysis, leaving firmly in place the principle that women properly could be the subject of discrimination based on their biological characteristics.

***

Questions

Can the majority's decision to engage in an equal protection analysis be justified?

The majority and the dissent disagreed as to the degree of deference to be afforded the EEOC. Who had the better argument and why?

What accounts for the majority's unwillingness to consider the lower courts' factual findings?

Should the Court have ruled at all on the constitutionality of General Electric's benefits plan?

17

KELO V. CITY OF NEW LONDON

Nor shall private property be taken for public use, without just compensation.
—U.S. Const., Amend. V

Summary

- In *Kelo*, the Court permitted the government to seize private property for private interests, provided that the government could demonstrate that the seizure served a public purpose, not a public use.
- The Court held that the state's broad interest in "promoting economic development" satisfied the "public purpose" standard and therefore justified the taking of private property for private interests.
- The Court's decision is contrary to the text of the Takings Clause, as well as its original meaning and purpose.

***

Introduction

In *Kelo*, the Court essentially rewrote the Fifth Amendment's Takings Clause to permit the government, through its eminent domain powers, to seize personal property for private interests, provided that the seizure served a public "purpose," *not* a public *use* as required by the Takings Clause.[1] The Court did not articulate the types of purposes that would be considered "public" or discuss whether the benefit to the public must be substantial and concrete or can merely be secondary and indirect. The Court also held that seizures intended to promote "economic development" are valid under the Takings Clause. However, the Court did not specify whether all seizures that seek

1 The quoted material in this chapter is taken from Kelo v. City of New London, 545 U.S. 469 (2005).

to promote economic development would be viewed as serving a public purpose, such as those providing a concrete financial benefit to identifiable members of the community. As a result, the Court's decision disregarded the text and purpose of the Takings Clause, dramatically expanded the scope of the government's eminent domain powers, and did not set forth workable limitations on the government's power to seize property for private interests.

***

The decision

In *Kelo*, the Court upheld the government's seizure of private property as part of a redevelopment project that included "a waterfront conference hotel anchoring a cluster of restaurants and shops," as well as "a marina, new homes, a museum, and office space."[2] Several local landowners objected to the taking, claiming that the seizure served primarily private interests and therefore ran afoul of the Takings Clause's requirement that the seizure of private property must be for a legitimate "public use."

The Court rejected the landowners' arguments. Writing for the majority, Justice Stevens noted that "the City would no doubt be forbidden from taking petitioners' land for the purpose of conferring a private benefit on a particular private party."[3] Similarly, the City would not be allowed "to take property under the mere pretext of a public purpose, when its actual purpose was to bestow a private benefit."[4] Justice Stevens acknowledged, however, that although the city was "not planning to open all of the condemned land for the general public's use," its seizure of the property was still permissible:

> [T]his is not a case in which the City is planning to open the condemned land – at least not in its entirety – to use by the general public. Nor will the private lessees of the land in any sense be required to operate like common carriers, making their services available to all comers. But although such a projected use would be sufficient to satisfy the public use requirement, this 'Court long ago rejected any literal requirement that condemned property be put into use for the general public.'[5]

For Justice Stevens, the relevant inquiry was not whether the seized property would be used by the public, but merely whether the seizure served a public purpose. In support of this conclusion, Justice Stevens noted that "[t]he relevant inquiry when this Court began applying the Fifth Amendment to the States at the close of the 19th century, it embraced the broader and more natural interpretation of public use as 'public purpose.'"[6] Additionally, Justice Stevens held that the seizures at issue were completed pursuant to a "carefully considered" development plan that served an overarching

2 Id. at 473.
3 Id. at 477.
4 Id.
5 Id. at 478–479 (internal citation omitted).
6 Id. at 480.

"public purpose."[7] Justice Stevens stated that the city's desire to "promote economic development [was] a traditional and long accepted function of government," even if part of the development would neither benefit nor be open to the public:

> The City has carefully formulated an economic development plan that it believes will provide appreciable benefits to the community, including – but by no means limited to – new jobs and increased tax revenue. As with other exercises in urban planning and development, the City is endeavoring to coordinate a variety of commercial, residential, and recreational uses of land, with the hope that they will form a whole greater than the sum of its parts. To effectuate this plan, the City has invoked a state statute that specifically authorizes the use of eminent domain to promote economic development. Given the comprehensive character of the plan, the thorough deliberation that preceded its adoption, and the limited scope of our review, it is appropriate for us . . . resolve the challenges of the individual owners, not on a piecemeal basis, but rather in light of the entire plan. Because that plan unquestionably serves a public purpose, the takings challenged here satisfy the public use requirement of the Fifth Amendment.[8]

In so holding, Justice Stevens rejected the landowners' argument that economic development was not a legitimate public purpose, stating that there was "no principled way of distinguishing economic development from the other public purposes that we have recognized."[9] Likewise, there was no basis for "exempting economic development from our traditionally broad understanding of public purpose," despite the fact that "the government's pursuit of a public purpose will often benefit individual private parties."[10]

In support of this decision, Justice Stevens emphasized that "[o]ur earliest cases in particular embodied a strong theme of federalism, emphasizing the 'great respect' that we owe to state legislatures and state courts in discerning local public needs." In so holding, the majority "eschewed rigid formulas and intrusive scrutiny in favor of affording legislatures broad latitude in determining what public needs justify the use of the takings power."[11]

***

Analysis

Justice Stevens's majority opinion was based on an overly broad view of the Takings Clause. Specifically, the opinion: (1) disregarded the clause's plain language and essentially read out of the clause the requirement that property be taken for public use, not merely a public purpose; and (2) allowed the government to seize property for the purpose of "economic development," which is an exceedingly broad and

7 Id. at 478.
8 Id. at 483–484.
9 Id. at 484.
10 Id. at 485.
11 Id. at 483.

difficult-to-define standard that arguably permits property to be seized to serve primarily private interests. At its core, Justice Stevens's opinion is inconsistent with the language and purpose of the Takings Clause and potentially subjects countless citizens to unwarranted seizures of their property.

Eliminating "public use" in favor of "public purpose"

The Takings Clause is not ambiguous: the government is prohibited from seizing private property for "*public use*, without just compensation."[12] On its face, therefore, the government must make a showing that seized property will be *used* by the public, not merely that property will benefit the public. As Justice O'Connor stated in her dissenting opinion:

> [T]o reason, as the Court does, that the incidental public benefits resulting from the subsequent ordinary use of private property render economic development takings 'for public use' is to wash out any distinction between private and public use of property – and thereby effectively to delete the words 'for public use' from the Takings Clause of the Fifth Amendment.[13]

In fact, the text of the Takings Clause leads to the ineluctable conclusion that "[g]overnment may compel an individual to forfeit her property for the *public's* use, but not for the *benefit* of another private person," which is a requirement that "promotes fairness as well as security."[14] The distinction between public "use" and public "purpose" is critical because the "public use" standard prevents the government from seizing property to serve primarily private interests, whereas the "public purpose" standard implies no such limitation, provided that the government can demonstrate that at least *some* public purpose will be served.

Furthermore, the "public purpose" standard is highly deferential, overly broad, and raises, rather than answers, many questions. What exactly is a "public purpose," and to what degree must the government's seizure of private property benefit the public? Must the benefit be direct and substantial or can it be merely secondary or tangential? What if the asserted public purpose is conditional or conjectural? What is the government's burden of proof, and what factual data must it adduce to show that a purpose is sufficiently public?

The Court's decision provides the government with extraordinary and nearly unchecked power to seize private property. In her dissenting opinion, Justice O'Connor stated as follows:

> Where is the line between 'public' and 'private' property use? We give considerable deference to legislatures' determinations about what governmental activities will advantage the public. But were the political branches the sole arbiters of the

12 U.S. Const. Amend. V (emphasis added).
13 Id. at 494 (O'Connor, J., dissenting).
14 Id. at 497 (emphasis added).

> public-private distinction, the Public Use Clause would amount to little more than hortatory fluff. An external, judicial check on how the public use requirement is interpreted, however limited, is necessary if this constraint on government power is to retain any meaning.[15]

Justice Stevens's opinion also disregarded the traditional bases upon which the Court deemed a "use" sufficiently public. For example, the government may "transfer private property to public ownership – such as for a road, a hospital, or a military base."[16] The government may also "transfer private property to private parties, often common carriers, who make the property available for the public's use – such as with a railroad, a public utility, or a stadium."[17] Finally, "although in certain circumstances . . . takings that serve a public purpose . . . satisfy the Constitution even if the property is destined for subsequent private use," the Court has never held that the government "may take private property . . . and give it over for new, ordinary private use, so long as the new use is predicted to generate some secondary benefit for the public – such as increased tax revenue, more jobs, maybe even esthetic pleasure."[18]

Moreover, nearly all seizures of private property can conceivably serve at least *some* public purpose. As Justice O'Connor stated, "nearly any lawful use of real private property can be said to generate some incidental benefit to the public."[19] Accordingly, "if predicted (or even guaranteed) positive side effects are enough to render transfer from one private party to another constitutional, then the words "for public use" do not realistically exclude *any* takings, and . . . do not exert any constraint on the eminent domain power."[20]

The vague and unduly broad "economic development" standard

In his majority opinion, Justice Stevens did not identify the types of "economic development" that would likely satisfy the "public purpose" standard. Does the public "benefit" merely because a redevelopment project will enhance community aesthetics, or must there be a concrete financial benefit to the community?

Unfortunately, Justice Stevens's general conclusion that "economic development" was a sufficient public purpose makes it possible that even the flimsiest public purposes may justify the government's seizure of private property. As Justice O'Connor noted:

> Under the banner of economic development, all private property is now vulnerable to being taken and transferred to another private owner, so long as it might

15 Id. at 497.
16 Id.
17 Id. at 498.
18 Id.
19 Id. at 501.
20 Id. (emphasis added).

> be upgraded – *i.e.*, given to an owner who will use it in a way that the legislature deems more beneficial to the public – in the process.[21]

Justice O'Connor also recognized that "[t]he trouble with economic development takings is that private benefit and incidental public benefit are, by definition, merged and mutually reinforcing. In this case, for example, any boon for Pfizer or the plan's developer is difficult to disaggregate from the promised public gains in taxes and jobs."[22]

Justice Thomas echoed this sentiment in his dissenting opinion, explaining that, if "'economic development' takings are for a 'public use,' any taking is, and the Court has erased the Public Use Clause from our Constitution."[23] Justice O'Connor also rejected the majority's argument that courts can identify unlawful takings by examining the government's motive:

> Even if there were a practical way to isolate the motives behind a given taking, the gesture toward a purpose test is theoretically flawed. If it is true that incidental public benefits from new private use are enough to ensure the "public purpose" in a taking, why should it matter, as far as the Fifth Amendment is concerned, what inspired the taking in the first place? How much the government does or does not desire to benefit a favored private party has no bearing on whether an economic development taking will or will not generate secondary benefit for the public. And whatever the reason for a given condemnation, the effect is the same from the constitutional perspective – private property is forcibly relinquished to new private ownership.[24]

For these reasons, "economic development takings 'seriously jeopardiz[e] the security of all private property ownership.'"[25] Most importantly, as Justice O'Connor explained, the Court's decision will have the likely effect of benefitting wealthy individuals and increasing the inequality gap:

> Any property may now be taken for the benefit of another private party, but the fallout from this decision will not be random. *The beneficiaries are likely to be those citizens with disproportionate influence and power in the political process, including large corporations and development firms.* As for the victims, the government now has license to transfer property from those with fewer resources to those with more. The Founders cannot have intended this perverse result.[26]

21 Id. at 494.
22 Id. at 502.
23 Id. at 506 (Thomas, J., dissenting).
24 Id. at 502–503.
25 Id. at 505 (internal citation omitted).
26 Id. (emphasis added).

For these reasons, Justice O'Connor stated that the majority's opinion was an "abdication of our responsibility . . . to enforce properly the Federal Constitution."[27] Justice O'Connor was undoubtedly correct.

***

Questions

What standards would you rely on to determine if property is seized for public use?

Can it be argued that all seizures that serve a public purpose inherently have a public use?

Is "economic development" a sufficient justification if the property will be used for private purposes? If so, are there any practical limitations on a state government's power to seize property for economic development?

27 Id. at 504.

PART V

The cases that encroached on state authority and individual autonomy

Let us never forget that government is ourselves and not an alien power over us. The ultimate rulers of our democracy are not a President and senators and congressmen and government officials, but the voters of this country.

—Franklin D. Roosevelt

18

LOCHNER V. NEW YORK

No State shall make or enforce any law which shall abridge the privileges or immunities of citizens of the United States; nor shall any State deprive any person of life, liberty, or property, without due process of law; nor deny to any person within its jurisdiction the equal protection of the laws.

—U.S. Const., Amend. XIV, Cl. 1

Summary

- The Court's opinion in *Lochner* fully embraced and articulated the concept that the Fourteenth Amendment could appropriately be construed to create certain unstated, yet "fundamental," rights, thereby paving the way for such decisions as *Roe* and *Griswold.*
- The *Lochner* court substituted its own beliefs in favor of those reflected in legislation derived through the democratic process, thereby exceeding its legitimate judicial role and weakening the democratic process.

***

Introduction

In *Lochner*, on a 5–4 vote, the Court struck down a New York law that limited the number of hours that bakers could work to no more than ten hours a day and sixty hours a week. Although the Court considered evidence in support of the claim that the regulation was enacted to address health and safety concerns regarding both the public and the bakers, the Court ruled that the regulation was unconstitutional because it interfered with the right of employers and employees to contract as they see fit. Specifically, the Court found that the right to so contract is "part of the liberty of the individual protected by the 14th Amendment of the Federal Constitution" and that, in its view, the state had failed to establish that the hours limitation constituted an appropriate exercise of its police powers. Rather, the Court determined that the New York law was completely unrelated to any legitimate attempt to regulate public safety or welfare. In so doing, the Court both created a substantive constitutional right out of whole cloth and disregarded the constraints on its Article III reviewing authority. Indeed, *Lochner* set the course for what would become an increasing, and inappropriate, willingness by the Court to create constitutional "rights" that are simply nowhere to be found in that document.

***

The decision

The New York regulation before the *Lochner* Court made it illegal for an employer to allow a baker to work in excess of sixty hours a week. The stated justification for the statute was the protection of the public health and welfare. In this regard, the Court considered evidence suggesting that a reduced workweek could have a positive health and safety impact on both the bakers and the public at large. The Court concluded, however, that the state had failed to show that the statute bore a close enough relationship to the public health to permit an infringement of the "liberty interest" to freely contract as to the number of hours to be worked. Specifically, the Court rejected the claim that the regulation legitimately spoke to the public health, concluding, "[c]lean and wholesome bread does not depend upon whether the baker works but ten hours per day or only sixty hours a week" and that the hours legislation constituted a "mere meddlesome interference [] with the rights of the individual."[1]

Stated another way, the Court determined that *Lochner*'s constitutional right to contract outweighed New York's power to legislate the appropriate number of hours that bakers and confectioners could work. In sum, the Court concluded that the right to contract regarding the terms of employment is generally protected by the Fourteenth Amendment against state interference.

The Court's decision rests on two significant assumptions. The first is that the Due Process Clause may appropriately be construed to identify substantive economic rights. In this regard, and citing to its prior decision in *Allgeyer v. Louisiana*, the Court announced its belief that the right to contract "is part of the liberty of the individual protected by the 14th Amendment of the Constitution"[2] and that "[t]he right to purchase or to sell labor is part of the liberty protected by this amendment."[3] The second is that it is an appropriate role for the Court to assess the fit between a piece of legislation and a state's exercise of its police powers. In this regard, the Court did not believe that the hours limitation had any real impact on public health, but instead saw the connection between the provision and health concerns to be "too shadowy and thin to build any argument for the interference of the legislature."[4] Because, in its

1 Id. at 545.
2 Id. at 541.
3 Id.
4 Id. at 545.

view, the legislation fell outside the limited scope of the state's ability to regulate the "safety, health, morals, and general welfare of the public,"[5] it constituted an improper interference with the constitutionally protected right to contract.

The dissent took issue with both assumptions. In his separate dissent, Justice Holmes contended that the majority erred in giving the word "liberty" in the Fourteenth Amendment a reading wide enough to encompass what he termed "an economic theory which a large part of the country does not entertain."[6] In particular, Holmes argued that the Court consistently had recognized the states' right to legislate in ways that affected parties' ability to contract, including Sunday and usury laws,[7] and that its unwillingness to do so in connection with an employment contract was tantamount to the Court embracing (and writing into the Fourteenth Amendment) an economic principle. "[A] Constitution," he insisted, "is not intended to embody a particular economic theory, whether of paternalism and the organic relation of the citizen to the State or of laissez faire." Indeed, he specifically cautioned:

> I think that the word 'liberty,' in the 14th Amendment, is perverted when it is held to prevent the natural outcome of a dominant opinion, unless it can be said that a rational and fair man necessarily would admit that the statute proposed would infringe fundamental principles as they have been understood by the traditions of our people and our law.[8]

Because a "reasonable man might think it [the statute] a proper measure on the score of health,"[9] Holmes concluded that the statute should not have been found unconstitutional.

Justice Harlan, joined by Justices White and Day, likewise dissented. Justice Harlan noted that the Court uniformly had recognized that a state's police power extends "at least to the protection of the lives, the health, and the safety of the public"[10] and that neither the Fourteenth Amendment, nor any other, was intended to intrude on this power. Rather, so long as a law has a real relation to the goal of protecting the general welfare, it should not be invalidated. Indeed, Justice Harlan further noted that

"if there be doubt as to the validity of the statute, that doubt must therefore be resolved in favor of its validity, and the courts must keep their hands off, leaving the legislature to meet the responsibility for unwise legislation."[11]

Because in Justice Harlan's view the statute plainly was enacted to protect the physical well-being of bakers, and because the statute reflected the belief of the people of

5 Id. at 543.
6 Id. at 546.
7 Id.
8 Id. at 547.
9 Id.
10 Id.
11 Id. at 548.

New York that working in excess of sixty hours a week might endanger a baker's well-being, the Court could not properly substitute its own understanding for that of duly elected state legislators:

> A decision that the New York statute is void under the 14th Amendment will, in my opinion, involve consequences of a far-reaching and mischievous character; for such a decision would seriously cripple the inherent power of the states to care for the lives, health, and well-being of their citizens. Those are matters which can be controlled by the states.[12]

In Justice Harlan's view, unless a legislative enactment is "plainly and palpably beyond all question in violation of the fundamental law of the Constitution,"[13] the will of the people, as expressed in such enactments, should not be disturbed by the judiciary.

***

Analysis

The Court's decision in *Lochner* is flawed on several levels. First, the Court inappropriately expanded the scope of the Due Process Clause by specifically injecting a "substantive" component into it. By identifying the right to make an employment contract on terms agreeable to the parties as an individual "liberty" interest, the Court ignored the fact that the text of the Constitution articulates no such protected interest. Indeed, the Due Process Clause identifies no substantive rights at all, but instead only guarantees that the fundamental rights to life, liberty, and property will not be taken in the absence of a fair process. The Court's willingness to recognize the unenumerated economic right to contract opened the door for what, in truth, did happen going forward – the creation of other kinds of "rights" through a broad (perhaps limitless) reading of what constitutes a "liberty" interest. Indeed, broad readings of the Due Process Clause and the recognition of nontextual rights are on full display in such cases as *Roe* and *Griswold*.

Further, the decision sanctioned the Court's ability to exchange the judgment of a state legislature (and, in turn, the will of the people who elected its members) with its own. Although the *Lochner* Court adamantly insisted that "[t]his is not a question of substituting the judgment of the court for that of the legislature,"[14] that is precisely what it did. In the face of evidence that the hours limitation was related to ensuring the health and safety of bakers and the public, the Court concluded that the provision had no such relationship. In so doing, the Court usurped the states' power to determine what is in the best interest of the public and their ability to choose the best measures for protecting those interests. In this regard, the opinion gave license to the Court to base its decisions on the Justices' own personal beliefs, political ideals, and moral judgments, rather than on the considered judgment of lawmakers who are in the best position to identify and solve problems affecting their constituents.

12 Id. at 551.
13 Id.
14 Id. at 543.

Moreover, the opinion undermined the democratic process, as it wrested control from elected state officials to implement solutions to problems affecting their citizens. The Court could have, and should have, deferred to the New York legislature's determination that the hours limitation was an appropriate response to a perceived health risk in the baking industry and left it to the voting public political to assess the validity of that determination.

Beyond these substantive issues, the opinion is also problematic because the Court likewise could have, but did not, give the statute a reading that would have rendered it constitutional. Although the Court acknowledged that there was evidence that supported New York's contention that the hours limitation was linked to its attempt to ensure the safety of bakers and the public, the Court opted to discredit that evidence in favor of a ruling that this statutory provision could not pass constitutional muster. It erred in this regard.

***

Questions

Did the Court have other avenues open to it for finding the legislation unconstitutional?

Was the New York statute actually designed to safeguard health and safety?

Should that matter, and who should be making that determination?

When, if ever, may the Court appropriately play the role of "expert" in construing a law?

Can the argument be made that the Court got it right in Lochner?

19

WICKARD V. FILBURN

The Congress shall have Power To . . . regulate Commerce with foreign Nations, and among the several States, and with the Indian Tribes.

—U.S. Const., Article I, Section 8, Cl. 3

Summary

- *Filburn* greatly, and improperly, expanded the scope of Congress's regulatory authority under the Commerce Clause.
- The Court's decision paved the way for increased congressional intrusion into areas historically, and properly, left to state control.

***

Introduction

In *Wickard v. Filburn* the Court upheld amendments to the 1938 Agricultural Adjustment Act that permitted Congress to limit the number of acres that could be cultivated for the production of wheat and to assess fines on those farmers who exceeded their allotted number of acres. Filburn exceeded his allotment and consequently was fined. He argued that because he grew wheat for his own family's consumption, Congress could not properly seek to regulate that production through its powers under the Commerce Clause. The Court disagreed, finding that the scope of Congress's authority under the Commerce Clause extends to all activities that substantially affect interstate commerce. Because the consumption of homegrown wheat could, in the aggregate, affect market prices, the Court found that Congress could properly regulate it. The Court's decision vastly expanded the scope of congressional power under the Commerce Clause and invited Congress to legislate in areas traditionally left to the states. In this regard, it disrupted the balance of powers envisioned by the Founders and chilled the ability of states to craft solutions to local problems and issues.

***

The decision

In *Filburn*, the Court considered whether the scope of the Commerce Clause extended to congressional controls on wheat grown for home consumption. Specifically, under the Agricultural Adjustment Act of 1938, Congress limited the number of acres that could be cultivated for the production of federally subsidized crops, including wheat. The act was designed to increase the market price of wheat by limiting, as necessary, the volume of domestically produced wheat. Filburn exceeded his allotment and harvested in excess of the number of permissible bushels of wheat for his farm. Filburn was assessed a penalty, and pending its payment, was unable to sell his wheat. Filburn challenged the penalty assessed against him, contending that, among other things, the wheat-marketing quota provisions of the Act fell outside the parameters of the Commerce Clause. In this regard, Filburn argued that the production and consumption of wheat consumed on the premises were activities local in nature, and therefore outside the reach of Congress's power to regulate interstate commerce. The Court disagreed, finding that although Filburn's activities alone might not appear to affect interstate commerce, the cumulative effect of the consumption of homegrown wheat did affect the price and market conditions of that commodity, thereby permitting congressional regulation. Specifically, the Court concluded that Congress may act regardless of whether the activity is local in nature and regardless of whether it may even be regarded as commerce if it "exerts a substantial economic effect on interstate commerce."[1]

In rendering its decision regarding the scope of the Commerce Clause, the Court focused heavily on the scope of the Act itself. Viewing the issue not as whether Congress could appropriately regulate home consumption, but instead whether Congress could properly control the available supply of wheat, and thereby regulate its pricing, the Court quickly determined that it needed to navigate away from prior "dicta" that limited the constitutional analysis to identifying whether the activities at issue were best categorized as relating to production (thereby being local in nature, only indirectly affecting commerce, and therefore generally beyond the scope of Congress's reach) or as relating to marketing (thereby historically falling within congressional control).[2] Instead, the Court eschewed such labeling, asserting:

> [Q]uestions of the power of Congress are not to be decided by reference to any formula which would give controlling force to nomenclature such as "production" and "indirect" and foreclose consideration of the actual effects of the activity in question upon interstate commerce.[3]

Articulating the question posed as turning on the economic effect of Filburn's activities rather than on their nature or locale, the Court turned to what, in its view, informed the nature of those effects. In this regard, the Court considered the "economics of the wheat industry" and its role not only domestically but also in the global market,[4] thereby signaling a shift away from any understanding that the focus of the

1 Wickard v. Filburn, 317 U.S. 111, 125 (1942).
2 Id. at 119–120.
3 Id. at 120.
4 Id. at 125–127.

economic effect inquiry should be only local in nature. Indeed, the Court made clear that the proper inquiry included consideration of the combined effect that home consumption had on the market as a whole. Accordingly, although Filburn's "own contribution to the demand for wheat may be trivial by itself,"[5] the Court determined that Congress might still appropriately limit production if, in the aggregate, wheat consumed on the farm would have a substantial impact on price and market conditions.[6] Noting that consumption of homegrown wheat "constitutes the most variable factor in the disappearance of the wheat crop,"[7] with farm consumption varying "in an amount greater than 20 percent of average production,"[8] the Court concluded that homegrown wheat necessarily "competes in the market,"[9] affects interstate commerce, and accordingly is the proper subject of regulation by Congress.

***

Analysis

> *The powers delegated by the proposed Constitution to the federal government are few and defined. Those which are to remain in the State governments are numerous and indefinite. The former will be exercised principally on external objects, as war, peace, negotiation and foreign commerce . . . The powers reserved to the several States will extend to all the objects which in the ordinary course of affairs, concern the lives and liberties, and properties of the people, and the internal order, improvement and prosperity of the State.*
>
> —James Madison

In ruling as it did, the Court invited an increasingly generous understanding of Congress's power under the Commerce Clause. Prior to *Filburn*, the Court had found relevant to its Commerce Clause analysis whether the legislation in question concerned production or consumption, as these activities suggested that the subject of the regulation was local and therefore a matter of state concern outside the scope of congressional control. Only if such activities were found to have a "direct" effect on interstate commerce could such activities be regulated by the Commerce Clause.[10] The Court's willingness to move away from these previously recognized restraints on congressional control has at its heart a broad perception of what constitutes commerce. Certainly the Court could have engaged in an analysis of the Founders' original intent and crafted a much more limited scope for congressional action. In this regard, the Court could have been particularly mindful of the Founders' concerns regarding federalism and the role of states as "laboratories of experimentation." Yet, with the exception of the Court's reference to Justice Marshall and its sweeping contention that this jurist "described the federal commerce power with a breadth never yet exceeded,"[11] the

5 Id. at 127.
6 Id. at 128.
7 Id. at 127.
8 Id.
9 Id. at 128.
10 Id. at 120, n.6.
11 Id. at 120.

Court paid little attention to the Founders' intent. The Court hints that such an analysis would be unproductive because, prior to the enactment of the Interstate Commerce Act in 1887, there had been few instances in which Congress had actually attempted to exercise its powers under the Commerce Clause, and therefore had little need to consider its scope.[12] Yet this hardly answers for a failure to acknowledge the text of the Constitution itself and its language limiting Congress's reach to regulating "commerce . . . among the several States." Nor does it speak to the Founders' expressed concern in preserving a balance between federal and state power.

The Court's movement toward consideration of the cumulative effects of a purely intrastate activity that, on its own, had little or no effect on interstate commerce paved the way for confusing the roles to be played by the states and the federal government with respect to matters traditionally falling within the realm of state control. What *Filburn* made clear is that Congress was not limited to legislating with respect to the movement of goods in commerce. Rather, under the effects test articulated in *Filburn* and its embrace of the aggregation concept, any activity taken as a whole – regardless of whether that activity was of a commercial nature, and regardless of whether that activity was purely intrastate in nature – could be regulated by Congress.

***

Questions

The Court suggests at the end of its Commerce Clause analysis that the resolution of conflicts regarding who is advantaged by a congressional regulation and who is not is best left to the "more flexible and responsible legislative process." Under what conditions can this contention be justified? When can it not?

Is there an argument that the substantial effects test makes sense in a modern economy?

Under Filburn, what activities can Congress not engage in pursuant to its powers under the Commerce Clause?

12 Id. at 121.

20

IMPORTANT CASES THAT DID NOT MAKE THE LIST

An activist court is a court that makes a decision you don't like.

—Justice Anthony Kennedy

Summary

- Two often-criticized decisions – *Bush v. Gore* and *National Federation of Independent Investors v. Sebelius* – did not make the list because they were based on a plausible, albeit controversial, interpretation of the Constitution. A third case, *Dred Scott v. Sandford*, did not make the list because it has been universally (and rightfully) criticized for years, thus rendering further examination redundant.
- Some commentators have argued that *Bush v. Gore* was a politically driven and outcome-based decision, but there was a legitimate legal basis upon which to reverse the Florida Supreme Court's decision.
- In *National Federation of Independent Investors v. Sebelius*, Chief Justice Roberts was severely criticized for basing his ruling on the Taxing Power, but there was a reasonable legal basis to construe the Affordable Health Care Act's individual mandate as a tax and to conclude that the Court appropriately deferred to the coordinate branches on a matter of social policy.
- The Court's decision in *Dred Scott* is universally denounced as one of the Court's worst decisions, but its effect on democracy is no longer significant.

***

Introduction

Many commentators have characterized the Court's decision in *Bush v. Gore* as among the worst in its history.[1] Critics allege that the Court's decision to overturn the Florida

1 The quoted material in this chapter is taken from Bush v. Gore, 531 U.S. 98 (2000); National Federation of Independent Investors v. Sebelius, 567 U.S., 132 S. Ct. 2566 (2012); and Dred Scott v. Sandford, 60 U.S. 393 (1857).

Supreme Court's ruling and effectively end the 2000 presidential election was driven by partisanship and ideology, not law. Upon closer analysis, the text of the Equal Protection Clause and 3 U.S.C. §5, which states that any controversy regarding a state's electors must be resolved within six days before the Electoral College votes on December 17 of each election year, provided at least some support for the Court's decision.

In fact, the Court voted 7–2 that the Florida Supreme Court's decision violated equal protection principles, and the majority included Justices identifying themselves as Republican and Democrat. The only remaining issue concerned the remedy for this violation. Dividing 5–4 on this question, the Court held that the recount procedure could not be completed in advance of the December 17 deadline, which as a practical matter ended the election. The text of the Equal Protection Clause and 3 U.S.C. §5 arguably supported the Court's holding, although, as Justice Breyer argued, an alternative and pro-democratic interpretation was possible. As such, *Bush v. Gore* is distinguishable from cases such as *Griswold*, where the Court invented constitutional "penumbras," and *Lawrence*, which was based in large part on liberty "in its more spatial and transcendent dimensions."

The same holds true for *National Federation of Independent Investors v. Sebelius*, where, on behalf of a 5–4 majority, Chief Justice Roberts upheld portions of the Affordable Health Care Act, including the act's individual mandate, which required all citizens who did not purchase health insurance to pay a fine. Although conservative-leaning commentators chastised Chief Justice Roberts's decision, most emphatically regarding the individual mandate, an examination of the decision reveals that the shared responsibility payment, which on its face appeared to be an unconstitutional penalty, could be construed as a "tax" and therefore a valid exercise of Congress's taxing power under Article I, Section 8. If anything, conservative commentators should be criticized because their disagreement with Chief Justice Roberts's decision was, at its core, based on an outcome that they disliked.

Finally, the Court's decision in *Dred Scott* is admittedly one of the worst in its history. But so much criticism has been directed at *Dred Scott* over the years (rightfully so), that its inclusion in this book would merely be revisiting territory that has been thoroughly explored. Suffice it to say that *Dred Scott* will – and should – always be considered one of the worst decisions in the Court's history, but its impact on democracy today, and value to the discussion here, is relatively insignificant.

***

The decisions

Bush v. Gore

By way of background, after one of the closest presidential elections in history, Democratic presidential candidate Al Gore requested a recount of Florida's ballots after losing to George W. Bush by only several hundred votes. During the lengthy and highly contested recount process, the Florida Supreme Court ordered a recount in Miami-Dade County of "9,000 ballots on which the machines had failed to detect a vote for President."[2] The

2 Id. at 100.

court also ordered that "215 and 168 legal votes for Vice President Gore be included in the certified election results."[3] George W. Bush appealed. The issues for review were whether "the Florida Supreme Court established new standards for resolving Presidential election contests," and whether the use of standardless manual recounts violates the Equal Protection and Due Process Clauses.[4]

In a 7–2 decision, the Supreme Court answered in the affirmative. The Court held that the standard governing whether a candidate voted for Al Gore or George Bush was not sufficiently specific to safeguard voters against arbitrary and unequal treatment:

> The recount mechanisms implemented in response to the decisions of the Florida Supreme Court do not satisfy the minimum requirement for nonarbitrary treatment of voters necessary to secure the fundamental right. Florida's basic command for the count of legally cast votes is to consider the "intent of the voter." This is unobjectionable as an abstract proposition and a starting principle. The problem inheres in the absence of specific standards to ensure its equal application. The formulation of uniform rules to determine intent based on these recurring circumstances is practicable and, we conclude, necessary.[5]

The Court acknowledged that "[t]he law does not refrain from searching for the intent of the actor in a multitude of circumstances." However, in the recount process, "the question is not whether to believe a witness but how to interpret the marks or holes or scratches on an inanimate object, a piece of cardboard or paper which, it is said, might not have registered as a vote during the machine count."[6]

As a result, because "[t]he factfinder confronts a thing, not a person," the search for a voter's intent must "be confined by specific rules designed to ensure uniform treatment."[7] Additionally, "the votes certified by the court included a partial total from one county, Miami-Dade," and therefore provided "no assurance that the recounts included in a final certification must be complete."[8]

For these reasons, the Court held that "the recount process, in its features here described, is inconsistent with the minimum procedures necessary to protect the fundamental right of each voter in the special instance of a statewide recount under the authority of a single state judicial officer."[9]

3 Id.
4 Id. at 103.
5 Id. at 105–106.
6 Id. at 106.
7 Id.
8 Id. at 108.
9 Id. at 109.

To be sure "when a court orders a statewide remedy, there must be at least some assurance that the rudimentary requirements of equal treatment and fundamental fairness are satisfied."[10]

Regarding the remedy for the equal protection violation, the Court held, in a 5–4 vote, that there was insufficient time within which to develop standards for and complete the recount process. Specifically, because "the legislature intended the State's electors to 'participat[e] fully in the federal electoral process,'" as provided in 3 U.S.C. §5, the deadline for selecting electors was December 12 – the day the Court's decision was announced.[11]

National Federation of Independent Investors v. Sebelius

Writing for a 5–4 majority, Chief Justice John Roberts held that the individual mandate was not a permissible exercise of Congress's power under the Commerce Clause. To begin with, "[t]he power to *regulate* commerce presupposes the existence of commercial activity to be regulated."[12] For this reason, "Congress has never attempted to rely on that power to compel individuals not engaged in commerce to purchase an unwanted product."[13] Indeed, "if the power to 'regulate' something included the power to create it, many of the provisions in the Constitution would be superfluous."[14]

The Court's precedents also "uniformly describe the [Commerce] power as reaching 'activity,'" but the individual mandate "does not regulate existing commercial activity," but instead "compels individuals to become active in commerce by purchasing a product, on the ground that their failure to do so affects interstate commerce."[15] Chief Justice Roberts stated as follows:

> Construing the Commerce Clause to permit Congress to regulate individuals precisely *because* they are doing nothing would open a new and potentially vast domain to congressional authority. Every day individuals do not do an infinite number of things. In some cases they decide not to do something; in others they simply fail to do it. Allowing Congress to justify federal regulation by pointing to the effect of inaction on commerce would bring countless decisions an individual could *potentially* make within the scope of federal regulation, and – under the Government's theory – empower Congress to make those decisions for him.[16]

In this way, concluding that the individual mandate regulated "activity" would invariably result in an unprecedented expansion of the Commercial Clause, as citizens could be "regulated under the Commerce Clause whenever enough of them are not

10 Id. at 110 (internal citation omitted).
11 Id.
12 132 S. Ct. 2566, 2586 (2012).
13 Id.
14 Id.
15 Id. at 2587.
16 Id. (emphasis added).

doing something the Government would have them do."[17] Essentially, upholding the individual mandate would enable "Congress to use its commerce power to compel citizens to act as the Government would have them act," a result that "is not the country the Framers of our Constitution envisioned."[18]

In a decision that surprised many commentators, Chief Justice Roberts held that the individual mandate was a valid exercise of Congress's taxing power, even though the statute used the word "penalty" to describe the fine individuals who did not obtain health insurance would pay. As the government asserted at oral argument, "if an individual does not maintain health insurance, the only consequence is that he must make an additional payment to the IRS when he pays his taxes."[19] As a result, the "mandate can be regarded as establishing a condition – not owning health insurance – that triggers a tax – the required payment to the IRS."[20] Therefore, the decision to forego health insurance would be "just another thing the Government taxes, like buying gasoline or earning income."[21]

Chief Justice Roberts agreed with the government's contention, stating that the "question is not whether that is the most natural interpretation of the mandate, but only whether it is a 'fairly possible' one," and "every reasonable construction must be resorted to, in order to save a statute from unconstitutionality."[22] Consequently, "[g]ranting the Act the full measure of deference owed to federal statutes, it can be so read."[23] Chief Justice Roberts stated as follows:

> The text of a statute can sometimes have more than one possible meaning. To take a familiar example, a law that reads "no vehicles in the park" might, or might not, ban bicycles in the park. And it is well established that if a statute has two possible meanings, one of which violates the Constitution, courts should adopt the meaning that does not do so. Justice Story said that 180 years ago: "No court ought, unless the terms of an act rendered it unavoidable, to give a construction to it which should involve a violation, however unintentional, of the constitution."[24]

To support this reasoning, Chief Justice Roberts relied on *Bailey v. Drexel Furniture, Co.*, in which the Court cited three primary factors the Court used to distinguish a tax from a penalty. In *Drexel Furniture*, the Court characterized a "so-called tax on employing child laborers" as a penalty for the following reasons:

> First, the tax imposed an exceedingly heavy burden – 10 percent of a company's net income – on those who employed children, no matter how small their

17 Id. at 2588.
18 Id. at 2589.
19 Id. at 2593–2594.
20 Id. at 2594.
21 Id.
22 Id. (internal citation omitted).
23 Id.
24 Id. at 2593 (internal citation omitted).

> infraction. Second, it imposed that exaction only on those who knowingly employed underage laborers. Such scienter requirements are typical of punitive statutes, because Congress often wishes to punish only those who intentionally break the law. Third, this "tax" was enforced in part by the Department of Labor, an agency responsible for punishing violations of labor laws, not collecting revenue.[25]

Applying this standard, Chief Justice Roberts held "the shared responsibility payment [individual mandate] may for constitutional purposes be considered a tax, not a penalty."[26] To begin with "for most Americans the amount due will be far less than the price of insurance, and, by statute, it can never be more."[27] Additionally, "the individual mandate contains no scienter requirement," and "the payment is collected solely by the IRS through the normal means of taxation – except that the Service is *not* allowed to use those means most suggestive of a punitive sanction, such as criminal prosecution."[28] As a result, "[t]he reasons the Court in *Drexel Furniture* held that what was called a 'tax' there was a penalty support the conclusion that what is called a 'penalty' here may be viewed as a tax."[29]

Moreover, the "exaction the Affordable Care Act imposes on those without health insurance looks like a tax in many respects," as the "'[s]hared responsibility payment' . . . is paid into the Treasury by 'taxpayer[s]' when they file their tax returns."[30] Also, "[f]or taxpayers who do owe the payment, its amount is determined by such familiar factors as taxable income, number of dependents, and joint filing status."[31] Likewise, the "requirement to pay is found in the Internal Revenue Code and enforced by the IRS, which – as we previously explained – must assess and collect it 'in the same manner as taxes.'"[32]

Additionally, although the "Act describes the payment as a 'penalty,' not a 'tax,' that fact alone does not determine whether the payment may be viewed as an exercise of Congress's taxing power."[33] In support of this proposition, Chief Justice Roberts cited the Court's precedent, noting that in the *License Tax Cases*, "we held that federal licenses to sell liquor and lottery tickets – for which the licensee had to pay a fee – could be sustained as exercises of the taxing power."[34] Likewise, in *New York v. United States*, the Court "upheld as a tax a 'surcharge' on out-of-state nuclear waste shipments, a portion of which was paid to the Federal Treasury."[35]

25 Id. at 2595.
26 Id.
27 Id. at 2595–2596.
28 Id. at 2596 (emphasis added).
29 Id. (internal citation omitted).
30 Id. at 2594. (internal citation omitted).
31 Id.
32 Id.
33 Id.
34 Id. at 2595.
35 Id. (internal citation omitted).

III. Dred Scot v. Sandford

In *Dred Scott v. Sandford*, the Court held that African Americans with ancestors who were sold as slaves could not become American citizens and therefore lacked standing to sue in federal court. The Court construed the naturalization law, "which was passed at the second session of the first Congress, March 26, 1790, and confines the right of becoming citizens '*to aliens being free white persons.*' "[36] The Court stated as follows:

> Now, the Constitution does not limit the power of Congress in this respect to white persons. And they may, if they think proper, authorize the naturalization of any one, of any color, who was born under allegiance to another Government. But the language of the law above quoted, shows that citizenship at that time was perfectly understood to be confined to the white race; and that they alone constituted the sovereignty in the Government.[37]

Based on this language, the Court held that there existed a "line of division which the Constitution has drawn between the citizen race, who formed and held the Government, and the African race, which they held in subjection and slavery, and governed at their own pleasure."[38] Stated differently, "[p]ersons of color, in the judgment of Congress, were not included in the word citizens, and they are described as another and different class of persons, and authorized to be employed, if born in the United States."[39]

***

Analysis

As stated earlier, many commentators have cited *Bush*, *National Federation of Independent Investors*, and *Dred Scott* as among the worst decisions in the Court's history. Regarding *Bush* and *National Federation of Independent Investors*, the majority of the criticism reflects disagreement with the outcome reached, and not necessarily the process by which the Court reached these decisions. Perhaps the best evidence of this fact is that (with the exception of *Dred Scott*), an individual's ideological disposition is the primary factor regarding whether one thinks *Bush v. Gore* was wrongly decided. Individuals affiliated with the Republican Party view the Court's decision in *Bush* favorably because it resulted in the election of President George W. Bush and corrected what many Republicans believed was overreaching by the Florida Supreme Court. Conversely, Democrats believed that the Court stole the election from presidential candidate Al Gore and that the Justices' political views, not the law, drove the decision. Regarding *National Federation of Independent Investors v. Sebelius*, many Republican commentators chastised Chief Justice Roberts for voting with the Court's

36 60 U.S. at 419 (internal citation omitted) (emphasis in original).
37 Id. at 419–420.
38 Id. at 420.
39 Id. at 421.

four liberal-leaning Justices, whereas Democratic commentators celebrated Chief Justice Roberts's decision to uphold the Affordable Health Care Act.

The criticism directed at both cases misses the mark because the criteria governing the legitimacy of a decision should not depend on whether the outcome was favorable from a policy perspective, but whether the process by which that outcome was reached resulted from sound principles of constitutional interpretation. On that question, the answer in *Bush v. Gore* and *National Federation of Independent Investors v. Sebelius* is arguably yes.

Bush v. Gore: The decision was predicated on a reasonable interpretation of the Constitution's text

As stated earlier, in *Bush v. Gore*, the Court voted by a 7–2 margin that the recount procedure mandated by the Florida Supreme Court violated the Equal Protection Clause. This conclusion was certainly justifiable, as there were no uniform standards within and across counties by which to discern the intent of the voter. As a result, there was a very real possibility that the standards adopted in each county would subject voters to differential and, ultimately, unequal treatment. For example, depending on the standard adopted, the same vote may reflect the intent of the voter in one county, but not in the other. This is precisely why the Court, by an overwhelming margin, held that the recount process violated the Equal Protection Clause.

Admittedly, the question regarding the proper remedy closely divided the Court, and by a bare 5–4 majority, the Court held that no time remained in which to continue and complete the recount process. The text of 3 U.S.C. §5 could be construed to support this conclusion, although it was not the only possible construction. This does not necessarily mean that the Court's decision was the proper one, that the outcome was desirable. It is to say that *Bush v. Gore* does not even approach the level of judicial overreaching that characterizes decisions such as *Griswold*, *Planned Parenthood*, and *Lawrence*.

Having said this, the Court could and probably should have interpreted 3 U.S.C. §5 in a manner that allowed Florida to complete the recount process. In his dissent, Justice Breyer focused on the principle of who should decide the election: Congress or the Court. In selecting the former, Justice Breyer explained that, given the "comprehensive scheme for counting electoral votes, there is no reason to believe that federal law either foresees or requires resolution of such a political issue by this Court."[40] Also, the "decision by both the Constitution's Framers and the 1886 Congress to minimize this Court's role in resolving close federal Presidential elections is as wise as it is clear," because "Congress, being a political body, expresses the people's will far more accurately than does an unelected Court."[41]

Justice Breyer's argument is compelling because the Court's decision, even if arguably supported by the text, created the perception that its decision was politically motivated, regardless of whether the five-member majority was so motivated. After all, by

40 531 U.S. at 155 (Breyer, J., dissenting).
41 Id.

only a one-vote margin, the Court ended a presidential election, and all five members of the majority, given their conservative judicial philosophy, probably shared the same political affiliation as George W. Bush. This fact made it inevitable that the Court's ruling would be criticized and, in the views of many, its legitimacy undermined. Had the Court allowed the recount to continue, the election would have been decided by the people democratically, or at least by a branch of government elected by the people.

In the final analysis, therefore, *Bush v. Gore* is not a decision that voters of any political persuasion should celebrate. For the reasons stated, however, it is not among the worst in the Court's history. The Court did not invent "penumbras." It did not invent a right to define "the mysteries of human life." And it certainly did not claim to have the authority to define "the liberty of all."

National Federation of Independent Investors v. Sebelius: Deferring to the coordinate branches and protecting the Court's institutional legitimacy

In *National Federation of Independent Investors*, Chief Justice Roberts was heavily criticized for casting the fifth and deciding vote to uphold the Affordable Health Care Act, including the act's mandate that all individuals purchase health insurance, the failure of which resulted in a "shared responsibility" payment.

Most commentators expected Chief Justice Roberts to side with the Court's conservative members and invalidate the Act. In fact, some commentators opined that Chief Justice Roberts had initially voted to uphold the Act, only to later change his mind. Whatever motivated Chief Justice Roberts, the critical question is whether the reasoning on which the opinion was based – holding that the shared responsibility payment was a tax, not a penalty – was constitutionally defensible. The answer to this question is yes – barely.

Certainly, the most reasonable interpretation of the "shared responsibility payment" would have been to declare it a penalty. To begin with, in various sections of the Act the payment was described as a penalty, and on its face it appears to function as a penalty. If individuals fail to obtain health insurance as required by the Act the payment they must make to the Internal Revenue Service (IRS) is a direct consequence of that failure and appears to be punitive in nature. In addition, there are very few instances in which individuals must pay a tax, rather than face a penalty, for failing to act. Motorists who fail to maintain an up-to-date license are typically cited for a traffic violation and must pay a fine. Business owners who fail obtain a liquor license, or citizens who do not complete their tax returns by the annual deadline, pay a fine. In each instance, the failure to comply with a law or regulation imposing a legal duty on an individual subjects them to a penalty. The individual mandate functions in the same way, and the most natural reading of the "shared responsibility" payment is that it operates as a penalty.

Nevertheless, Chief Justice Roberts explained that this was not the only possible construction. Article I, Section 8, which gives Congress the authority to "lay and collect taxes, duties, imposts and excises, to pay the debts and provide for the common defense and general welfare," is ambiguous on its face. The precedent on which Chief Justice Roberts relied arguably provides at least some support for the proposition that, given the relatively modest fine imposed on individuals who did not procure health insurance, the lack of a *scienter* requirement, and the Internal Revenue Service's involvement, the shared responsibility payment could be construed as a tax. This is certainly not the most natural reading, but when considering the textual ambiguity and relevant case law, it is a possible reading. This is what differentiates *National Federation of Independent Investors* from *Griswold*, *Roe*, and *Planned Parenthood*. No interpretation of the Constitution supported the rulings in those cases.

A compelling argument can be made that Chief Justice Roberts's decision to uphold the act's individual mandate was consistent with Roberts's overarching judicial philosophy – promoting judicial restraint – and furthered one of his primary goals – preserving the Court's institutional legitimacy. Chief Justice Roberts likely felt reticent to invalidate a law that was passed by both houses of Congress and signed by the president when the law on its face did not necessarily violate the Constitution. Given that the Act's constitutionality was a "close" question and that reasonable minds could differ regarding the outcome, deferring to the coordinate branches made sense, both from an institutional and a democratic perspective.

Consequently, in upholding the individual mandate, the Court's decision did not appear to be politically motivated and helped to insulate the Court from attacks on its institutional legitimacy. The decision also left intact a policy that, regardless of one's view of its soundness, was passed by a democratic institution. As a result, the Court's decision accomplished precisely what *Citizens United*, *McCutcheon*, and *Clinton* did not: it deferred to Congress (and the people) on a policy matter that was not facially unconstitutional and enabled democratic choice to trump judicial activism. For these reasons, the Court's decision can be considered one of the most pragmatic, but certainly not the worst, in its history. After all, unless a law facially violates an express provision in the Constitution's text, why should constitutional ambiguity ever be construed in a manner that impedes progress toward political and democratic equality and fiscal responsibility?

How can *National Federation of Independent Investors* be reconciled with *Shelby County v. Holder*?

One can certainly argue that Justice Roberts's decision in *National Federation of Independent Investors*, if truly based on a desire to defer to the coordinate branches, cannot be squared with his majority opinion in *Shelby County v. Holder*, where the Court, again by a 5–4 margin, invalidated two provisions of the Voting Rights Act even though the Senate had voted 98–0 in favor of reauthorization.[42] Section Five of the Act required state and local governments with a history of voter discrimination to obtain preclearance from the federal government before implementing changes to their voting laws.[43] Section Four set forth a coverage formula to identify states that would be subject to the preclearance requirement.[44]

42 133 S. Ct. 2612 (2013).
43 Id. at 2615.
44 Id. at 2615.

How can the Court's holding in *Shelby County* – in which not a single senator voted against reauthorization – be reconciled with the Court's reasoning in *National Federation of Independent Investors*, which involved a law that deeply divided Congress? In *Shelby County*, the legislative branch could not adequately confront this issue because it was politically unpopular to do so. As Justice Scalia stated during oral argument, members of Congress likely feared the political fallout that such a vote would engender. Justice Scalia stated as follows:

> I don't think there is anything to be gained by any Senator to vote against continuation of this act. And I am fairly confident it will be reenacted in perpetuity unless – unless a court can say it does not comport with the Constitution . . . *It's – it's a concern that this is not the kind of a question you can leave to Congress.* There are certain districts in the House that are black districts by law just about now. And even the Virginia Senators, they have no interest in voting against this. The State government is not their government, and they are going to lose – they are going to lose votes if they do not reenact the Voting Rights Act. Even the name of it is wonderful: The Voting Rights Act. Who is going to vote against that in the future?[45]

Simply put, when political considerations make it difficult, if not impossible, for the legislature to pass corrective legislation, judicial intervention is necessary – no matter how lopsided the vote. The Court's decision is not anomalous: federal courts have often intervened to decide legal issues where the legislative branch is either unable or unwilling to remedy cognizable legal harms.

Dred Scott: awful decision, but there is not much more to say than has already been said

Few would disagree that the Court's decision in *Dred Scott* was one of the worst in its history. The Court's decision embedded racism, inequality, and white supremacy into the law and stamped African Americans with the label "inferior." No explanation could even remotely excuse such a morally vacant and intentionally demeaning decision.

At the same time, *Dred Scott* has been roundly criticized by commentators for decades, and there is minimal, if any, value in repeating such criticism at great length. Also, given the subsequent developments in the Court's jurisprudence, including its decisions in *Brown v. Board of Education* and *Regents of the University of California v. Bakke*, coupled with policies striving to increase equal opportunity for members of all minority groups, the impact of *Dred Scott* on democracy is no longer significant. Suffice it to say that *Dred Scott* was a dark moment in the Court's history and will remain so permanently.

***

45 See Transcript of Oral Argument at 47–48, Shelby Cty. v. Holder, 133 S. Ct. 2612 (2013) (No. 12-96), available at http://www.supremecourt.gov/oral_arguments/argument_transcripts/12-96_7648.pdf (emphasis added).

Questions

Was Bush v. Gore an outcome-driven decision motivated by partisan ideology? If so, what part of the Court's reasoning should have been different, and why?

If the Court reached the opposite result, would it nonetheless have faced the same criticism from conservative commentators?

Was the Court's decision based in part on the perception that the Florida Supreme Court had overreached?

In National Federation of Independent Investors v. Sebelius, why did Chief Justice Roberts hold that the individual mandate was not a valid exercise of Congress's power under the Commerce Clause?

PART VI

The landmark cases that promoted democracy, respected federalism, strengthened the rule of law, and preserved the Court's institutional legitimacy

What should be targeted is a concept of organic, and not just mechanic, democracy that preserves the rule of law, separation of powers, and that is participatory and pluralistic.

—Recep Tayyip Erdogan

21

BROWN V. BOARD OF EDUCATION

No State shall make or enforce any law which shall abridge the privileges or immunities of citizens of the United States; nor shall any State deprive any person of life, liberty, or property, without due process of law; nor deny to any person within its jurisdiction the equal protection of the laws.

—U.S. Const., Amend. XIV, Cl. 1

Summary

- *Brown* marks a high point in the Court's jurisprudence, as it correctly identified the evils permeating the "separate but equal" doctrine and clearly articulated that the doctrine has no place in the public schools.
- The Court appropriately exercised its power by intervening to protect minority rights in the face of racial discrimination.

***

Introduction

In *Brown v. Board of Education* the Court held that state laws establishing segregated public schools violate the Equal Protection Clause of the Fourteenth Amendment because "separate educational facilities are inherently unequal."[1] In so ruling, the Court overturned its 1896 decision in *Plessy v. Ferguson* in so far as that decision could be construed as sanctioning state-sponsored racial segregation in the public schools. The decision opened the door to the Civil Rights Movement, advanced the movement toward racial integration, and brought the nation one step closer to realizing the promise of equal rights for all of its citizens.

***

1 Brown v. Board of Education, 347 U.S. 483, 495 (1954).

The decision

The issue before the *Brown* Court was whether separate, but essentially equal, educational facilities could be provided to black Americans without running afoul of the Fourteenth Amendment's Equal Protection Clause. In a 9–0 decision, the Court held that separate educational facilities are inherently unequal and, accordingly, that segregation in the public schools denies equal protection of the laws.

In formulating its ruling, the Court began by addressing its previous holding in *Plessy v. Ferguson*, where the Court had concluded that equality under the Constitution exists when the races are afforded separate facilities so long as those facilities are substantially equal. Thus, the issue before the Court in *Brown* was whether segregated, but similarly equipped, schools could properly be understood as being "equal." In answering that question, the Court employed a two-prong inquiry. First, it sought to determine whether the history of the Fourteenth Amendment could assist, and readily concluded that the history was too inconclusive to render any meaningful insights, particularly because at the time of the amendment's adoption the nation's public school system was virtually nonexistent.[2] The Court then considered whether features beyond what it termed "tangible factors" such as buildings, curricula, and teacher qualifications and salaries influence whether, and to what degree, an educational facility is, in fact, equal for purposes of the Equal Protection Clause. In this regard, the Court determined that it had to look at the "effect of segregation itself on public education."[3]

The Court's examination of the "effect" of segregation began with its contention that education is vital to the proper functioning of the nation and critical to an individual's ability to succeed in life:

> Today, education is perhaps the most important function of state and local governments. Compulsory school attendance laws and the great expenditures of education both demonstrate our recognition of the importance of education in our democratic society. It is required in the performance of our most basic public responsibilities, even service in the armed forces. It is the very foundation of good citizenship. Today it is a principal instrument in awakening the child to cultural values, in preparing him for later professional training, and in helping him to adjust normally to his environment. In these days, it is doubtful that any child may reasonably be expected to succeed in life if he is denied the opportunity of an education. Such an opportunity, where the state has undertaken to provide it is a right which must be made available to all on equal terms.[4]

Employing this logic, the operative question for the Court quickly became whether the same educational opportunity was possible if students were separated from one another on the basis of race. In concluding that it was not, the Court specifically noted

2 Id. at 489–90.
3 Id. at 492.
4 Id. at 493.

the negative psychological impact visited on minority students in a segregated system. Specifically, the Court drew on findings in the following cases, showing that segregation breeds a sense of inferiority in minority children that handicaps their educational development and, consequently, necessarily deprives them of the same opportunity they would be afforded in a racially integrated school.[5] Given such a lost opportunity, the Court concluded, "in the field of public education the doctrine of 'separate but equal' has no place. Separate educational facilities are inherently unequal."[6] The Court went on to hold that segregation in public education "is a denial of the equal protection of the laws."[7]

***

Analysis

There can be no reasonable dispute that the *Brown* decision was a powerful step toward turning the tide on what had been hundreds of years of segregationist thought and practice in the United States, and in that regard certainly reached the correct result. But did it do so by following an appropriate process? In reaching its result, the Court quite correctly sought to identify what evidence, if any, it could find in the history of the Fourteenth Amendment that might shine a light on the intent of its drafters. Having found the language of the amendment silent as to the question posed by the case and the history of the amendment to be inconclusive, the Court arguably could have declined to rule on the constitutionality of segregation in the public schools. It could have concluded instead that the states themselves should be left to make determinations about the nature and scope of education within their boundaries and to permit the legislative process to address any problems attendant to the same.

The Court's decision to intervene, however, can be justified. Although the text and original purpose of the Due Process and Equal Protection Clauses did not expressly support the Court's ruling, they nonetheless could be construed as they were because the underlying motive behind school segregation, regardless of the Court's prior articulation of the "separate but equal" doctrine, was an animus toward African Americans and an attempt to deprive this group of citizens educational opportunities available to others solely on the basis of race. The Court quite appropriately recognized that the effect of the states' segregationist policies was to discriminate on the basis of race. In such an instance, the Court had an obligation to step in to protect the rights of a politically marginalized group. To have ruled otherwise would have permitted the nation to continue to ignore the problems being engendered by segregation and the toll it was taking on the country as a whole, as well as on the individuals suffering under its weight.

***

5 Id. at 494.
6 Id. at 495.
7 Id.

Questions

Should the Court have expressly overruled Plessy? Why didn't it?

Why did the Court come so close to identifying education as a constitutional right, but ultimately shy away from doing so?

What parallels and differences can be drawn between Brown and Lochner?

Did the Court have to focus on the psychological effects of segregation to rule as it did? Should it have?

22

WASHINGTON V. GLUCKSBERG

No State shall make or enforce any law which shall abridge the privileges or immunities of citizens of the United States; nor shall any State deprive any person of life, liberty, or property, without due process of law; nor deny to any person within its jurisdiction the equal protection of the laws.

—U.S. Const., Amend. XIV, Cl. 1

Summary

- In *Washington v. Glucksberg*, the Court interpreted the Due Process Clause narrowly, holding that the Fourteenth Amendment only protects unenumerated rights that are "deeply rooted in the Nation's history and traditions."
- The Court's process-based exposition on substantive liberty enabled citizens to decide whether to legalize assisted suicide through the democratic process.
- The Court rejected the broad definition of liberty adopted in *Planned Parenthood v. Casey*, recognizing that this approach would lead the Court to hold that nearly every asserted right was worthy of constitutional protection.

***

Introduction

In *Glucksberg*, the Court's reasoning bore no resemblance to the broad and open-ended rhetoric that characterized its decisions in *Griswold*, *Roe*, and *Planned Parenthood*.[1] Rather than adopting a nebulous and imprecise definition of liberty "in its more transcendent dimensions," the Court relied primarily on the historical record regarding the permissibility of assisted suicide. In doing so, the Court retained the

1 The quoted material in this chapter is taken from Washington v. Glucksberg, 521 U.S. 702 (1997).

flexibility to recognize new rights in appropriate circumstances, yet simultaneously avoiding a rights-creation enterprise that is based solely on subjective values or normative considerations. The Court's decision in *Glucksberg* underscores the importance of process-based decision making and shows that legitimate decision-making processes need not prevent judges from considering the utility of a particular outcome. Most importantly, the decision promotes bottom-up lawmaking as a cornerstone of American constitutionalism – a desirable outcome in and of itself.

***

The decision

In *Glucksberg*, four terminally ill patients challenged the constitutionality of the state of Washington's ban on assisted suicide, alleging that the ban violated their substantive liberty interests under the Due Process Clause. Writing for a 7–2 majority, former Chief Justice William Rehnquist held that the Due Process Clause did not include a right to assisted suicide. Although conceding that the clause "guarantees more than fair process, and the 'liberty' it protects includes more than the absence of physical restraint," Chief Justice Rehnquist explained that the Court has "always been reluctant to expand the concept of substantive due process because guideposts for responsible decision-making in this unchartered area are scarce and open-ended."[2]

The majority's primary concern was that "[b]y extending constitutional protection to an asserted right or liberty interest, we, to a great extent, place the matter outside the arena of public debate and legislative action."[3] For this reason, the Court must "exercise the utmost care whenever we are asked to break new ground in this field," lest the liberty protected by the Due Process Clause be subtly transformed into the policy preferences of the Members of this Court."[4]

Against this backdrop, Chief Justice Rehnquist applied the Court's two-part test for determining whether the Due Process Clause protects the right to assisted suicide. First, the Court inquired whether the asserted right is "deeply rooted in this Nation's history and tradition."[5] Second, the Court required "in substantive-due-process cases a 'careful description' of the asserted fundamental liberty interest."[6] In conducting this inquiry, Chief Justice Rehnquist emphasized that "[o]ur Nation's history, legal traditions, and practices . . . provide the crucial 'guideposts for responsible decision-making' that direct and restrain our exposition of the Due Process Clause."[7]

In adopting a relatively narrow view of the Due Process Clause, Justice Rehnquist rejected an alternative test that would "ask 'whether [Washington's] statute sets up one

2 Id. at 719–720 (internal citation omitted).
3 Id. at 720.
4 Id. (internal citation omitted).
5 Id. (internal citation omitted).
6 Id. at 721 (internal citation omitted).
7 Id. (internal citation omitted).

of those 'arbitrary impositions' or 'purposeless restraints' at odds with the Due Process Clause of the Fourteenth Amendment."[8] Chief Justice Rehnquist explained as follows:

> In our view . . . the development of this Court's substantive-due-process jurisprudence . . . has been a process whereby the outlines of the "liberty" specially protected by the Fourteenth Amendment-never fully clarified, to be sure, and perhaps not capable of being fully clarified-have at least been carefully refined by concrete examples involving fundamental rights found to be deeply rooted in our legal tradition. This approach tends to rein in the subjective elements that are necessarily present in due-process judicial review. In addition, by establishing a threshold requirement-that a challenged state action implicate a fundamental right-before requiring more than a reasonable relation to a legitimate state interest to justify the action, it avoids the need for complex balancing of competing interests in every case.[9]

Applying this framework, Chief Justice Rehnquist held that the Due Process Clause did not protect a right to assisted suicide. Emphasizing the "almost universal tradition that has long rejected the asserted right . . . even for terminally ill, mentally competent adults," Chief Justice Rehnquist held that "to hold for respondents, we would have to reverse centuries of legal doctrine and practice, and strike down the considered policy choice of almost every State."[10]

Additionally, Chief Justice Rehnquist noted that the petitioners' reliance on *Planned Parenthood v. Casey*, including the Court's dicta concerning liberty and autonomy, did not support the creation of a right to assisted suicide. Specifically, the fact that "many of the rights and liberties protected by the Due Process Clause sound in personal autonomy does not warrant the sweeping conclusion that any and all important, intimate, and personal decisions are so protected."[11] Moreover, because "the history of the law's treatment of assisted suicide in this country has been and continues to be one of the rejection of nearly all efforts to permit it," there was no basis to recognize assisted suicide as a fundamental constitutional right.[12] Perhaps most importantly, because citizens "are engaged in an earnest and profound debate about the morality, legality, and practicality of physician-assisted suicide," the Court holding appropriately "permits this debate to continue, *as it should in a democratic society*."[13]

***

Analysis

The Court's interpretation of substantive liberty under the Fourteenth Amendment is in stark contrast to the ethereal rhetoric – and exceedingly broad definition of

8 Id. (internal citation omitted).
9 Id. at 722.
10 Id. at 723.
11 Id. at 727.
12 Id. at 728.
13 Id. at 735 (emphasis added).

liberty – espoused in *Griswold*, *Roe*, and *Planned Parenthood*. Although acknowledging that "liberty" under the Due Process Clause includes a substantive component, the Court (1) relied on history and tradition to ensure that its decision was not predicated on subjective values; (2) emphasized that an asserted right must be "carefully described"; and (3) promoted citizen participation in democracy.

A process-based decision-making framework: rights creation through the lens of history and tradition

The Court's framework for determining whether to create a new right under the Fourteenth Amendment was process based rather than outcome driven, showed respect for the democratic process, and embraced a modest view of the Court's reviewing authority. By focusing on whether an asserted right is consistent with the country's history and tradition, the Court understood that its decisions must be grounded in a legitimate source of constitutional authority and that the desirability of a particular outcome was not, by itself, a sufficient basis upon which to invent a new right. In short, *Glucksberg* is a textbook example of judicial humility – a concept wholly foreign to the *Griswold* majority.

If the Court had relied on the sweeping definition of liberty set forth in *Planned Parenthood*, no conceivable obstacle would have prevented the Court from creating whatever "rights" that a majority of the Justices deemed most desirable. For example, a constitutional right "to define one's own concept of existence . . . and the mystery of human life" can encompass nearly *any* right whatsoever, such as a constitutional right to polygamy, to use hallucinogenic drugs, to commit suicide at any stage of life, and to engage in revenge killings.[14] After all, what aspect of *Planned Parenthood*'s dicta suggests even the slightest limitation on the rights encompassed within the word liberty, or on the Court's power to define "the liberty of all"?

The *Glucksberg* Court's reliance on history and tradition provides a workable "middle ground" in which to create rights without usurping the democratic process, because history and tradition do not limit the Court to recognizing only those rights that existed at the time the Constitution was adopted. Rather, they enable the Court to consider whether public attitudes and opinions have evolved over time and therefore provide a historical basis to support the creation of a new right. At the same time, history and tradition constrain the Court from inventing law that is entirely unmoored from the Constitution's text, the values it expresses (e.g., decentralization, federalism, separation of powers), and the United States' legal traditions. This enables the Court to consider the utility of an outcome, but only to the extent that there exists legitimate legal authority to justify that outcome.

In cases such as *Griswold* and *Planned Parenthood*, no such limitations existed, as the Court's broad exposition on liberty left judges "free to roam where unguided speculation might take them" absent some constraint on its power. That is precisely why the Court should never rely on imprecise words such as liberty, autonomy, and

14 Planned Parenthood, 505 U.S. at 851.

dignity to create new rights – it gives the Court license to discard process-based decision making into the "graveyard of the forgotten past."[15]

The importance of carefully (and narrowly) describing a right

The interesting aspect of *Glucksberg* is that, of all the rights created under *Griswold*-liberty, the one that most likely warrants constitutional protection is the right to assisted suicide. The most sincere expression of liberty, autonomy, self-determination, and dignity would seem to support permitting terminally ill citizens to end their lives in a manner and at a time of their choosing. After all, if women are constitutionally entitled to terminate a pregnancy, why are they prohibited from terminating their own lives to avoid prolonged suffering from cancer?

Nevertheless, had the Court created a right to assisted suicide, it would have entirely disregarded – and disrespected – the values and judgments made by citizens and their elected representatives over 200 years. Additionally, the Court would have substituted normative (not legal) judgment for the democratic choices of voters and legislators through the country. Similarly, if, under the guise of "liberty," the Court had created a right to assisted suicide for terminally ill cancer patients, its decision would have engendered the same problems as the *Griswold*-liberty line of cases: citizens would have relied on *Glucksberg* to assert new constitutional rights. Why should the right to assisted suicide be restricted to terminally ill patients? Should not all citizens have the right to end their lives if they suffer a severe handicap or mental illness? Should citizens who are permanently disabled after a traumatic accident have the right to assisted suicide? In fact, why should citizens be prohibited from ending their lives at any stage and for any reason? Would not this be the precise expression of liberty and equal dignity that Justice Kennedy championed in *Obergefell*? The answer is yes.

Some might posit that, in the latter examples, the government's interest in protecting and preserving human life is stronger and that the individual's interest in ending his or her life is weaker. But the basis for making these distinctions is moral, not legal or constitutional, and the Court possess no unique expertise, regardless of how "reasoned" its judgment, to make moral judgments, and certainly has no authority to invent rights that no reasonable reading of the text can support. Doing so would impermissibly conflate legal and moral decision making and lay the foundation for an entirely outcome-driven jurisprudence. That is a prescription for judicial overreaching of the most undemocratic kind – as *Griswold*, *Roe*, and *Planned Parenthood* so clearly demonstrated.

Democracy is a desirable outcome

The Court's decision has no bearing on the question of whether such a right should be recognized and does not imply that the Justices are personally opposed to assisted suicide. The relevant question is: *Who* should be responsible for making this decision? In *Glucksberg*, the Court correctly held that where the country has throughout history

15 Application of Gault, 387 U.S. 1, 24 (1967).

rejected an asserted right and where the Constitution's text does not provide a basis to recognize such a right, citizens have the authority to make this decision through their elected representatives.

By respecting the structural constraints on its lawmaking power, the Court furthered a bedrock component of American constitutionalism: bottom-up lawmaking through the democratic process, which in and of itself is a desirable outcome because the Constitution's text states that powers not reserved to the government belong to the people. After *Glucksberg*, some states may decide to allow terminally ill citizens to end their lives. Others may decide to enact a blanket prohibition on assisted suicide. That is precisely how democracy should work – citizens have the right to advocate for and adopt different policies, which is the essence of self-determination. In other words, sometimes it is better to be divided, not united.

***

Questions

What arguments can be made that the Court should have relied on the "arbitrariness" test instead of history and tradition? What standards should be used to determine if a law is "arbitrary"?

Does reliance on history and tradition unduly constrain the Court's Article III power? If so, what other interpretive approaches should be used to determine if a right should be afforded constitutional protection?

Can the desirability of an outcome ever justify manipulating or disregarding the Constitution? What criteria would you use to determine if an outcome is "desirable"?

Are there instances where adherence to legitimate decision-making processes leads to unjust or draconian outcomes? What criteria would you use to determine if an outcome is "unjust"?

23

AUSTIN V. MICHIGAN CHAMBER OF COMMERCE

Congress shall make no law respecting an establishment of religion, or prohibiting the free exercise thereof; or abridging the freedom of speech, or of the press; or the right of the people peaceably to assemble, and to petition the Government for a redress of grievances.
—U.S. Const., Amend. I

Summary

- In *Austin*, the Court held that the state of Michigan could restrict corporate expenditures for the purpose of preventing corporations from gaining unfair access to and influence over elected officials.
- Contrary to *Citizens United* and *McCutcheon*, the Court held that unfair access and undue influence are forms of corruption because they have a "corrosive effect" on the democratic process.
- The Court appropriately deferred to the coordinate branches because the Constitution's text was ambiguous and the legislation at issue enabled elected officials to reduce the effects of corruption (or the appearance thereof) in the electoral process.
- The Court's decision improved the fairness and integrity of elections and enhanced citizens' ability to meaningfully participate in the political process.

***

Introduction

In *Austin*, a plurality of the Court held that states may regulate corporate speech to prevent corporations from gaining unfair access to and undue influence over elected officials.[1]

1 The quoted material in this chapter is taken from Austin v. Michigan Chamber of Commerce, 494 U.S. 652 (1990).

The Court's decision reduced the "corrosive influence" of money in politics; promoted a marketplace, not a monopoly, of ideas; and enabled the Michigan legislature to address the harms that result when citizens' ability to meaningfully participate in government is compromised.

***

The decision

In *Austin*, the Court addressed the constitutionality of §54(1) of the Michigan Campaign Finance Act, which prohibited corporations from "using corporate treasury funds for independent expenditures in support of, or in opposition to, any candidate in elections for state office."[2] In recognition of the fact that corporations are protected under the First Amendment, the act permitted corporations to make such expenditures from segregated funds dedicated solely to political purposes.

Writing for a plurality of the Court, Justice Thurgood Marshall held that the Act did not violate the First or Fourteenth Amendment. Justice Marshall began by recognizing that corporations are entitled to First Amendment protection and that money is a form of political speech. Justice Marshall explained that a speaker's status as a corporation "does not remove its speech from the ambit of the First Amendment,"[3] that "the use of funds to support a political candidate is 'speech,'" and that "independent campaign expenditures constitute "political expression 'at the core of our electoral process and of the First Amendment freedoms.'"[4]

Justice Marshall also acknowledged that the Act although permitting corporations to make expenditures through a segregated fund, nonetheless implicated free speech concerns because "the corporation is *not* free to use its general funds for campaign advocacy purposes."[5] Accordingly, to withstand constitutional scrutiny, the Act had to further a compelling state interest and be narrowly tailored to achieve that interest. In stark contrast to the Court's later decisions in *Citizens United* and *McCutcheon*, the plurality held that the purpose of the Act – to prevent corporations from gaining an unfair advantage in elections – satisfied this demanding standard. Justice Marshall stated as follows:

> State law grants corporations special advantages – such as limited liability, perpetual life, and favorable treatment of the accumulation and distribution of assets – that enhance their ability to attract capital and to deploy their resources in ways that maximize the return on their shareholders' investments. *These state-created advantages not only allow corporations to play a dominant role in the Nation's economy, but . . . permit them to use "resources amassed in the economic marketplace" to obtain "an unfair advantage in the political marketplace."*[6]

2 Id. at 654.
3 Id. at 657.
4 Id. (internal citation omitted).
5 Id. at 658 (internal citation omitted).
6 Id. at 658–659 (internal citation omitted) (emphasis added).

Also, "[t]he resources in the treasury of a business corporation . . . are not an indication of popular support for the corporation's political ideas," and the "availability of these resources may make a corporation a formidable political presence, even though the power of the corporation may be no reflection of the power of its ideas."[7]

Consequently, "a legislature might demonstrate a danger of real or apparent corruption posed by such expenditures when made by corporations to influence candidate elections."[8] In other words, the legislature need not show that a danger of *quid pro quo* corruption exists, but may instead focus on "the corrosive and distorting effects of immense aggregations of wealth that are accumulated with the help of the corporate form and that have little or no correlation to the public's support for the corporation's political ideas."[9] Thus, although the act "does not attempt 'to equalize the relative influence of speakers on elections,'" it "ensures that expenditures reflect actual public support for the political ideas espoused by corporations."[10] In short, the act's purpose responds to the reality that "[c]orporate wealth can unfairly influence elections when it is deployed in the form of independent expenditures, just as it can when it assumes the guise of political contributions."[11]

Moreover, the Act was "precisely targeted to eliminate the distortion caused by corporate spending while . . . allowing corporations to express their political views."[12] In fact, "[a]lthough some closely held corporations, just as some publicly held ones, may not have accumulated significant amounts of wealth, they receive from the State the special benefits conferred by the corporate structure and present the potential for distorting the political process."[13]

Accordingly, the antidistortion interest – not *quid pro quo* corruption – supported applying the Act to all corporations. In further support of its constitutionality, the Court noted that the Act does not "impose an *absolute* ban on all forms of corporate political spending but permits corporations to make independent political expenditures through separate segregated funds."[14] In this way, "[b]ecause persons contributing to such funds understand that their money will be used solely for political purposes, the speech generated accurately reflects contributors' support for the corporation's political view."[15]

***

Analysis

The plurality's decision in *Austin* furthers several important principles concerning constitutional interpretation and the scope of free speech rights. Specifically, the plurality

7 Id. at 659 (internal citation omitted).
8 Id.
9 Id. at 660.
10 Id.
11 Id.
12 Id.
13 Id. at 689 (internal citation omitted).
14 Id. at 660.
15 Id. at 660–661.

(1) recognized that unfair access to or influence over public officials is a form of corruption subject to regulation; (2) construed the First Amendment's ambiguous language in a pro-democracy fashion; (3) adopted a contextual reading of the First Amendment; and (4) furthered the First Amendment's original purposes.

Unfair access and influence *is* a form of corruption

The most important and pro-democracy aspect of *Austin* was the plurality's conclusion that the use of corporate expenditures to gain unfair access and undue influence in the political process *is* a form of corruption. As the majority recognized, restricting the definition of corruption to only *quid pro quo* corruption (bribes) disregards the realities of electoral politics, notably the vital role that money plays in a candidate's chances of winning an election.

It is widely known that state and federal campaigns can be very costly, forcing candidates to depend heavily on private and often wealthy donors to amass a "war chest" of financial resources to outspend their political rivals. But corporate (and individual) donations come at a price. Corporate donors expect that, if elected, the candidates they support advocate for policies favorable to the corporation's interest, even though such interests do not necessarily represent the views of a majority, or even minority, of citizens – or constitute wise public policy.

As a result, upon taking office successful candidates will be expected to "pay back" their donors by casting favorable votes on legislation that is not necessarily in the best interests of the country, or even representative of the candidate's views. And elected officials will have every reason to do so because they will depend in substantial part on retaining wealthy corporate donors to win reelection. Given the Supreme Court's decision in *U.S. Term Limits v. Thornton*, this cycle can and often does continue in perpetuity. In short, the path to power requires money, which means that those who donate the most money wield the most, and perhaps the only, influence.

Ultimately, the connection between wealth and access to elected officials creates a governance structure motivated by self-interest (e.g., elected officials cast votes favorable to their donors) and dominated by a small group of wealthy individuals, the combination of which is the essence of corruption and a prescription for inequality. In addition, a corporation's ability to gain unfair access to and influence over public officials all but eliminates the need to engage in *quid pro quo* corruption because the same result can be achieved through entirely legal means. That is why *Austin*, not *Citizens United*, was correctly decided. Corporate expenditures are inherently antidemocratic because they represent little more than an attempt to purchase influence, votes, and power.

Pro-democracy decisions in the face of constitutional ambiguity

Although the First Amendment prohibits the government from "abridging the freedom of speech," it does not answer the question of whether restricting corporate speech constitutes an abridgement of speech. Likewise, neither the First Amendment nor its purposes provide sufficient guidance concerning whether the government may restrict corporate speech for the purpose of reducing unfair access to and influence in the political process. In the face of such ambiguity, when confronted with "close" questions regarding the constitutionality of campaign finance reform, the Court should make every attempt to uphold a law that strives to reduce political favoritism – the *sine qua non* of political inequality. The Court may (1) deny *certiorari* and defer to the legislative branch, absent a showing that a law is facially unconstitutional; or (2) issue decisions that enhance meaningful citizen participation in government and therefore reduce political inequality. In *Austin*, the Court chose the latter option and provided the legislative branch with sufficient latitude to experiment with solutions that improved the fairness, integrity, and transparency of elections. Unfortunately, in *Citizens United* – by a 5–4 vote – the Court overruled *Austin* and returned electoral politics to those with the most money, not the best ideas.

Contextualizing the First Amendment

The plurality's decision rested in part on a contextual interpretation of the First Amendment because the plurality considered the effect that a corporation's free speech rights would have on other citizens and the electoral process. As discussed in Part VII, and as evidenced in *Austin*, a contextual approach to constitutional interpretation enhances equal and collective liberty for all citizens because it considers not only the relationship between citizens and government, but also the relationship among citizens.

In particular, the plurality emphasized the "corrosive influence" on democracy that would result if corporations, including the wealthiest, were permitted to gain undue influence over elected officials by making substantial political contributions. Specifically, corporate expenditures can, and often do, diminish the voices of ordinary citizens (e.g., reducing the practical value of their First Amendment rights) and create the perception of corruption. Consequently, although the law at issue in *Austin* did not expressly strive to equalize First Amendment rights – and the plurality stated that such a purpose was not constitutionally permissible – the effect of regulating corporate speech is to reduce the marginalization of ordinary voters. By giving citizens a more egalitarian voice in governance, the plurality's decision enhanced ordinary citizens' ability to exercise First Amendment rights in a manner that promotes a participatory democracy.

The original purpose of the First Amendment

Even though the language of the First Amendment is broadly phrased and therefore ambiguous in some cases, its original purpose is clear. The right to freely express one's views enables all citizens to contribute to public debate on matters of political and social importance, which creates a robust "marketplace of ideas" in which all viewpoints, including those that are offensive and unpopular, are heard. Nowhere is this more important, both for the health of democracy and the goal of ensuring political equality, than in the context of state and federal elections, where citizens confront a myriad of issues affecting their liberty and autonomy.

Giving corporations such as Soros Fund Management and Euclidean Capital the ability to unduly influence elections (and elected officials) undermines this core value because the "marketplace of ideas" transforms into a monopoly of wealthy donors who use money to access power and influence public policy. This state of affairs offends the basic principles upon which the Constitution and democracy are based – liberty, equality, and collective governance. This, again, is why *Citizens United* was wrongly decided.

***

Questions

Do you agree with the Court's decision in Austin or Citizens United? Why?

In cases such as Citizens United and Austin, should the Court require the parties to provide factual evidence regarding the extent to which money has a "corrosive influence" on the democratic process?

Should states be permitted to restrict corporate expenditures for the purpose of equalizing speech, or would that constitute impermissible discrimination on the basis of the speaker's identity?

Might it be preferable to allow corporations and interest groups to influence elections? For example, would progress toward racial equality have been slowed if groups such as the NAACP and ACLU were prohibited from donating money within thirty and sixty days of primary and presidential elections, respectively?

24

UNITED STATES V. NIXON

After Watergate we learned what generations before us have known; our Constitution works. And during Watergate years it was interpreted again so as to reaffirm that no one – absolutely no one – is above the law.

—Leon Jaworski

Summary

- In *Nixon* the Court appropriately declined to expand executive power to permit the cloaking of potential criminal conduct and to impede the fair and orderly operation of the criminal justice system.
- The Court correctly construed the Constitution to clarify that the president of the United States is not above the law.

***

Introduction

In 1974 a grand jury of the United States District Court for the District of Columbia returned an indictment charging a number of individuals with, among other things, a conspiracy to defraud the United States. Although not specifically identified as such in the indictment, President Richard Nixon was named as an unindicted co-conspirator. A subpoena was later issued upon the request of the special prosecutor demanding the production of certain documents, including tape recordings, relating to meetings between the president and his aides and advisors. The president moved to quash the subpoena, asserting that the materials were subject to executive privilege. In a unanimous decision, the Court ruled that the president was required to comply with the subpoena. Specifically, the Court concluded that although the president may assert a constitutionally protected privilege under certain circumstances related to military, diplomatic, or national security, the president does not enjoy an absolute privilege.

Rather, the Court ruled that claims of privilege by the executive branch are reviewable by the judiciary and are to be weighed against the Court's interest in the fair administration of justice.

***

The decision

The president urged three major arguments in connection with this challenge of the subpoena. The first was that the court lacked jurisdiction to issue the subpoena in the first instance because the matter concerned an intrabranch dispute that was not properly subject to judicial resolution.[1] Specifically, the president argued that his refusal to comply with the special prosecutor's demands under the subpoena did not present a "case" or "controversy" subject to judicial resolution, but instead involved a dispute within the executive branch between a subordinate and his superior officer and thus posed a political question.[2] The president also urged that the subpoena failed to satisfy the requirements of Fed. R. Crim. P. 17(c).[3] Finally, the president asserted that the subpoena should be quashed because the separation-of-powers doctrine precluded judicial review of a president's claim of executive privilege, as such a privilege was necessary for the executive branch to properly perform its duties.[4] The Court rejected each of the president's arguments.

With respect to the president's jurisdictional claim, the Court first noted that the mere fact that counsel had determined to identify the matter as an "intrabranch" dispute was not sufficient to defeat federal jurisdiction.[5] Rather, the Court looked to the nature of the action and concluded that the issue was one that courts traditionally resolve because, among other things, the matter arose in the regular course of a federal criminal prosecution.[6] The Court likewise quickly disposed of the president's contention that the subpoena failed to comply with Rule 17, finding that the subpoena suffered from none of the alleged deficiencies (lack of relevancy, admissibility, and specificity) identified by the president's counsel.[7]

As to the president's claim of absolute executive privilege, the Court ruled that it properly could consider the validity of such a claim and rejected the contention that the president enjoyed such a privilege. Counsel for President Nixon had asserted that the Court could not properly hear the case in the first instance because under the separation-of-powers doctrine, the judicial branch may not interfere with the functions of the executive branch. In this regard, counsel urged that the president's claim of absolute privilege under the Constitution was not subject to judicial review. The Court disagreed. Although the Court acknowledged that each of the governmental branches must interpret its constitutional powers in order to perform its assigned duties and

1 The quoted material in this chapter is taken from United States v. Nixon, 418 U.S. 683, 692–693 (1974).
2 Id.
3 Id. at 697.
4 Id. at 703.
5 Id. at 693.
6 Id. at 696–697.
7 Id. at 700.

that such interpretations are "due great respect from the others,"[8] the Court reiterated *Marbury*'s assertion that the Court's duty is to "say what the law is."[9] Accordingly, because the president's claim of privilege raised an issue regarding constitutional interpretation, the Court ruled that it fell within its province. In rejecting the president's claim of absolute privilege, the Court declined to embrace counsel's contention that the concept of executive privilege afforded the president the power to withhold information from the other governmental branches to keep confidential communications between high-level employees and officers of the executive branch confidential. Although the Court acknowledged the need for candor and the value of keeping high-level communications secret in certain circumstances, the Court declined to recognize an absolute, unqualified presidential privilege of immunity under all circumstances. Rather, the Court indicated that a qualified privilege might exist in the context of a need "to protect military, diplomatic, or sensitive national security secrets."[10] But where, as in the case of a criminal proceeding, the executive's interest in maintaining confidentiality conflicts with the judiciary's duty to ferret out the truth, the latter is to be given greater weight:

> In this case we must weigh the importance of the general privilege of confidentiality of Presidential communications in performance of the President's responsibilities against the inroads of such a privilege on the fair administration of criminal justice. . . . A President's acknowledged need for confidentiality in the communications of his office is general in nature, whereas the constitutional need for production of relevant evidence in a criminal proceeding is specific and central to the fair adjudication of a particular criminal case in the administration of justice. . . . We conclude that when the ground for asserting privilege as to subpoenaed materials sought for use in a criminal trial is based only on the generalized interest in confidentiality, it cannot prevail over the fundamental demands of due process of law in the fair administration of criminal justice.[11]

Accordingly, "[t]he generalized assertion of privilege must yield to the demonstrated, specific need for evidence in a pending criminal trial."[12]

***

Questions

Was the Court correct to identify the existence of an executive privilege?

What is the textual support for such a privilege?

Was the Court correct to conclude that it could challenge the president's interpretation of his powers and prerogative under the Constitution?

8 Id. at 703.
9 Id.
10 Id. at 706.
11 Id. at 712–713.
12 Id.

25

UNITED STATES V. LOPEZ

The Congress shall have Power To . . . regulate Commerce with foreign Nations, and among the several States, and with the Indian Tribes.

—U.S. Const., Article I, Section 8, Cl. 3

Summary

- In *Lopez* the Court appropriately declined to expand Congress's power under the Commerce Clause to regulating crime and education – two areas traditionally left to state control.
- In construing the scope of the Commerce Clause, the *Lopez* Court correctly tethered itself to the text of the Constitution and appropriately considered the Framers' stated intent to create a balance of power between federal and state government.

***

Introduction

In 1990 Congress passed the Gun-Free Zones Act, which made it a federal offense for anyone to knowingly possess a firearm in a school zone. In 1992, Lopez was arrested for carrying a concealed handgun at a high school in San Antonio, Texas, and was subsequently charged with violating the act and ultimately indicted by a federal grand jury under Section 922(q) of the act. He challenged the indictment, contending that Section 922(q) was unconstitutional "as it is beyond the power of Congress to legislate control over public schools."[1] The Court agreed, finding that Section 922(q) exceeded Congress's authority under the Commerce Clause to "regulate Commerce . . . among the several States."[2] In so ruling, the Court correctly reasserted the long-neglected

1 The quoted material in this section is taken from United States v. Lopez, 514 U.S. 549, 551 (1995).
2 Id.

principle that congressional power under the Commerce Clause is limited in nature and clarified the appropriate inquiry for analyzing whether a particular activity falls within the scope of the clause. The decision marked a needed retreat from the Court's prior grants of expanded congressional power.

***

The decision

The powers delegated by the proposed Constitution to the federal government are few and defined. Those which are to remain in the State governments are numerous and indefinite.
—James Madison

The precise issue in *Lopez* was whether Section 922(q) of the 1990 Gun-Free Zones Act, which sought to eliminate firearms from school zones, was an appropriate exercise of Congress's power to regulate commerce under the Commerce Clause. In a 5–4 decision, the Court held that it was not.

In so ruling, the Court began with what it termed "first principles."[3] These included the dual concepts that the powers delegated to the federal government are limited in nature and that the division of powers between the federal government and the states was designed by the Framers to protect fundamental liberties.[4] The Court then turned to the text of the Constitution itself to highlight that the power delegated to Congress under the Commerce Clause is expressly limited to regulating commerce and, for the purposes of the issue at hand, limited to doing so among the states.[5] Having identified the parameters of the analysis to follow, Justice Rehnquist then briefly reviewed the Court's Commerce Clause jurisprudence and noted that even under its more recent precedents – cases that he acknowledged as having expanded congressional power – the Court confirmed that congressional power under the Commerce Clause "is subject to its outer limits."[6] The remainder of the decision sets out the three categories that, in the Court's view, define Congress's regulatory authority. These include the power to "regulate the use of the channels of interstate commerce"; the power to regulate and protect "the instrumentalities of interstate commerce, or persons or things in interstate commerce"; and the power to regulate those activities that have "a substantial relation" to interstate commerce."[7] With respect to the third category, and recognizing that the case law had not always been consistent in this regard, the Court clarified that the proper Commerce Clause analysis requires an inquiry into whether the regulated activity "substantially affects" interstate commerce.[8] In Justice Rehnquist's view, the operative question was whether Section 922(q) "substantially affected" commerce.[9]

3 Id. at 552.
4 Id.
5 Id.
6 Id. at 557.
7 Id. at 558–559.
8 Id. at 559.
9 Id.

Distinguishing *Wickard v. Filburn*, a case in which the Court found that Congress properly could regulate the production of wheat for home consumption because such consumption, in the aggregate, affected the market pricing of wheat on a whole, and identifying *Filburn* as "perhaps the most far reaching example of Commerce Clause authority over intrastate activity,"[10] Justice Rehnquist quickly opined that "[s]ection 922(q) is a criminal statute that by its terms has nothing to do with 'commerce' or any sort of economic enterprise, however broadly one might define those terms."[11] Further, the Court noted that Section 922(q) did not contain a jurisdictional statement articulating Congress's belief that the firearm ban did, in fact, affect interstate commerce.[12] Finally, the Court pointed out that the government had not come forward with any legislative or congressional committee findings regarding the ban's effects on interstate commerce.[13]

The Court next addressed the government's arguments as to why Section 922(q) could properly be understood to substantially affect interstate commerce. The government contended that the possession of firearms in a school zone affected the national economy in two ways. First, it urged that such activity results in violent crime that, in turn, imposes substantial economic costs on the nation in the form of higher insurance costs. The government likewise asserted that violent crimes deter travelers from willingly going into areas that experience such crime.[14] Second, the government argued that the presence of guns in schools threatens the learning environment itself, which ultimately leads to a less informed, less productive workforce and, consequently, a weaker national economy.[15] The Court rejected both arguments, finding that to embrace them would both sanction congressional control over law enforcement and education – two areas traditionally left to regulation by the states[16] – as well as leave completely open ended the activities that Congress could control. Specifically, the Court opined, "[I]f we were to accept the Government's arguments, we are hard pressed to posit any activity by an individual that Congress is without power to regulate."[17] Because the government's position would render Congress's authority under the Commerce Clause tantamount to "a general police power of the sort retained by the States,"[18] as well as "eliminate the distinction between 'what is truly national and what is truly local' envisioned by the Founders, the Court specifically declined to permit any further expansion of Congress's powers under the Commerce Clause.",[19] the Court specifically declined to permit any further expansion of Congress's powers under the Commerce Clause.

Justice Kennedy, joined by Justice O'Connor, concurred. Noting that the transition from the economic system in place at the time of drafting and the "single, national

10 Id. at 560.
11 Id. at 561.
12 Id.
13 Id. at 562.
14 Id. at 563–564.
15 Id. at 564.
16 Id.
17 Id. at 566.
18 Id. at 567.
19 Id. at 567.

market" driving the modern economy is still taking place,[20] Justice Kennedy cautioned that rulings invalidating congressional action under the Commerce Clause should be issued with "great restraint."[21] Despite his articulated support of Congress's broad power to regulate in the national market and his stated concern that the *Lopez* decision be understood as a necessary but limited holding,[22] Justice Kennedy nonetheless opined on the important issues of federalism raised by the case. In this regard, he discussed the Court's role in preserving the balance between federal and state power, of protecting areas of traditional state concern, and in ensuring that the states continue to function as "laboratories for experimentation."[23]

Justice Thomas likewise concurred, but expressed his concern that the Court's decision had "drifted far from the original understanding of the Commerce Clause."[24] Specifically, he urged that the "substantial effects" test be reevaluated and a new standard developed to better reflect the "text and history of the Commerce Clause."[25] In Justice Thomas's view, the "substantial effects" test cannot be squared with either the language of the clause or its history.

***

Analysis

Lopez marks a clear move by the Rehnquist Court to try to more closely define the powers that Congress may properly exercise under the Commerce Clause and to slow, if not put a complete halt to, what the Court saw as an unprincipled expansion of that power into a "general police power of the sort retained by the States."[26] In doing so, the Court quite properly directed its focus to the language of the text itself and to the Founders' intent in structuring a dual state and federal system. In this regard, the Court appropriately framed the analysis by highlighting that the Constitution creates a federal government of limited, enumerated powers and that language of the Constitution itself specifically delineates that the powers afforded to Congress under the Commerce Clause are expressly limited to regulating commerce. As Justice Rehnquist accurately noted, the Court's prior decisions could be read to invite unlimited congressional activity under the clause – as evidenced by the government's inability to identify any activity that the states could regulate but that Congress could not. Certainly there can be little dispute that banning firearms from schools is a laudable goal, but the Court quite correctly resisted achieving that goal through improper means. Specifically, and as the Court recognized, to style Congress's attempt to legislate with respect firearms in the school would require a reading of the text that it simply could not support. It would also wholly ignore the Framers' attempt to limit congressional infringement into areas best controlled by the states. As Justice Kennedy correctly

20 Id. at 568.
21 Id.
22 Id.
23 Id. at 581.
24 Id. at 584.
25 Id. at 585.
26 Id. at 567.

stated, the act's ban on firearms deprived the states from experimenting with solutions to the problem of gun violence tailored to their individual needs and circumstances. Imposing a federal response would, as Justice Kennedy noted, "contradict [] the federal balance the Framers designed and that [the] Court is obliged to enforce."[27]

***

Questions

Is Justice Thomas's concern that the "substantial effects" test is unworkable and at odds with the original understanding of the Commerce Clause justified?

Does the Court's distinction between economic and noneconomic activities make sense? How strong is that distinction?

Can the majority's rationale be squared with the Court's prior decisions embracing federal civil rights legislation?

Does looking to original intent make sense in construing the Commerce Clause in light of our modern, global economy?

27 Id. at 583.

26

TEXAS V. JOHNSON

Congress shall make no law respecting an establishment of religion, or prohibiting the free exercise thereof; or abridging the freedom of speech, or of the press; or the right of the people peaceably to assemble, and to petition the Government for a redress of grievances.

—U.S. Const., Amend. I

Summary

- In *Johnson* the Court correctly applied well-established precedent to arrive at an unpopular, but correct, result.
- The Court properly exercised its power to "say what the law is" and resisted the temptation to say what it believed the law should be, and in so doing preserved the Court's institutional legitimacy.

***

Introduction

During the 1984 Republican National Convention in Dallas, Gregory Johnson participated in a political demonstration protesting the policies of the Reagan Administration. Following the demonstration, with protestors looking on and chanting, Johnson doused an American flag with kerosene and set it on fire. Johnson was subsequently charged and convicted under a Texas statute that prohibited the desecration of state or national flags. The statute defined desecration to include physically mistreating a flag "in a way that the actor knows will seriously offend one or more persons likely to observe or discover his action." Although no person was physically injured or threatened with injury, several witnesses to the flag burning reported that they were seriously offended. Johnson appealed his conviction. The Court of Appeals for the Fifth District of Texas affirmed the conviction, but the Texas Court of Criminal Appeals reversed, finding that Johnson's conduct was expressive speech protected by the First Amendment and that the statute was unconstitutional as it applied to him. The Supreme

Court affirmed. In so doing, the Court adhered to the text of the Constitution and its prior rulings construing it, thereby preserving its institutional legitimacy.

***

The decision

In a 5–4 decision, the Court concluded that Johnson's conviction violated his rights under the First Amendment. In so ruling, the Court began by analyzing whether Johnson's act of burning of the flag was expressive conduct entitled to First Amendment protection. In concluding that it was, the Court first noted the context in which the burning took place, including that Johnson burned the flag as part of a political demonstration. In light of the state's concession that Johnson's conduct was expressive speech, coupled with the "overtly political nature" of his conduct, the Court readily concluded that the flag burning was sufficiently communicative to implicate the First Amendment.[1] The Court then sought to determine whether Texas's interest in support of Johnson's conviction was unrelated to the suppression of expression – a finding that would trigger the relatively lenient *O'Brien* standard. The state had asserted two interests in support of Johnson's conviction. The first was its claimed interest in preventing breaches of the peace. The Court found this interest not to have been implicated because, among other reasons, no disturbance or threatened disturbance had actually occurred.[2] The Court also rejected the state's contention that the offensive nature of the expression was likely to incite a disturbance of the peace. In this regard, the Court found nothing in the circumstances to suggest that Johnson's acts were tantamount to "fighting words" or an invitation to lawlessness.[3] Accordingly, it concluded that the state's interest in maintaining order was not implicated under the facts.[4]

Texas also contended that it had an interest in preserving the flag as a symbol of nationhood and national unity.[5] The Court quickly concluded that this interest was related to expression, as the state necessarily must have understood Johnson's burning of the flag as a call to people to doubt what the flag actually stands for. The Court found that this concern could arise only when "a person's treatment of the flag communicates some message."[6] Accordingly, the Court found the *O'Brien* test to be inapplicable.

Finally, the Court considered whether Texas's interest in preserving the flag as a symbol of nationhood and national unity justified Johnson's conviction. In concluding that it did not, the Court first noted that Johnson's political expression was restricted because of its content. Specifically, the Court determined that Johnson was convicted because his flag burning was designed to send a politically charged message of dissatisfaction with the government.[7] The Court then noted that the state's asserted interest was subject to "the most exacting scrutiny."[8] Because the Court understood

1 The quoted material in this section is taken from Texas v. Johnson, 491 U.S. 397, 406 (1989).
2 Id. at 407.
3 Id. at 409.
4 Id. at 410.
5 Id.
6 Id.
7 Id. at 411.
8 Id. at 412.

the state's real interest to be preserving a particular meaning for the flag – a meaning contrary to Johnson's – it found that Johnson's conviction flew in the face of the First Amendment's "bedrock principle" that the government "may not prohibit the expression of an idea simply because society finds the idea itself offensive or disagreeable."[9] The Court therefore affirmed the judgment of the Texas Court of Criminal Appeals.

Chief Justice Rehnquist dissented, arguing that "The American flag . . . has come to be a visible symbol embodying our nation. . . . The Flag is not simply another 'idea' or 'point of view' competing for recognition in the marketplace of ideas."[10] Given the "almost mystical reverence"[11] it has garnered, Justice Rehnquist believed that its public burning did have the tendency to incite a breach of the peace, thus permitting Texas to prohibit that conduct.[12] Justice John Paul Stevens also dissented, concluding that the case had "nothing to do with 'disagreeable ideas,'" but instead involved "disagreeable conduct" that, in Justice Stevens's opinion, "diminishes the value of an important national asset."[13]

***

Analysis

In ruling as it did, the Court correctly applied its well-established First Amendment principles – despite arriving at an outcome that many found to be personally distasteful. As Justice Kennedy aptly noted in his concurrence, the Court was presented with a "clear and simple statute to be judged against a pure command of the Constitution."[14] Although, as Justice Kennedy correctly remarked, the holding was not one that many would like, it was right "in the sense that the law and the Constitution . . . compel[ed] the result."[15]

***

Questions

Chief Justice Rehnquist noted in his dissent that forty-eight of the fifty states had criminalized the public burning of the flag. Should the Court have given any deference to these legislative pronouncements?

Justice Rehnquist also noted that Johnson had a "full panoply of other symbols and every conceivable form of verbal expression to express his deep disapproval of national policy." Should this matter?

According to Johnson, what is "symbolic speech"?

9 Id. at 414.
10 Id. at 429.
11 Id.
12 Id. at 431.
13 Id. at 438.
14 Id. at 420.
15 Id. at 420–421.

27

GIDEON V. WAINWRIGHT

> *In all criminal prosecutions, the accused shall enjoy the right to a speedy and public trial, by an impartial jury of the State and district wherein the crime shall have been committed, which district shall have been previously ascertained by law, and to be informed of the nature and cause of the accusation; to be confronted with the witnesses against him; to have compulsory process for obtaining witnesses in his favor, and to have the Assistance of Counsel for his defence.*
>
> —U.S. Const., Amend. VI

Summary

- In *Gideon* the Court correctly recognized the right to counsel as a fundamental right protected by the Fourteenth Amendment.
- The Court appropriately intervened in an area traditionally regulated by the states to protect minority rights.

***

Introduction

In 1961 Clarence Earl Gideon was arrested and charged in a Florida state court with breaking and entering a pool hall with the intent to commit a misdemeanor – a non-capital felony. Gideon, an indigent defendant, pled not guilty and asked for an attorney. His request for a court-appointed lawyer was denied on the ground that Florida law permitted the appointment of counsel in capital cases only. Gideon subsequently represented himself, was convicted, and sentenced to five years in prison. Gideon then filed a habeas corpus petition with the Florida Supreme Court, contending that his conviction and incarceration violated his federal constitutional rights. The Florida Supreme Court denied Gideon's request for relief. He received a different reception in the U.S. Supreme Court. Writing for the Court, Justice Black concluded that the right of an indigent criminal defendant to counsel is a fundamental right, is critical to a fair trial, and Gideon's trial and conviction in the absence of counsel violated the Fourteenth Amendment. In so ruling, the Court embraced an appropriate reading of the Constitution and correctly intervened to protect the rights of a marginalized group.

***

The decision

The issue before the *Gideon* Court was whether a defendant's federal constitutional right to counsel in a criminal case extended to state court criminal actions.[1] The Court began its inquiry by questioning whether its previous decision in *Betts v. Brady* required reconsideration. In *Betts*, a case that likewise concerned an indigent defendant charged in state court with a felony, the Court held that the refusal to appoint counsel to such a defendant did not necessarily violate the Fourteenth Amendment's Due Process Clause. Rather, under *Betts*, the appointment of counsel under such circumstances turned on whether the particular facts and circumstances in the case suggested that it would be fundamentally unfair not to do so.[2] The *Gideon* Court quickly concluded that *Betts* should be overruled because the decision was based on the erroneous conclusion that the appointment of counsel is a not a fundamental right, essential to a fair trial.[3] Specifically, the Court determined that had the *Betts* Court concluded that the appointment of counsel was such a right, "it would have held that the Fourteenth Amendment requires appointment of counsel in a state court, just as the Sixth Amendment requires in a federal court."[4]

In concluding that the Sixth Amendment right to counsel is a fundamental guarantee obligatory on the states, the Court turned to its prior holdings, including *Powell v. Alabama*. In *Powell*, the Court upheld the right to appointed counsel under a Fourteenth Amendment "fundamental fairness" analysis. According to *Powell*, the right to appointed counsel had its genesis in the due process right to a fair hearing. Finding that the right to a fair hearing entailed a right to be heard, and that such a right in turn was linked to having counsel, the *Powell* Court determined that the state had a due process obligation to provide the indigent defendant with counsel, at least where the facts showed that the presence of counsel was essential to obtaining a fair hearing. Although Justice Black acknowledged that *Powell* was specifically limited to its facts,[5] he nonetheless determined that the Court had, in fact, concluded that the right to counsel is fundamental.[6] Relying on *Powell*, as well as *Johnson v. Zerbst*, a case in which the Court had held that the right to appointed counsel was found in the Sixth Amendment and was fundamental,[7] the *Gideon* Court held that *Betts* had "made an abrupt break with [the Court's] own well-considered precedents."[8] Recognizing this break, and

1 The quoted material in this section is taken from Gideon v. Wainright, 372 U.S. 335 (1963).
2 Id. at 339.
3 Id. at 340.
4 Id.
5 Id. at 343.
6 Id.
7 Id.
8 Id. at 343–344.

endeavoring to restore "constitutional principles established to achieve a fair system of justice,"[9] the *Gideon* Court stated:

> Not only these precedents but also reason and reflection require us to recognize that in our adversary system of criminal justice, any person hauled into court, who is too poor to hire a lawyer, cannot be assured a fair trial unless counsel is provided for him. This seems to use to an obvious truth.[10]

Because Gideon was convicted in violation of his rights under the Constitution, the Court reversed the Florida Supreme Court's judgment.

Justice Douglas joined in the opinion, but wrote separately to express his view that the Fourteenth Amendment fully incorporated the Bill of Rights and made those rights applicable to the states.

Justice Clark likewise concurred, but wrote to state that he understood *Gideon* to do nothing more than erase the prior distinction between capital and noncapital cases and the right to counsel with respect to each.[11] Specifically, Justice Clark pointed out that the Sixth Amendment's plain language requirement that counsel be appointed in all criminal prosecutions, coupled with the Court's prior decisions finding that counsel is required for capital offenses, merely highlighted that the Constitution "makes no distinction between capital and noncapital cases" requiring that indigent defendants be provided with counsel in all cases.[12]

***

Analysis

Although the Court concluded that *Betts* had been an "abrupt break" with its prior precedents, Justice Harlan disagreed. Rather, he noted that in *Powell*, a capital case, the Court had specifically declared that it was the particular facts of the case – the defendants' ignorance, illiteracy, youth, and public hostility – that imposed a duty on the state court to assign counsel to ensure due process of law.[13] Accordingly, in Justice Harlan's view, the *Betts* decision did no more than clarify the possibility that in a noncapital case, special circumstances might be shown to establish a denial of due process. In this regard, *Betts* was "not a departure from, but an extension of, existing precedent."[14] Noting, however, that the "special circumstance" rule was "no longer a reality"[15] in light of the Court's recognition that the serious nature of a criminal charge itself constituted such a "special circumstance,"[16] Justice Harlan agreed with the Court that the right to counsel is a fundamental right embraced by the Fourteenth

9 Id. at 344.
10 Id.
11 Id. at 348.
12 Id. at 349.
13 Id. at 349–350.
14 Id. at 350.
15 Id. at 351.
16 Id. at 351.

Amendment.[17] He went on to observe, however, his view that in finding the right to counsel to be "implicit in the concept of ordered liberty,"[18] and thus valid against the states, the Court was not suggesting that the Fourteenth Amendment "incorporates" the Sixth Amendment "as such."[19]

Inherent in the Court's decision was the veil of federalism and a nod toward its understanding that the state legislatures were not in the best position to ensure fairness at trial and to protect the liberty interests of indigent defendants. The Court certainly could have determined that it should be left to the states to decide when counsel is required and how counsel should be obtained. Indeed, taking such a position would have been consistent with the view that the states should be free to experiment with crafting solutions, including in the area of criminal procedure.

***

Questions

Is there an argument to be made that the Court's seeming rejection of the circumstance-specific approach taken in Betts is, in fact, inconsistent with the Fourteenth Amendment's concept of due process?

Why didn't the Gideon Court specifically address the issues of federalism raised by the decision? Should it have?

Should the Court have been more specific about whether the ruling was based on the Due Process Clause or the Equal Protection Clause of the Fourteenth Amendment? Why wasn't it?

Can the majority's rationale be squared with the Court's prior decisions embracing federal civil rights legislation?

17 Id. at 352.
18 Id.
19 Id.

PART VII

An interpretive theory that promotes federalism, separation of powers and principled judicial review

The government, which was designed for the people, has got into the hands of the bosses and their employers, the special interests. An invisible empire has been set up above the forms of democracy.

—Woodrow Wilson

We always hear about the rights of democracy, but the major responsibility of it is participation.

—Wynton Marsalis

28

IS DEMOCRACY A GOOD THING? THE ARGUMENTS – AND THE PRACTICALITIES

> *—Democracy substitutes election by the incompetent many for appointment by the corrupt few.*
>
> —George Bernard Shaw

The utility of developing a pro-democracy jurisprudence turns on a fundamental question: Is democracy a desirable form of government?

It depends.

Theoretically, the answer is yes, but *only* if citizens reside in a *democratic republic*, in which majoritarian rule is constrained by the rights granted in a constitution or charter. Because a government that combines democratic and republican components intrinsically promotes basic human values, including equality, individual liberty and autonomy, self-determination, and self-governance.

The United States: a hybrid of democracy and republicanism

The distinction between a republican and democratic form of government is not insignificant, particularly regarding individual versus collective power. Broadly speaking, in a democracy, whether direct (the people vote directly on policy initiatives) or indirect (where elected representatives enact legislation that governs all citizens in a state or country), the majority is considered the governing body, and majority will is paramount in lawmaking. As a result, the minority may be left with little, if any, legal protections. For this reason, democracy has the potential to devolve into tyranny, in which the majority controls all aspects of governance, disregards minority rights, and, in effect, disenfranchises a substantial number of citizens. This is commonly referred to as the "tyranny of the majority."

Conversely, in a republic, power resides in the people as individuals, and citizens have *inalienable* rights that the majority cannot infringe. Such rights are typically enumerated in a constitution or charter. As a result, in a republic, protections for minority rights are typically stronger because there is an increased focus on ensuring liberty and equality for *all* citizens through enforcement of inalienable rights.

The United States is a hybrid of a democratic and republican form of government. The will of the majority, whether directly (e.g., through a ballot initiative) or indirectly (e.g., through elected representatives), still controls, but the majority's power is constrained by the rights citizens possess under the Constitution. The Preamble to the Constitution underscores the fact that a republican form of government is integral to American democracy:

> *We the people of the United States, in order to form a more perfect union*, establish justice, insure domestic tranquility, provide for the common defense, promote the general welfare, and secure the blessings of liberty to ourselves and our posterity, do ordain and establish this Constitution for the United States of America.

As stated in the Declaration of Independence, "[w]e hold these truths to be sacred & undeniable; that all men are created equal [and] independent, that from that equal creation they derive rights *inherent and inalienable*, among which are the preservation of life, [and] liberty, [and] the pursuit of happiness."

Importantly, however, although republicanism enhances the legal and constitutional protections for all citizens, including the minority, it does not sanction blatant manipulations of the Constitution to create rights that no reasonable reading of the text could support. Otherwise, republicanism would, in effect, destroy democracy and nullify majoritarian rule. Although this would prevent democracy from devolving into the "tyranny of the majority," it would simultaneously risk transforming governing into the "tyranny of the minority" (e.g., rule by unelected, life-tenured judges).

A functioning democratic republic

A democratic republic must be practiced correctly if its ideals are to be realized. For example, in a society that calls itself democratic, does greed trump compassion? Does corruption triumph over fairness? Does government answer to the few or the many? Do privilege and power dominate over equality and dignity? In the United States, the answer to all four questions should be no, but the reality yields a different answer. Social and economic inequality is rampant. Schools remain segregated. The wealthiest individuals and corporations use vast amounts of money to influence elected officials. Government answers to the elite, not the middle class; the gap between the wealthy and the poor is widening, not narrowing; and upward mobility for many is an aspiration, not a reality. Put simply, when democracy is dysfunctional, the answer is to fix the problems. That, in a nutshell, summarizes the flaws in the Court's jurisprudence. It does not solve the problems. It makes them worse, and more difficult to fix.

American democracy has now morphed into a hybrid of three other forms of government: a plutocracy, in which corporate donors unduly influence elected officials; an oligarchy, in which unelected judges invent rights out of thin air; and an aristocracy, in which a handful of citizens control most of the country's wealth. For this reason, some might argue democracy is – or has become – an illusion and that the United States is entirely divorced from the values upon which democracy is based.

Specifically, some may assert that democracy is inherently, and thus irreparably, flawed and little more than an illusion. Others may claim that democracy is unsustainable and inevitably morphs into socialism, gives decision-making power to a largely ignorant and uninformed population, and is itself the cause of social and economic inequality, primarily because it is based on rule by the majority, which fails to provide any protections for the minority. These arguments are addressed next.

The illusion of democracy

> *The difference between a democracy and a dictatorship is that in a democracy you vote first and take orders later; in a dictatorship you don't have to waste your time voting.*
>
> —Charles Bukowski

> *What difference does it make to the dead, the orphans and the homeless, whether the mad destruction is wrought under the name of totalitarianism or in the holy name of liberty or democracy?*
>
> —Mahatma Gandhi

Perhaps democracy is an illusory concept that is designed to convince citizens that they have a voice in governance, thereby allowing government to control citizens, prevent disillusionment (or the perception of it), and promote stability. Assuming *arguendo* that democracy is illusory, consider whether the illusion itself has value because, for most individuals, their perception is their reality. By way of analogy, why do individuals who have extramarital affairs conceal such affairs from their spouses? If the spouse discovered the affair, it would likely cause tremendous hurt and be accompanied by feelings of anger and betrayal. In many cases, the marriage may end – a relationship's equivalent of a revolt. The same is true in a democracy. When citizens discover that democracy is plagued by elitism, corruption, and greed, they become disillusioned, apathetic, and alienated. They may develop a collective desire to revolt like the Founding Fathers, secede from the Union like the Confederate states, or, as has occurred recently, some states may advocate for a second constitutional convention. Put simply, what citizens do not know does not hurt them, just like the spouse who is unaware of her husband's mistress can live in temporary bliss.

For these and other reasons, some commentators assert that democracy – and majority rule – is a scam. The will of the majority is merely a euphemism for the tyranny of the majority, leaving those who lose elections or policy disputes without any rights whatsoever and rendering all citizens subservient to a powerful – and unaccountable – federal government. Furthermore, the electoral process is plagued by corruption, and the concept of a participatory democracy disregards the realities of how elections function. In the United States, for example, the federal government is dominated by a two-party system – Republican and Democratic – and candidates who seek office as independent third parties have virtually no chance of succeeding. The two-party system has become so entrenched in American democracy that third-party candidates are often stigmatized as "outside the mainstream" and implicitly branded as unelectable. In other words, potential candidates must first join the entrenched political establishment before they can be considered viable, which prevents any candidate from challenging the very establishment that some contend is plagued by corruption and elitism.

Additionally, the staggering cost of elections prevents many individuals from campaigning for public office, and those that do seek office may sacrifice integrity for the advantages that wealthy campaign donors provide. The practical effect is that, if successful, many elected officials are accountable to and dependent on a small population composed of corporations and lobbyists, not average voters who went to the ballot box and cast a vote they believed was real, not symbolic.

Consequently, when one considers the realities of federal elections, voters arguably do not have a meaningful choice among candidates for public office. Members of the Republican and Democratic Party choose their "establishment" candidate long before a primary or general election begins, and this candidate receives all of the benefits that "establishment" status brings – money, endorsements, and name recognition. These advantages make it difficult, if not impossible, for candidates within either party (or outside of both parties) to successfully challenge the establishment candidate. In other words, voters are presented with a choice that, in actuality, is no choice at all, a proposition supported by the fact that citizens typically vote overwhelmingly for each party's "establishment" candidate. In this way, it does not matter whether and to what extent citizens "participate" in an election because the outcome, for all intents and purposes, is predetermined. Put bluntly, democracy is merely a show – one must suspend disbelief to believe that democracy meaningfully engages the typical voter.

What's more, there is no limit on the number of terms that a congressman may serve, which strengthens the already formidable power of incumbency (and the name recognition and "establishment" support it brings) to a level that makes it difficult for anyone – within or outside the two-party system – to successfully challenge a sitting congressman. And members of the majority party at the state level who are responsible for drawing "district" lines (based on each state's demographics) will often do so in a manner that favors the party's incumbent candidates, a practice known as political gerrymandering. The practical effect is that, in some circumstances, the voting power of citizens who support the opposing party's candidate is diluted, the effect of which is to undermine their ability to challenge the status quo. Finally, extreme partisanship in the United States Congress has resulted in gridlock, government shutdowns, and a legislative process dominated by political gamesmanship and favoritism, wasteful government spending, and a staggering national debt.

When one considers the practical problems with democratic governance, it is not difficult to understand how democracy can be overrun by elitism, corruption, inequality, and a lack of accountability and morph into a plutocracy. Given these facts, the question that one must ask is whether this state of affairs is inevitable for democracy.

No.

The causes of dysfunction in democracy are readily identifiable, did not occur overnight, and certainly did not arise from an unknown source. Corruption and pervasive inequality, along with the Court's decisions in a number of landmark cases, is a substantial contributor to the current state of American democracy, including decisions that blocked remedial attempts by Congress to address political and democratic inequality. In *Citizens United* and *McCutcheon*, the Court – by a 5–4 vote – enabled wealthy corporations and individuals to continue to unduly influence the electoral process and have unfair access to public officials, the effect of which is to render citizens' votes at the ballot box more symbolic than real. In *U.S. Term Limits* the Court facilitated party entrenchment (and tyranny of the majority) by allowing incumbents, who already enjoy a substantial advantage in elections, to serve a potentially limitless number of terms in office. In *Griswold*, *Roe*, *Planned Parenthood*, and *Lawrence*, the Court invented "rights" and, in a flagrant example of top-down lawmaking, removed divisive social policy issues from the democratic process. *San Antonio School District* made it more difficult to remedy social and economic inequality, and the majority of wealth is now concentrated in the top 2% of the population. The Court's decision in *U.S. Term Limits* prompted Justice Thomas to draft a scathing dissent, in which he argued as follows:

> It is ironic that the Court bases today's decision on the right of the people to "choose whom they please to govern them." Under our Constitution, there is only one State whose people have the right to "choose whom they please" to represent Arkansas in Congress . . . *Nothing in the Constitution deprives the people of each State of the power to prescribe eligibility requirements for the candidates who seek to represent them in Congress. The Constitution is simply silent on this question. And where the Constitution is silent, it raises no bar to action by the States or the people.*[1]

Few could gainsay that *U.S. Term Limits* was undemocratic and that the Court has repeatedly frustrated federal and state attempts to effectuate accountability in government and equality for all citizens. For example, in *Clinton* the Court interpreted an ambiguous provision in the Constitution (the Presentment Clause) to prevent, rather than permit, Congress to enhance fiscal accountability. In *San Antonio School District*, the Court permitted states to condition the quality of education on wealth, and in *Milliken* made it harder, not easier, to eradicate de facto segregation. Moreover, the Court's reticence to hear cases alleging improper political gerrymandering has enabled states to continue drawing district lines in a manner that gives an advantage to the party that controls the legislative branch. Put bluntly, the United States is now a shadow democracy that is infected with plutocracy's greed, oligarchy's elitism, and aristocracy's inequality. The Founders would turn in their graves if they witnessed a government that, for all intents and purposes, now mirrors the monarchy from which they revolted.

These cases demonstrate that the deficiencies in democracy do not support the conclusion that democracy is an undesirable form of government per se. What can be said is that democracy will not work if the executive, legislative, and judicial branches of federal and state governments fail to promote equal participation, accountability, and a political milieu in which elected officials are responsible to the needs of their

1 514 U.S. at 845 (Thomas, J., dissenting) (emphasis added).

constituents, not merely to corporate donors. The Court's jurisprudence has turned a blind eye to these objectives, and for reasons that neither the Constitution nor common sense can justify. For example, instead of inventing constitutional "penumbras" in *Griswold*, the Court should have upheld the limits on corporate expenditures in *Citizens United*. Instead of creating a right to abortion in *Roe*, the Court should have upheld aggregate limits on individual contributions in *McCutcheon*. Instead of defining "liberty" in the most broad and unworkable terms in *Planned Parenthood*, the Court in *Clinton* should have held that the Presentment Clause was ambiguous and therefore did not compel invalidation of the Line Item Veto Act. This type of "activism" would have strengthened democracy, promoted bottom-up lawmaking, and made elected officials more accountable to the people, not simply the powerful. Sadly, the Court allowed elitism, corruption, entrenchment, partisan gridlock, and political inequality to remain endemic. As a result, democracy in the United States has become illusory for many citizens.

Of course, no society should be satisfied with an illusory democracy. In fact, citizens have already begun to discover the truth behind the illusion because the deleterious effects of inequality and the appearance of corruption are difficult to ignore and impossible to accept. As stated earlier, the answer is not to abandon democracy, but to make it work effectively and efficiently. This process begins by recognizing that liberty, political and democratic equality, and autonomy depend on facilitating meaningful participation in the democratic process and constricting, not expanding, the scope of the judicial branch's power. When citizens cast a vote at the ballot box, criticize elected officials at town hall meetings, or decide whether to support a referendum, they should trust that their voices will be heard, not silenced; that their opinions have real, not symbolic, value; and that their capacity to effectuate change is shared equally with fellow citizens. After all, to achieve true equality, liberty, and self-determination, the process of governance should reflect respect for the dignity of every human being and vindicate the principle that "all men are created equal."

Ensuring that democracy exists in this form prevents society from devolving into a government akin to tyranny, a society characterized by inequality, and a citizenry plagued by disillusionment. As such, the government's primary and enduring obligation should be to safeguard the integrity and vibrancy of democracy, protect citizens from the tyranny of an unelected majority, and resist the temptation to choose power over principle.

***

Democracy is unsustainable

> *Democracy while it lasts is more bloody than either aristocracy or monarchy. Remember, democracy never lasts long. It soon wastes, exhausts, and murders itself. There is never a democracy that did not commit suicide.*
>
> —John Adams

Democracy only "murders itself" when greed trumps compassion; corruption triumphs over fairness; and when social, economic, and educational inequality undermines equal opportunity. It should not be surprising that when the vast majority of wealth and power is concentrated in a small percentage of the population, this is precisely what happens. The result is that citizens become disconnected from the democratic and political process and, concomitantly, disenchanted with government.

To make matters worse, wealth-based inequality leads to injustice of the most undemocratic – and intolerable – kind. For example, low-income citizens receive an inferior education at the grade and high school level because the resources dedicated to public education are based on property taxes, which obviously favors residents of affluent communities. Additionally, many low-income citizens lack access to basic health care services, and members of minority groups, such as African Americans, are treated unfairly in the criminal justice system. For example, in many communities law enforcement's investigatory practices include targeting impoverished and minority-dominated neighborhoods to fill prisons and increase revenue, and many arrestees lack the resources to afford high-quality legal representation in criminal cases.

Put bluntly, pervasive social and economic inequality results in a welfare state in which the government bears the cost of providing basic services to its citizens. In the United States, the government supplies low-income citizens with health insurance through Medicaid, offers unemployment and disability compensation for an extended period, and provides a monthly allowance to purchase food. Likewise, all citizens are eligible to fund the cost of higher education with federal loans, and upon retirement citizens receive a monthly social security payment. In this way, socioeconomic inequality directly undermines democracy because it creates a quasi-socialist welfare state, and the causes of such inequality are traceable to four causes: the accumulation of wealth by a small percentage of the population, the political marginalization (and de facto disenfranchisement) of citizens, the lack of equal opportunity, and the unfulfilled promise of upward mobility.

In this regard, John Adams's statement is correct because, as history reveals, the vicissitudes of human existence all too often favor greed and power over shared responsibility and egalitarianism. This is not to say, of course, that the devolution of democracy is inevitable. Rather, it results in significant part from decisions by elected and unelected officials who wield power in government. For example, had one Justice voted differently in *Citizens United*, *McCutcheon*, and *U.S. Term Limits*, corporations and individuals would not be able to purchase access and influence with large donations, and elected officials would be prohibited from serving limitless terms in office. Contrary outcomes in both cases would have enhanced accountability and incentivized elected officials to advocate for purposeful legislation that benefited their constituents, not corporate donors from Goldman Sachs. In short, a single vote had an immeasurable – and harmful – impact on American democracy by ensuring that, for many citizens, political and democratic equality would remain illusory. Put differently, the Court's decisions in cases such as *Citizens United* give new meaning to the concept of "one person, one vote" because the direction of an entire country was fundamentally altered – and possibly irreparably damaged – by the decision of a single, unelected, and life-tenured judge.

If the Founders knew that American democracy would be subject to the vagaries of one individual, particularly in cases with far-reaching ramifications, they would have almost certainly done something to prevent this state of affairs. The Founders' silence in this instance speaks volumes: they likely never imagined that democracy would disintegrate into a dictatorial regime that bears more resemblance to the government from which they revolted, not the government they created. Ironically, Justice Kennedy – and four other Justices on the Court – see nothing wrong with the aggrandizement of power in an unelected branch of government. What's worse, citizens across the United States know that nothing whatsoever can be done to stop the Court from deciding cases in any manner it desires, regardless of what the Constitution says, what common sense dictates, or what the citizens of each state believe. The powerlessness – and helplessness – that results is anathema to democracy, inimical to liberty, and incompatible with equality.

To be blunt, rather than exercising "reasoned judgment" in the "heady days of the here and now" to reach indefensible outcomes that the "convenience of the moment" demands, the Court should strive to reach outcomes that safeguard the principles upon which democracy is founded. This requires the Court to embrace a decision-making process that gives life to the Constitution's text and underlying purposes, not to the Justices' subjective values, and remedy the causes of procedural and substantive inequality. Until the causes of inequality are remedied, the United States will continue to prove John Adams correct – perhaps permanently – and lend credence to the statement that "[t]here is never a democracy that did not commit suicide."

***

Rule by the masses is tantamount to government by the ignorant

> *The best argument against democracy is a five-minute conversation with the average voter.*
>
> —Winston Churchill

> *Democracy is a pathetic belief in the collective wisdom of individual ignorance.*
>
> —H. L. Mencken

Some may assert that democracy gives decision-making power concerning issues affecting the rights and liberties of citizens across the United States to a largely uneducated and uninformed citizenry. Inevitably, entrusting such power to a largely ignorant population has and will continue to result in unwise and unfair public policy, such as slavery, segregation bans on inter-racial and same-sex marriage, and a prohibition on contraception use. Many would assert that to avoid the injustices that flow from arbitrary and discriminatory legislation, the Court should remove certain policy questions, such as whether a woman should have the right to obtain abortion services and whether same-sex couples should have a right to marriage, from the democratic process and reach outcomes that promote liberty, ensure equal protection of the law, and protect politically marginalized groups. In other words, when the Court intervenes to effectuate desirable policy outcomes, it serves an inherently democratic institution by remedying the injustices and inequities that democracy (and majority rule) causes, and therefore creating a more egalitarian society for all citizens.

This argument lacks merit and is predicated on dangerous, arrogant, and misguided assumptions. Although in any society a portion of citizens may lack a formal education or struggle to understand the complexities of many political and social issues, this does not mean that citizens should be prohibited from participating in democracy or that they will necessarily make unwise policy choices. First, in many countries, including the United States, democracy is not direct, as policy decisions are made by elected officials acting on behalf of their constituents, the vast majority of whom are highly educated. Second, prohibiting allegedly "uninformed" and "uneducated" citizens from having a voice in governance presupposes that one can identify criteria to define these terms with precision, that rationality and logic are necessary and sufficient tools upon which to participate in self-governance, that a lack of knowledge or education correlates highly with unwise policy choices, and that a select group of individuals, based solely on an evaluation of educational or intellectual capacity, can make "better" policy choices to further the collective good. This view is mistaken.

Many policy decisions involve distinctly moral issues, which renders one's educational level or intelligence level largely irrelevant. For example, issues such as whether women should have the right to terminate a pregnancy, whether same-sex couples should have a right to marry, whether the death penalty is cruel and unusual, and whether individuals should have a right to assisted suicide implicate deeply personal beliefs regarding morality, religion, and the sanctity of human life. The operative word in these areas is *should*, which signifies that one's view on these matters is primarily, even entirely, subjective. Reasonable people can – and do – disagree on whether the death penalty is cruel and unusual, and no individual, regardless of his or her intelligence, is in a superior decision to make a value judgment on behalf of the "ignorant." That is precisely why *Griswold*, *Roe*, and *Planned Parenthood* were wrongly decided. The answer to whether abortion should be permitted does not lie in invisible penumbras or the transcendent dimensions of liberty. It lies in the individual and collective conscience of citizens who have the right to define "the collective good" through the democratic process.

This argument also begs a fundamental question: to the extent that citizens can, with any degree of certainty, be characterized as "uneducated" or "ignorant," one must ask why this is so, particularly in a country of substantial wealth. The answer is attributable in substantial part to the United States' long and sordid history of slavery, segregation, racism, and bigotry and to the Court's decisions in several landmark cases that made it harder to remedy the harms resulting from these intolerable practices. For example, in *San Antonio School District*, the Court upheld the financing of public education based on property taxes and concluded that the Constitution does not protect a fundamental right to education. In so holding, the Court enshrined educational inequality, along with inequality of opportunity, into the law based on wealth because the most affluent – and predominantly Caucasian – communities were able to devote far more resources to public education than low-income communities. Similarly, in *Milliken* the Court held that states need not desegregate schools unless they had historically and intentionally supported segregation, which, as a practical matter, ensured that de facto segregation would persist in many states and that the promise of *Brown v. Board of Education* would be unfulfilled.

Considering these facts, it is arrogant and misguided to label citizens "ignorant," inexcusable to rely on the nefarious effects of discriminatory practices to justify disenfranchising citizens who may have been harmed by such practices, and intolerable to base criticisms of democracy on an overly broad and not necessarily correlative generalization. The emphasis should be on fixing the problem that past injustices have caused and remedying their impact on political and democratic inequality. In so doing, the benefits of democracy can, as they should, flow all the way down to the people, and the promise of equal opportunity can germinate from the bottom up. As Thomas Jefferson stated:

> Educate and inform the whole mass of the people . . . [t]hey are the only sure reliance for the preservation of our liberty.

A quality education is essential to achieving equality of opportunity, which is a necessary predicate to individual and collective liberty. Unfortunately, decisions such as *San Antonio School District*, along with the Court's invention of constitutional penumbras in *Griswold* and Justice Kennedy's soaring rhetoric regarding liberty in *Lawrence* and *Obergefell*, have made liberty itself an endangered species.

***

Democracy causes social and economic inequality

Democracy is beautiful in theory; in practice it is a fallacy.

—Benito Mussolini

One may argue that democracy in any form, whether direct or indirect, is inherently unjust because it is based on "majority rule" and therefore provides the minority with no legal protections. Given this concern, some assert that the Court should not interpret the law in a formalistic and rigid manner, but should strive to protect minority rights and, more broadly, politically marginalized groups. Proponents of this argument assert that deferring to the democratic process as a default position, such as when confronted with constitutional ambiguity, can weaken democracy because, in some cases, excessive deference enables entrenched majorities to abuse the rights of citizens who lack political power. Put simply, the Court's role is to protect citizens from the "tyranny of the majority" and effectuate equality for all citizens.

To an extent, this argument has merit, but it does not rebut a fundamental proposition: although the Court must protect minority rights by invalidating arbitrary and discriminatory laws, it must do so in a manner that is consistent with the Constitution's text and underlying purpose(s). Also, for purposes of this discussion one must first distinguish between procedural and substantive inequality. Procedural inequality refers to citizens' inability to participate equally and meaningfully in the democratic process, not to achieve equal outcomes. In the United States, procedural inequality is pervasive. Although all citizens have a right to vote, it can hardly be denied that a small percentage of citizens – wealthy individuals and corporations – have disproportionate influence in the electoral and political process. Notwithstanding, procedural inequality is not an intrinsic feature of democracy. Rather, procedural inequality can be traced to, among other things, the Court's decisions in *Citizens United* and *McCutcheon*, the influence of money in obtaining access to and influencing elected officials, and redistricting plans that favor incumbents. In this way, procedural inequality is not intrinsic to democracy, but rather is traceable to the actions of elected and unelected government officials.

On the other hand, substantive inequality is, to a degree, an inherent consequence of majoritarian rule. After all, democracy does not entitle all citizens to equal *outcomes*, but instead gives citizens an equal *opportunity* to achieve the outcomes they prefer. Put simply, American democracy, although incorporating a republican form of government, is nonetheless predicated on the idea that there will be "winners" and "losers" and that liberty promises a "fair fight," not a medal for every participant. For example, assume that every citizen in the United States had a relatively equal voice – not merely an equal vote – in deciding whether a woman should have the right to terminate a pregnancy. If, by a margin of 51 percent to 49 percent, citizens in one state answered in the negative, a substantial (and nearly equal) percentage of citizens, particularly women, would "lose" the debate and, concomitantly, would be denied the ability to access abortion services. Now, the *only* way to ensure the legitimacy of this result, and majority rule generally, is to ensure that citizens have *procedural* equality (e.g., a right to participate in governance and have their voices heard). It is precisely for this reason that *Citizens United* was so injurious to democracy; the Court's decision enshrined *procedural* and political inequality into the electoral process, thereby undermining the fairness – and legitimacy – of majority rule and democratic self-governance.

Of course, the existence of substantive inequality in a majority rule–based democracy does not mean that the minority is powerless or that the Court should not intervene in some cases to protect minority rights. For example, the minority can seek policy changes through the legislature and vote for candidates who support their views. In addition, as is consistent with the republican component of American democracy, the Court can – and should – invalidate state and federal laws that infringe on *enumerated* constitutional rights, provided that the Court does so in an intellectually honest manner.

For some, however, the Court should take a far more "activist" role and issue decisions that effectuate desirable policy outcomes for all citizens, regardless of whether the Constitution's text supports such decisions. Proponents of this view would argue that although this may result in top-down lawmaking and may increase procedural inequality (e.g., citizens' right to self-governance), it significantly remedies *substantive* inequality, thus making the trade-off worthwhile and counseling in favor of a *purely* republican, rather than purely democratic, form of government. As stated earlier, a republican form of government has inherent risks that threaten to undermine the core values of equality and liberty because it can empower the government, namely the Court, to manipulate the Constitution and invent "rights" that eviscerate majoritarian rule and the Constitution's structural constraints, including separation of powers, decentralization, and federalism. Stated simply, a society that values liberty and autonomy must ensure that government does not devolve into tyranny or oligarchy. Democracy and republicanism achieve this objective because both inherently act as a check on the other and therefore avoid the risks that they independently pose.

Protecting minority rights in an intellectually honest manner

The Constitution is the guide which I never will abandon.

—George Washington

Article III gives the Court power to adjudicate certain categories of cases arising under the Constitution, and as such empowers the Court to interpret the Constitution's text. This authority necessarily includes invalidating state and federal laws that infringe on citizens' fundamental rights, ensuring a fair and participatory democracy, and protecting minority rights. Throughout its history, the Court has consistently intervened to protect minority rights. In *Brown v. Board of Education*, for example, the Court correctly held that the "separate but equal" doctrine, which segregated African American and Caucasian children in public schools, violated the Equal Protection Clause of the Fourteenth Amendment. In *Loving v. Virginia*, the Court correctly invalidated a ban on interracial marriage, emphasizing that such a law was motivated by animus against African Americans. The Court stated as follows:

> There is patently no legitimate overriding purpose independent of invidious racial discrimination which justifies this classification. The fact that Virginia prohibits only interracial marriages involving white persons demonstrates that the racial classifications must stand on their own justification, as measures designed to maintain White Supremacy. We have consistently denied the constitutionality of measures which restrict the rights of citizens on account of race. There can be no doubt that restricting the freedom to marry solely because of racial classifications violates the central meaning of the Equal Protection Clause.[2]

The Court emphasized that bans on interracial marriage are "so directly subversive of the principle of equality at the heart of the Fourteenth Amendment," that they "deprive all the State's citizens of liberty without due process of law."[3]

Likewise, in *Skinner v. Oklahoma*, the Court invalidated a law authorizing the forced sterilization of habitual criminals because it contained an exemption for individuals convicted of "white collar" crimes. The majority held that the law improperly discriminated against individuals convicted of similar crimes:

> Oklahoma makes no attempt to say that he who commits larceny by trespass or trick or fraud has biologically inheritable traits which he who commits embezzlement lacks. We have not the slightest basis for inferring that line has any significance in eugenics, nor that the inheritability of criminal traits follows the neat legal distinctions which the law has marked between those two offenses. In terms of fines and imprisonment, the crimes of larceny and embezzlement rate the same under the Oklahoma code. Only when it comes to sterilization are the pains and penalties of the law different.[4]

2 388 U.S. 1, 11–12 (1967).
3 Id. at 12.
4 316 U.S. 535, 541–542 (1942).

As the Court noted, the "equal protection clause would indeed be a formula of empty words if such conspicuously artificial lines could be drawn."

This discussion underscores the fact that there are many instances in which the Court has – and should – intervene to safeguard minority rights and the fundamental rights of individuals who are subjected to unlawful state action. For example, the Court should protect the rights of public employees who are terminated without notice or an opportunity to be heard because such terminations violate the Due Process Clause of the Fourteenth Amendment. Likewise, the Court should overturn state laws that, among other things, restrict speech on the basis of disagreement with the speaker's viewpoint, authorize unreasonable searches and seizures, impose barbaric punishments, or allow prosecutors to infer guilt based on the defendant's Fifth Amendment right to remain silent. The Court should also strike down laws that violate well-settled precedent, such as a law outlawing all first-trimester abortions except in cases of rape or incest (in violation of *Roe v. Wade*). Such laws constitute an abuse of the state's authority because, absent intervention by the Court, the minority (and politically marginalized groups) would have no avenue by which to challenge arbitrary – and unconstitutional – state conduct.

The Court's duty to protect minority and individual rights, however, should not be construed as a license to ignore or manipulate the Constitution's text to achieve a desired outcome. Regardless of how noble the Court's intentions or virtuous the result, doing so would fundamentally alter the balance of power between the federal and state governments and vest lawmaking authority with nine unelected, unaccountable, and life-tenured judges. Unfortunately, even a cursory analysis of decisions such as *Griswold*, *Roe*, and *Planned Parenthood* demonstrate that the Court has paid mere lip service to these propositions and has invented "rights" out of thin air to protect newly recognized minorities. For example, in *Griswold* the Court invented constitutional "penumbras" because no provision in the text supported the invalidation of Connecticut's admittedly unwise law. Similarly, in *Roe*, the Court relied on an implied (and judicially created) right to privacy to "discover" a right to abortion under the Fourteenth Amendment, despite the fact that no reasonable reading of the amendment's language justified this interpretation. In *Planned Parenthood*, the Court relied on "living constitutionalism," substantive due process, and a right to "define the mysteries of human life" to reaffirm a right that that neither the Founders nor the Court (until *Roe*) had contemplated. No amount of legal jujitsu – and certainly not the interest in protecting minority rights – can justify these decisions, all of which made a mockery of American constitutional law. What's worse, when the Court, by a 5–4 majority, issues landmark decisions creating a new "right" or invalidating a federal or state statute, a single Justice (in recent years, most often Justice Kennedy) is responsible for imposing law on an entire country. The fact that *Roe* and *Planned Parenthood* were decided by the thinnest of margins and involved an intellectually dishonest interpretation of the Constitution's text suggests that the outcomes were illegitimate and that the Court should have never agreed to hear these cases.

In the final analysis, the price that citizens must pay for such outcomes is akin to making a deal with the devil, as all citizens, regardless of political persuasion, sacrifice the right to self-governance and self-determination. As Justice Scalia stated in *Obergefell*,

> [t]his practice of constitutional revision by an unelected committee of nine, always accompanied . . . by extravagant praise of liberty, robs the People of the

> most important liberty they asserted in the Declaration of Independence and won in the Revolution of 1776: the freedom to govern themselves.[5]

Decisions such as *Griswold*, *Roe*, and *Obergefell* send a message to citizens that they can seek policy changes through the judicial, rather than legislative, process. In so doing, the Court transforms the judiciary into a political rather than legal branch of government and sows the seeds of illegitimacy into the rule of law. Put differently, the majority in *Griswold*, *Roe*, and *Planned Parenthood* would transform democracy into a society ruled by philosopher kings, in which the rule of law would be replaced by rule by the few. One must wonder if the Court, including Justice Kennedy, was so concerned about minority rights and politically powerless citizens in *Obergefell*, why it ruled in favor of wealthy corporations in *Citizens United* – an opinion authored by Justice Kennedy – and wealthy individuals in *McCutcheon* – an opinion Justice Kennedy joined.

To be sure, it is no response to justify such rulings by citing *Marbury v. Madison*, where Justice Marshall said that the Court has the power to "say what the law is." This statement means that the Court has the power to interpret *existing* laws, not to *create* laws. Ignoring this distinction transforms the Court into a lawmaking institution that encroaches on power reserved to the legislative branch, undermines the separation of powers, and infringes on authority traditionally entrusted to state governments. In other words, the power to say what the law is does not allow the Court to say what the law should be, no matter how strongly the Justices believe in the utility of a particular outcome.

Put simply, in a democracy, there are winners and losers. Citizens cast votes in support of candidates and, either directly or through their elected representatives, a majority decides whether to adopt specific laws. When such laws, even if unwise, do not violate an express provision in the Constitution, the Court has no basis to intervene. The fact that citizens not in the majority will "lose" an election or public policy dispute does not in and of itself create a "minority" that requires protection by the Court. Those in the minority have the right to seek policy changes through the legislature or to support candidates who oppose the incumbent. In other words, a remedy for a non-constitutional harm still exists through the political process. That is how democracy works. As Justice Scalia explained, "[i]t's not up to the courts to invent new minorities that get special protections."

The line between legitimate and illegitimate interpretation of the Constitution depends on the answer to a straightforward question: Does the text of a particular provision, when ascribed a meaning that the words can reasonably support and its original purpose, justify the reasoning upon which an outcome is based? If the answer is yes, a decision is legitimate. If the answer is no, such a decision constitutes an abuse of the Court's reviewing authority, an attack on the rule of law, a threat to democracy, and a usurpation of powers reserved to the people. For these reasons, the Court should not intervene to protect minority rights unless it makes a threshold determination that (1) there is a procedural defect regarding the manner in which a particular law was adopted

5 135 S. Ct. at 2627 (Scalia, J., dissenting).

or a right deprived (in violation of the Due Process Clause); (2) duly enacted legislation exceeds the federal or state governments' enumerated powers, such as where a state law is preempted by federal law, or where legislation exceeds Congress's authority to regulate interstate commerce, or where a law infringes on a fundamental constitutional right; (3) the political process is not a viable avenue by which to seek redress for cognizable harms; or (4) a law violates the Court's precedent. Unless one of these threshold considerations is satisfied, the invalidation of a state law constitutes an abuse of the Court's Article III powers.

More fundamentally, the Court should view process-based decision making and the pragmatic, outcome-based considerations as interdependent, not independent, components of judicial review. When the Court adheres to a legitimate decision-making process, desirable outcomes naturally follow, along with the realization that protecting minority rights and construing the Constitution in an intellectually honest manner are not mutually exclusive. For example, and as discussed in Chapter 20, in *National Federation of Independent Investors v. Sebelius*, Justice Roberts protected "minority rights," safeguarded the Court's legitimacy, and respected the coordinate branches' lawmaking powers. In *Sebelius*, the Court held that the Affordable Health Care Act, which imposed a fine on individuals who did not purchase health insurance, was a valid exercise of Congress's taxing powers, even though the law, on its face, arguably penalized individuals for noncompliance with the mandate and appeared to be an impermissible penalty, not a tax. Writing for a 5–4 majority, Justice Roberts argued that (1) where possible, the Court should defer to the policy judgments of the coordinate branches; (2) the Act could reasonably be construed as a tax, not a penalty; (3) the Act could not be justified under the Commerce Clause; and (4) although certain parts of the Act were unconstitutional, this did not require invalidation of the entire Act. Roberts was correct – regarding both the reasoning and result. As discussed later, Justice Roberts's decision reconciled a number of competing constitutional interests, such as respecting the coordinate branches' policy choices, grounding decisions in a reasonable interpretation of the text, and maintaining the separation of powers through judicial restraint. Developing a jurisprudence that reconciles these and other interests and that merges process-based decision making with pragmatic, outcome-based considerations is essential if the Court is to retain its legitimacy and relevance.

Striking the proper balance: reconciling competing constitutional harms

In most cases, the Court must reconcile the myriad and often competing constitutional interests that are implicated in a given case, especially where the text arguably supports alternative outcomes and where the results of any outcome will have both benefits and drawbacks that will engender criticism from a segment of the population. For example, had the Court reached the opposite conclusion in *Griswold*, it would have arguably furthered principles of federalism, most notably the authority of states to legislate in areas not reserved to the federal government, promoted judicial restraint by deferring to the democratic process on a matter that the Constitution does not address, and respected the Constitution's visions for decentralized governance.

Concededly, a contrary result in *Griswold* would not have been immune to criticism, and it would have resulted in a different type of harm. For example, married couples would potentially be subjected to severe invasions on their privacy, allowed states to have de facto oversight over married couples' reproductive choices, and likely caused some women to seek illegal abortions. Likewise, had the Court reached a different outcome in *Citizens United*, the integrity of the electoral process would have been enhanced, the influence of money in politics would have been reduced, and elected officials would have been more responsive to ordinary voters. At the same time, the Court would have upheld a law that targeted corporations as speakers and discriminated against corporate speech merely because such speech accomplished its intended goal of influencing public officials.

These cases reveal that, in most instances, the Court will confront competing and seemingly irreconcilable interests, all of which have significant and lasting implications for, among other things, individual liberty and separation of powers, federalism, and decentralized governance. Reconciling these competing concerns in a manner that promotes the Constitution's core values – autonomy, equality, and democratic self-governance – is essential if the Court is to retain institutional legitimacy in an ever-changing society. The next chapter sets forth a proposal to develop such a jurisprudence.

29

FOUNDATIONAL PRINCIPLES FOR A PRO-DEMOCRACY, PROCESS-ORIENTED, AND PRAGMATIC JURISPRUDENCE

We the people are the rightful masters of both Congress and the courts, not to overthrow the Constitution but to overthrow the men who pervert the Constitution.

—Abraham Lincoln

***

A functioning, robust democracy requires a healthy educated, participatory followership, and an educated, morally grounded leadership.

—Chinua Achebe

In many landmark cases, the Court – often by bare 5–4 majorities –has undermined the integrity of the democratic, political, and electoral process and exacerbated procedural and substantive inequality. As a consequence, in these cases the Court compromised the fundamental values underlying American constitutionalism: equality, federalism, separation of powers, decentralization, checks and balances, and government by the people, not the powerful. To remedy the damage caused by decisions such as *Citizens United* and *Roe*, the Court should embrace an interpretive framework that promotes equal protection of, and equal liberty under, the law; that facilitates a participatory, not paternalistic, democracy; and that rewards citizens based on effort, not birthright. As discussed later, to achieve these objectives, the Court should (1) identify the competing constitutional interests or "tensions" that exist in most cases; (2) reconcile them in a manner that furthers democracy's underlying values; and (3) embrace the concepts of "contextualism" and "collective liberty" when interpreting the Constitution. The objective in all cases should be to develop, as Harvard law professor Lani Guinier states, a "demosprudence."

Competing constitutional interests

The competing constitutional interests that affect the structure of governance, individual rights, and the integrity of the democratic process should inform the Court's analysis and, ultimately, its decision in a given case. These interests are as follows.

Structural considerations

- *Judicial Restraint*. Adhering to legitimate decision-making processes (e.g., basing decisions on the Constitution's text, the purpose(s) underlying a particular provision, the historical record, and tradition without eschewing pragmatic, outcome-based considerations).
- *Federalism*. Ensuring that the Court's decisions respect the powers reserved to the states.
- *Separation of Powers*. Issuing decisions that respect the limits on the Court's Article III power and defer to the coordinate branches when the text arguably supports upholding the legislation at issue and when doing so would promote respect for democratically and duly enacted legislation.
- *Decentralization*. Resolving legal issues in a manner that promotes decentralized governance and bottom-up lawmaking through the democratic and legislative process.
- *Checks and Balances*. Invalidating federal laws that exceed the coordinate branches' enumerated powers.
- *Severance*. Retaining the constitutional provisions of laws that are unconstitutional, in part if doing so would be consistent with (and further) the purposes underlying such law.
- *Redressability*. Considering whether a remedy is available through the political process, including whether the legislature is able or willing to address a matter through the legislative process.
- *Appropriate Judicial Activism*. Invalidating arbitrary legislation that infringes on citizens enumerated constitutional rights, thus protecting minorities and politically disenfranchised groups from the "tyranny of the majority."
- *Workability*. Developing rules that effectively guide lower courts, legislators, and litigants.

Individual rights considerations

- *Procedural Equality*. Promoting political and democratic equality.
- *Substantive Equality (Enumerated Rights Protection)*. Ensuring that all citizens receive equal protection – and equal liberty – under the law.
- *Unenumerated Rights Protection*. Protecting individuals, the minority, and politically disenfranchised groups from arbitrary and unconstitutional legislation, either through the Ninth Amendment or the Privileges and Immunities Clause.
- *Unjust Outcomes*. Avoiding draconian and wholly unjust outcomes provided that the text reasonably supports such outcomes.

In most cases, several constitutional interests are implicated and, at first glance, appear entirely irreconcilable. For example, in *Clinton*, some would argue the Court's decision furthered the interest in "checks and balances" by prohibiting Congress from transferring lawmaking power to the executive branch. Others may posit that the decision undermined separation-of-powers principles because, in the face of constitutional ambiguity (the Presentment Clause), the Court unnecessarily prohibited the coordinate branches from experimenting with a solution that addressed wasteful government spending. In *Obergefell*, some may assert that the Court's decision effectuated substantive equality for a marginalized minority (same-sex couples), whereas others could argue that by prohibiting the people from resolving this issue through the democratic process, the Court compromised principles of federalism and decentralization.

Additionally, some may argue that the decision-making process itself is often (and inherently) imperfect, particularly when a constitutional provision or statute is ambiguous, or where the historical record provides little, if any, guidance. There are also instances where a law appears to be arbitrary, without a rational justification, and unjust but a reasonable reading of the text would not support an outcome that would remedy the alleged harms. In such situations, what should the Court do? Is there a "right" result? Also, given that the Court has the final word concerning a law's constitutionality, is it preferable to uphold unjust laws simply to remain faithful to the text?

The answer depends in substantial part on the Court's actual or perceived role in government and, more specifically, a democracy. If the Justices believe that their role is to reach just outcomes, the text should be disregarded if it would prevent the Court from doing so. However, if the Court's role is to strengthen democracy and the values upon which it rests, then ignoring or manipulating the text (as in *Griswold* and *Roe*) can never be justified. Put differently, the Court may reach a "good" outcome in a given case, but the injury inflicted on the people's right to autonomy, self-determination, and self-governance is irreparably harmed. That is precisely why the text – and judicial humility – matters. It prohibits the Court from assaulting democracy and the rule of law with the "mystical aphorisms of the fortune cookie."

Resolving these issues depends in substantial part on the specific language in the text, its purposes, and the Court's jurisprudence throughout history. It also turns on the various "default" positions that the Court should adopt when competing interests collide with constitutional ambiguity. As discussed later, these "default" positions should include promoting meaningful participation in democracy, ensuring fairness in the electoral and political process, embracing bottom-up lawmaking (while protecting citizens from arbitrary state legislation), and preserving the Court's institutional legitimacy by issuing textually based and intellectually honest opinions. By adopting this approach, the Court's jurisprudence would further one of the most fundamental principles in democracy: equal participation – and an equal voice – in governance, the *sine qua non* of liberty. To achieve this goal, the Court should adopt specific interpretive frameworks for each constitutional interest and rely on these frameworks to guide the decision-making process when faced with one or more competing interests. The recommended interpretive approaches are provided later. The objective is to enhance the integrity of, and egalitarianism in, the democratic process, avoid prioritizing some citizens' interests over others, and recognize that ensuring equal liberty under the law is necessary to achieve "equal justice under the law."

Foundational principles for constitutional interpretation: structural principles

Principle one

Judicial restraint

The Court should adhere to legitimate decision-making processes (e.g., basing decisions on the Constitution's text, the purpose[s] underlying a particular provision, the historical record, and tradition without eschewing pragmatic, outcome-based considerations).

Principle of interpretation

The Court should interpret the Constitution's text to include all meanings that the text can reasonably support, but it should never ignore the text (as in *Griswold*) or alter its meaning (as in *Planned Parenthood*).

Principle two

Federalism

The Court should ensure that its decisions respect the powers reserved to the states.

Principle of interpretation

When interpreting the scope of the federal government's (including the judiciary's) enumerated power over the states, the Court should reject an expansive view of the federal government's authority, including where states experiment with solutions that will strengthen democratic and political equality.

Principle three

Separation of powers

The Court should issue decisions that respect the limits on its Article III power and defer to the coordinate branches when the text arguably supports upholding the legislation at issue and when doing so would promote respect for democratically and duly enacted legislation.

Principle of interpretation

When faced with constitutional ambiguity, the Court should typically defer to the coordinate branches at the state and federal level, particularly in cases where legislation strives to promote fairness, transparency, efficiency, and accountability in the democratic and political process.

Principle four

Decentralization

The Court should resolve legal issues in a manner that promotes decentralized governance and bottom-up lawmaking through the democratic and legislative process.

Principle of interpretation

The Court should uphold state laws unless such laws, on their face or as applied, violate an enumerated constitutional right, violate due process of law, or resulted from a corrupt political process.

Principle five

Checks and balances

The Court should invalidate federal laws that, based on a reasonable (not opportunistic) reading of the text and historical record, exceed the coordinate branches' enumerated powers.

Principle of interpretation

The Court should construe the federal government's enumerated constitutional authority narrowly and invalidate laws that infringe on powers reserved to the states or that impermissibly transfer executive or legislative power to another branch or government institution.

Principle six

Severance

The Court should retain the constitutional provisions of laws that are unconstitutional, in part if doing so would be consistent with (and further) the purposes underlying such law.

Principle of interpretation

If a federal or state law is partially unconstitutional, the Court should uphold the portions that can be reasonably be interpreted to withstand constitutional scrutiny, if doing so would be consistent with the law's purposes.

Explanation of principle six

Judicial "activism," a term often used by "conservative" commentators to criticize decisions with which they disagree (these same commentators also celebrate *Bush* and *Citizens United*), is not necessarily problematic if it is directed toward pro-democracy ends. Stated differently, the Court should not adopt a minimalist or inconsequential role in government or automatically defer to the coordinate branches (or state governments) whenever confronted with constitutional ambiguity. One method by which the Court can develop an appropriately "activist" and pro-democracy jurisprudence is by embracing the concept of "severance," in which it would invalidate *only specific provisions of* laws that violate the Constitution, while upholding other provisions that withstand constitutional scrutiny, *if* doing so would further the purpose underlying such laws. Chief Justice Roberts's opinion in *National Federation of Independent Investors* is a paradigmatic – and pro-democratic – example of severance.

On balance, the Court has shown a reluctance to adopt this approach. For example, in *United States v. Stevens* the Court invalidated legislation that made it a crime to "produce, sell or distribute images depicting animal cruelty." The primary purpose of the legislation was to criminalize "crush videos," in which an animal is crushed to death by the heel of a person's shoe. In an 8–1 decision, the Court held that the legislation was unconstitutionally overbroad because it potentially criminalized the depiction of legal conduct, such as hunting or the slaughtering of animals for food. Although the Court was correct in this regard, it should not have invalidated the entire act. Rather, the Court could merely have struck the language it deemed overbroad yet retain the provisions that prohibited depictions of "crush videos." In other words, the Court could have issued a narrow holding that would have effectuated the statute's purposes and avoided impermissible infringements on First Amendment freedoms. *Griswold*, and the cases that followed in its wake, eschewed this framework in favor of an approach to constitutional interpretation that placed the Court, not citizens, atop the constitutional hierarchy.

Principle seven

Redressability

The Court should consider whether a remedy is available through the political process, including whether the legislature is able or willing to address a matter through the legislative process.

Principle of interpretation

The Court should invalidate legislation even if it may be interpreted to withstand constitutional scrutiny if citizens cannot realistically petition the legislature for redress, such as the legislature lacks political will or is composed of an entrenched majority.

Principle eight

The Court should invalidate arbitrary legislation that infringes on citizens' enumerated constitutional rights, which will protect minorities and politically disenfranchised groups from the "tyranny of the majority."

Principle of interpretation

The Court should invalidate arbitrary laws, but only to the extent that such laws are consistent with a reasonable reading of the text and its underlying purpose(s).

Principle nine

Workability

The Court should develop rules that effectively guide lower courts, legislators, and litigants.

Principle of interpretation

The Court should create workable rules that resolve conflicts among the lower courts, clarify the law, result in a cohesive jurisprudence, and in many cases, and avoid ad hoc, case-by-case decision making.

Individual rights principles

Principal one

Procedural equality

The Court should promote political and democratic equality.

Principle of interpretation

The Court should reach outcomes that promote meaningful participation in the democratic, political, and electoral process and that strive to remedy corruption, including undue influence on, and unequal access to, elected officials, and inequality.

Principal two

Substantive equality (enumerated rights protection)

The Court should ensure that all citizens receive equal protection – and equal liberty – under the law.

Principle of interpretation

The Court should interpret each provision in the Bill of Rights as broadly as a reasonable reading of the text and its purpose(s) will allow and rely on the Equal Protection Clause (not unsupportable manipulations of the text) to invalidate legislation that draws arbitrary distinctions between groups, is motivated by animus toward a particular group, or, absent a rational justification, disparately affects specific groups.

Principle three

Unenumerated rights protection

The Court should protect individuals, the minority, and politically disenfranchised groups from arbitrary and unconstitutional legislation, either through the Ninth Amendment or the Privileges and Immunities Clause.

Principle of interpretation

The Court should rely on the Privileges and Immunities Clause and the Ninth Amendment to identify and protect rights that are "implicit in the concept of ordered liberty" and thus retained by the people.

Principle four

Unjust outcomes

The Court should avoid draconian and wholly unjust outcomes, provided that the text reasonably supports such outcomes.

Principle of interpretation

Where alternative yet reasonable interpretations of the text are possible (e.g., where constitutional ambiguity exists), the Court should select the interpretation – and reach an outcome – that does not have unjust and draconian consequences.

***

Against this backdrop, the difficult task is to discern how these principles should be applied in specific legal and factual contexts. As discussed in Chapter 30, two broad principles should guide this inquiry: collective (or equal) liberty and contextualization, both of which will lead to equal participation in democracy and equal justice under the law. These concepts, and the interpretive principles proposed in this chapter, are applied to the cases discussed in Chapters 1 through 19. The result is better outcomes and a legitimate, intellectually honest, and pro-democracy decision-making process.

30

APPLYING THE FOUNDATIONAL PRINCIPLES TO THE "WORST" SUPREME COURT DECISIONS AND ARRIVING AT NONIDEOLOGICAL, PROCESS-ORIENTED, AND PRO-DEMOCRACY OUTCOMES

Freedom is never voluntarily given by the oppressor; it must be demanded by the oppressed.
—Martin Luther King, Jr.

The workability of the interpretive principles proposed in Chapter 29, both in reconciling competing constitutional concerns in a given case and amalgamating process-based concerns with pragmatic, outcome-based considerations, is best evaluated by applying them to the cases discussed throughout this book. As illustrated later, applying the structural and individual rights principles would have led the Court to reach different – and better – outcomes in every case. For example, the Court would have enhanced fairness in the electoral process, promoted equal participation in democracy, facilitated accountability and efficiency in governance, and ensured that citizens are treated equally under the law. Ultimately, the application of these principles is predicated on a novel theory of constitutional interpretation: contextualism and collective liberty.

Contextualism and collective liberty

When the Court evaluates whether a state or federal law infringes on fundamental constitutional rights, it focuses primarily on the relationship between citizens and the government. For example, in *Church of Lukumi Babalu Aye v. Township of Hialeah*, the Court held that a law prohibiting the ritual slaughter of animals infringed on the petitioners' right to freely exercise their religion. In *McCullen v. Coakley*, the Court held that a law prohibiting protestors from walking on a public road within thirty-five feet of an abortion facility violated the First Amendment. In these and other cases, the Court's analysis concerned the permissibility of governmental conduct against citizens as individuals or groups.

On the other hand, the Court rarely, if ever, emphasizes the relationship between citizens *qua* citizens and ignores, for example, the question of whether the recognition or protection of rights for one group of citizens will infringe on *other citizens'* constitutional rights. In other words, the Court does not sufficiently consider the *effect* that an individual's exercise of a constitutional right has on the collective ability of citizens to exercise the same (or other) rights. Affording at least some weight to this concern would fit perfectly with a pro-democracy framework because it is guided by the principle that all citizens should enjoy equal liberty under the law and in the exercise of fundamental constitutional freedoms.[1]

Contextualism in *Citizens United* and other cases

Citizens United is illustrative of how contextualism would have led the Court to a contrary result and promoted equal liberty for all citizens. The most troubling and antidemocratic aspect of *Citizens United* was the portion of the Court's opinion holding that "[f]avoritism and influence are not . . . avoidable in representative politics," and that the only "reason *to make a contribution to, one candidate over another is that the candidate will respond by producing those political outcomes the supporter favors*" (emphasis added). As a result, the Court rejected Congress's interest in "equalizing the relative ability of individuals and groups to influence the outcome of elections."

As discussed in Chapter 1, this reasoning disregards the fact that when a wealthy corporation engages in free speech, it can (and often does) diminish the impact of speech exercised by average citizens, in part because it enables corporations to gain unfair access to elected officials, who in turn become accountable to a very small segment of the population. In other words, corporations reap substantial benefits from exercising their free speech rights, whereas citizens enjoy a benefit that is more symbolic than real, which frustrates the original purposes of the First Amendment and sows the seeds of political inequality. Put simply, the Court's opinion enabled corporations, particularly the wealthiest, to "speak" in a manner that constructively muted the voices of millions of citizens. It is precisely for this reason that, although corporations and citizens retain equal First Amendment rights in the abstract, the First Amendment protections afforded to corporations should be viewed pragmatically or contextually. Had the Court done so in *Citizens United*, it would have most likely reached the same conclusion as the majority in *Austin*, and in so doing vindicated the principle that *equal* or collective liberty is essential to ensuring democratic equality.

The same holds true in other landmark cases. In *McCutcheon*, the potentially corrosive effects of money on both the integrity of the political process and the free speech rights of middle- and low-income citizens counseled in favor of upholding aggregate limits on individual contributions. In *U.S. Term Limits*, the effects of allowing elected officials to serve a limitless number of terms in Congress – most notably entrenchment and a lack of accountability to the average voter – supported upholding a constitutional amendment denying ballot access to elected officials who had already served three terms. In *Milliken*, the injurious effects of de facto segregation, both in perpetuating racial stereotypes and exacerbating inequality, justified a rule requiring

1 Although citizens may bring suit in state and federal courts to recover for private wrongs (e.g., negligence, assault), very little consideration is given to whether the protection of one individual's constitutional right may lead to the infringement of another's right.

all states to desegregate public schools. In *San Antonio School District*, the impact of a property tax–based education system on creating wide disparities in the quality of secondary education and contributing to *in*equality of opportunity supported a rule requiring states to fund public schools in affluent and poor communities at a reasonably similar level. In *McCleskey*, the disproportionate imposition of the death penalty on African Americans, many of whom reside in impoverished communities and cannot afford high-quality legal representation, supported a finding that the death penalty was arbitrarily imposed.

In *Korematsu*, the harmful effects of, and discriminatory motives underlying, internment should have compelled the Court to hold that such a practice "falls into the ugly abyss of racism" and therefore violates the Fourteenth Amendment. Similarly, in *General Electric Co.*, the Court should have held that excluding pregnancy-related conditions from employer health insurance plans constituted impermissible gender-based discrimination in violation of the Equal Protection Clause. Finally, in *Kelo*, the Court should have held that allowing municipalities to seize private property for a public purpose, rather than a public use, constituted an unprecedented threat to citizens' private property rights. Perhaps most troubling is that, in each of these cases, the constitutional provision at issue was ambiguous and therefore did not compel the Court to reach a specific outcome. Given this fact, the Court's decision, for example, to uphold laws authorizing the internment of Japanese Americans and basing the quality of public education on wealth, and to invalidate laws that addressed corruption in the electoral process and entrenchment in Congress demonstrates that its judgment was anything but reasoned. Had the Court reached contrary outcomes, it would have furthered democracy's core values – equality, liberty, and autonomy – and recognized that the rights of one citizen, corporation, or group should not function to undermine the basic civil liberties of third parties. In short, liberty is best expressed as a collective, not individual, value.

Contextualism has been implicitly recognized in amendment-specific contexts

The First Amendment and free speech

A contextualist paradigm would present the Court with a workable standard to interpret most provisions of the Constitution, including the First Amendment. In fact, the Court has implicitly embraced a contextual approach to constitutional interpretation. For example, in *McCullen*, the Court cited precedent, holding that although political speech is afforded the highest level of constitutional protection, the Court permits the states to regulate the time, place, and manner in which speech is expressed. Likewise, in *City of Renton v. Playtime Theaters*, the Court held that states may restrict speech based upon its harmful "secondary effects." Similarly, in *Central Hudson Gas & Electric Corporation v. Public Utilities Commission*, the Court held that commercial speech (e.g., advertisements) receives lesser First Amendment protection and businesses may be held liable for speech that deceives or misleads consumers. In fact, as the Court concluded in *Chaplinsky v. New Hampshire* and *Miller v. California*, states may prohibit certain forms of speech altogether, including "fighting words" and obscenity.

The varying levels of constitutional protection afforded to various types of speech are based in large part on the deleterious effects that some speech has on other citizens. Obscenity, which often involves depictions of child pornography, materially harms children. Fighting words, which are often motivated by hatred and prejudice, can subject individuals or groups to physical violence. Likewise, a misleading advertisement deceives and causes harm to unsuspecting consumers. A contextualist paradigm avoids these results by recognizing that one citizen's exercise of a constitutional right should not function to deprive other citizens of basic civil rights and liberties.

The First Amendment and religious liberty

The Free Exercise Clause of the First Amendment states that "Congress shall make no law respecting an establishment of religion, or prohibiting *the free exercise thereof*" (emphasis added). In the United States, the Court has struggled to develop a cohesive doctrine regarding the scope of religious liberty, including in situations where an individual's religious beliefs infringe on other citizens' right to equal protection of the law. For example, should the owners of a bakery be permitted to refuse to serve a wedding cake to a same-sex couple on the ground that doing so would violate their religious beliefs? Should a county clerk be allowed to refuse to issue a marriage license to a same-sex couple because it violates the clerk's religious beliefs? The answer should be no. To hold otherwise would be to enable one citizen's exercise of religious liberty to infringe on another citizen's right to equal protection of the law, and therefore to prevent all citizens from enjoying liberty in an equal and collective sense. After all, if the government had engaged in precisely the same conduct, the Court would unquestionably hold that the government violated the Equal Protection Clause of the Fourteenth Amendment. Why should the result be any different when a constitutional harm is caused by a citizen rather than the government? Of course, this argument should not be interpreted to mean that private citizens should have a legal duty to avoid infringing on other citizens' constitutional rights. It is to say that citizens do not exercise rights in a vacuum and that, in some contexts, the effect of protecting one citizen's constitutional right can – and does – lead to cognizable legal harm.

The Fourth Amendment

The Court has interpreted the Fourth Amendment in a quasi-contextualist manner by affording differing levels of privacy protection to citizens based on the place where a search or seizure occurs and on law enforcement's interest in protecting public safety. For example, before law enforcement officers may conduct a search of a home, they must, absent exigent circumstances, have probable cause and a warrant. Searches of vehicles traveling on public roads, however, only require officers to have reasonable suspicion that a motorist is violating the law. Finally, officers may view objects that are placed in open fields, search items placed in the trash, and observe citizens who are traveling in public places without any suspicion whatsoever. The rationale undergirding the Court's Fourth Amendment jurisprudence is predicated in substantial part on the fact that, in some situations, personal privacy rights must yield to the interest in protecting public safety. This implicitly recognizes that the degree to which privacy rights receive constitutional protection depends on countervailing community interests.

Applying contextualism – and the proposed interpretive framework – to each case discussed in prior chapters

As demonstrated in the following table, if the Court had applied, or at least given significant weight to, the proposed interpretive frameworks discussed in Chapter 29 to the cases discussed in Chapters 1 through 20, it would have reached different – and more desirable – outcomes through a legitimate and constitutionally defensible decision-making process. The result is a society that is more egalitarian, just, and fair, in which all citizens enjoy the right to equal protection – and liberty – under the law.

Case	*Interpretive Principle*	*How the Court Should Have Ruled*	*Impact on Democracy*
Citizens United v. Federal Election Commission	(Separation of Powers) When faced with constitutional ambiguity, the Court should typically defer to the coordinate branches at the state and federal level, including in cases where legislation strives to promote fairness, transparency, efficiency, and accountability in the democratic and political process.	Independent expenditures by corporations may be prohibited within 30 and 60 days or primary and presidential elections, respectively.	Reducing undue influence in the electoral process and unfair access to elected officials.
McCutcheon v. Federal Election Commission	(Separation of Powers) When faced with constitutional ambiguity, the Court should typically defer to the coordinate branches at the state and federal level, including in cases where legislation strives to promote fairness, transparency, efficiency, and accountability in the democratic and political process.	Aggregate limits on individual contributions are permissible to reduce unfair access to and influence over elected officials.	Reducing undue influence in the electoral process and unfair access to elected officials.
Clinton v. New York	(Separation of Powers) When faced with constitutional ambiguity, the Court should typically defer to the coordinate branches at the state and federal level, including in cases where legislation strives to promote fairness, transparency, efficiency, and accountability in the democratic and political process.	The Line Item Veto Act does not violate the Presentment Clause.	Curbing wasteful government spending; promoting efficiency in governance; allowing the coordinate branches to experiment with solutions that address governance problems.

(*Continued*)

Case	*Interpretive Principle*	*How the Court Should Have Ruled*	*Impact on Democracy*
U.S. Term Limits v. Thornton	(Federalism) When interpreting the scope of the federal government's (including the judiciary's) enumerated power over the states, the Court should reject an expansive view of the federal government's authority, including where states experiment with solutions that will strengthen democratic and political equality. (Separation of Powers) When faced with constitutional ambiguity, the Court should typically defer to the coordinate branches at the state and federal level, most notably in cases where legislation strives to promote fairness, transparency, efficiency, and accountability in the democratic and political process.	Statutes establishing term limits are constitutional.	Promoting greater accountability; reducing power of incumbency and likelihood of entrenchment.
Chevron, Inc., v. Natural Resources Defense Council	(Checks and Balances) The Court should construe the federal government's enumerated constitutional authority narrowly and invalidate laws that infringe on powers reserved to the states or impermissibly transfer executive or legislative power to another branch or government institution.	Federal agencies' interpretation of existing laws and constitutional provisions, particularly where ambiguous, are not entitled to deference unless the interpretation is the most reasonable interpretation.	The Court's Article III powers include close oversight of agency interpretations of law, as federal regulations have the force of law and therefore the potential to infringe on state and individual rights.
Korematsu v. U.S.	(Substantive Equality – Enumerated Rights Protection) The Court should interpret each provision in the Bill of Rights as broadly as a reasonable reading of the text and its purpose(s) will allow and the Equal	The forced detainment of Japanese Americans exceeds the executive branch's powers and violates the Due Process and Equal Protection	Prohibiting the government from enacting laws that are motivated by animus and prejudice toward a particular group.

Case	*Interpretive Principle*	*How the Court Should Have Ruled*	*Impact on Democracy*
	Protection Clause to invalidate legislation that draws arbitrary distinctions between groups, is motivated by animus toward a particular group, or, absent a rational justification, disparately affects specific groups. (Unjust Outcomes) Where alternative yet reasonable interpretations of the text are possible (e.g., where constitutional ambiguity exists), the Court should select the interpretation – and reach an outcome – that avoids unjust and draconian consequences.	Clauses of the Fourteenth Amendment.	
Griswold v. Connecticut	(Judicial Restraint) The Court should interpret the Constitution's text to include all meanings that the text can reasonably support, but it should never ignore the text (as in *Griswold*) or alter its meaning (as in *Planned Parenthood*). (Decentralization) The Court should uphold state laws unless such laws, on their face or as applied, violate an enumerated constitutional right, violate due process of law, or resulted from a corrupt political process. (Appropriate Judicial Activism) The Court should invalidate arbitrary laws, but only to the extent that such laws are consistent with a reasonable reading of the text and its underlying purpose(s).	Laws banning contraception, although unwise, do not violate any provision in the Constitution.	Citizens must seek policy change through the legislature to correct laws that, although improvident, do not violate the Constitution.

(*Continued*)

Case	*Interpretive Principle*	*How the Court Should Have Ruled*	*Impact on Democracy*
Roe v. Wade	Same as above	The Fourteenth Amendment's text and original purpose do not contemplate a right to abortion.	The judiciary cannot recognize unenumerated rights that the Constitution's text does not support or on which the Constitution is silent. Such rights must be created through the democratic process.
Planned Parenthood v. Casey	Same as above	*Roe v. Wade* was wrongly decided and is therefore overruled.	The judiciary cannot recognize unenumerated rights that the Constitution's text does not support or on which the Constitution is silent. Such rights must be created through the democratic process.
Lawrence v. Texas	(Substantive Equality – Enumerated Rights Protection) The Court should interpret each provision in the Bill of Rights as broadly as a reasonable reading of the text and its purpose(s) will allow and rely on the Equal Protection Clause (not unsupportable manipulations of the text) to invalidate legislation that draws arbitrary distinctions between groups, is motivated by animus toward a particular group, or, absent a rational justification, disparately affects specific groups.	Statutes banning sodomy among same-sex couples violate the Equal Protection Clause of the Fourteenth Amendment.	All citizens are entitled to equal protection under the law. States may not enact legislation motivated by moral disapproval and animus of a particular group.

Case	*Interpretive Principle*	*How the Court Should Have Ruled*	*Impact on Democracy*
Obergefell v. Hodges	Same as above	Statutes banning same-sex marriage violate the Equal Protection Clause.	States may not deprive citizens of equal rights and liberties under the law unless there is, at the very least, a rational basis underlying challenged legislation.
The Slaughterhouse Cases	(Appropriate Judicial Activism) The Court should invalidate arbitrary laws only to the extent that such laws are consistent with a reasonable reading of the text and its underlying purpose(s). *Or* (Unenumerated Rights Protection) The Court should rely on the Privileges and Immunities Clause and Ninth Amendment to identify and protect rights that are "implicit in the concept of ordered liberty" and thus retained by the people.	Laws creating a state-sponsored monopoly violate the Equal Protection Clause. The distinction between state and federal citizenship impermissibly subjects citizens to abuses of state power. In addition, the Privileges and Immunities Clause, when read together with the Ninth Amendment, provides a textual basis upon which to recognize *some* unenumerated rights.	The Court has the authority to invalidate laws that infringe on basic civil rights and liberties and that protect politically marginalized minorities from arbitrary legislation and entrenched majorities.
Milliken v. Bradley	(Procedural Equality) The Court should interpret each provision in the Bill of Rights as broadly as a reasonable reading of the text and its purpose(s) will allow and rely on the Equal Protection Clause (not unsupportable manipulations of the text) to invalidate legislation that draws arbitrary distinctions between groups, is motivated by animus toward a particular group, or, absent a rational justification, disparately affects specific groups.	Regardless of whether racial segregation is *de facto* or *de jure*, states must take concrete steps to eliminate segregation in public schools.	Reducing disparities in the quality of public education and therefore enhancing equality of opportunity for citizens of all backgrounds.

(*Continued*)

Case	*Interpretive Principle*	*How the Court Should Have Ruled*	*Impact on Democracy*
San Antonio School District v. Rodriguez	(Substantive Equality – Enumerated Rights Protection) The Court should interpret each provision in the Bill of Rights as broadly as a reasonable reading of the text and its purpose(s) will allow and rely on the Equal Protection Clause (not unsupportable manipulations of the text) to invalidate legislation that draws arbitrary distinctions between groups, is motivated by animus toward a particular group, or, absent a rational justification, disparately affects specific groups.	States may not base the funding of public education on property tax revenue unless specific and concrete steps are taken to ensure relative parity in the quality of public education.	Reducing disparities in the quality of public education and therefore enhancing equality of opportunity for citizens of all backgrounds.
McCleskey v. Kemp	Same as above.	Disparate impact in the administration of the death penalty is arbitrary and therefore violates the Eighth and Fourteenth Amendments.	Citizens are entitled to equal treatment under and due process of law, unless the state can demonstrate by clear and convincing evidence that the disparate impact is justified.
General Elec. Co. v. Gilbert	(Appropriate Judicial Activism) The Court should invalidate arbitrary laws, but only to the extent that such laws are consistent with a reasonable reading of the text and its underlying purpose(s). (Substantive Equality) The Court should interpret each provision in the Bill of Rights as broadly as a reasonable reading of the text and its purpose(s) will allow and rely on the Equal Protection Clause (not unsupportable	Employers must cover pregnancy-related conditions in their health insurance plans.	Promoting gender disparity and equal treatment under the law.

Case	*Interpretive Principle*	*How the Court Should Have Ruled*	*Impact on Democracy*
	manipulations of the text) to invalidate legislation that draws arbitrary distinctions between groups, is motivated by animus toward a particular group, or, absent a rational justification, disparately affects specific groups.		
Kelo v. City of New London	(Unjust Outcomes) Where alternative yet reasonable interpretations of the text are possible (e.g., where constitutional ambiguity exists), the Court should select the interpretation – and reach an outcome – that avoids unjust and draconian consequences.	The government may not seize private property unless the seizure is for a legitimate public use.	Citizens may not be subject to regulatory takings that are primarily intended to benefit private economic interests and indirectly promote economic and social inequality.
Lochner v. New York	(Decentralization) The Court should uphold state laws unless such laws, on their face or as applied, violate an enumerated constitutional right, violate due process of law, or resulted from a corrupt political process.	States may enact regulations to protect workers from harmful employment practices.	The state's police powers include authority to protect individual citizens from harmful or abusive conditions in the workplace.
Wickard v. Filburn	(Federalism) When interpreting the scope of the federal government's (including the judiciary's) enumerated power over the states, the Court should reject an expansive view of the federal government's authority, including where states experiment with solutions that will strengthen democratic and political equality.	The Commerce Clause does not give Congress the authority to regulate economic activity that is exclusively local in nature.	The national government may not regulate *local* economic activity unless such activity has a direct and substantial impact on commerce.

Comparing this table to the one on pages x–xii which appears more promising for democracy, and which more effectively gives citizens, not the Court, the authority to identify the rights under which they will be governed? The answer is obvious. Most importantly, this analysis demonstrates that by adopting a contextualist view of constitutional interpretation, the Court can reach desirable outcomes through legitimate and constitutionally defensible decision-making processes.

CONCLUDING THOUGHTS

The tree of liberty must be refreshed from time to time with the blood of patriots and tyrants.

—Thomas Jefferson

Four score and seven years ago our fathers brought forth on this continent, a new nation, conceived in Liberty, and dedicated to the proposition that all men are created equal.

—Abraham Lincoln

The United States Constitution was drafted by principled men who aspired to form "a more perfect union," in which the individual pursuits of free men triumphed over the collective power of government. The Founders recognized the intuitive, almost instinctual, human craving for liberty that is driven by the power of the human spirit, the promise of free will, the preservation of self-autonomy, and the primacy of *the people*. The Founders' vision for American democracy embodied equality, not elitism, championed fairness, not favoritism, and emphasized autonomy, not aristocracy.

Unfortunately, the "heady days of the here and now" and the "transcendent dimensions of liberty" have blinded many to the Founders' vision. We have become a nation of men, not laws, governed by an unelected Supreme Court and an unaccountable federal government. We are a country defined by party, not patriotism, by selfishness, not sacrifice, and by corruption, not compassion. Today, the United States does not resemble the country in which the Founders lived and continues to drift from the values upon which the Constitution rests. American democracy now resides in the shadows of elitism, buried under the intolerable burden of inequality and disillusioned by the false promise of liberty. Until this changes, the future will not be brighter than the past, and the winds of change will stall under the weight of cynicism.

To restore democracy and create a government for and by the people, the United States Supreme Court – and all institutions of government – must renew the vision embodied in the Constitution, which Patrick Henry so eloquently captures:

> *The Constitution is not an instrument to restrain the people, it is an instrument for the people to restrain the government – lest it come to dominate our lives and interests.*

Heeding these words and giving life to their meaning is essential if American democracy is to survive. After all, "[w]hen the past no longer illuminates the future, the spirit walks in darkness," and the Founders' dream for a "more perfect union" vanishes.

INDEX